About This Book

Why is this topic important?

Although training games have been around for a long time, everybody's raving about their power and potency in recent times. Even when you drastically discount the hype and the exaggeration, you have to agree that simulation, games, and similar activities are becoming mainstream methodologies in education and training. The claims about the strength of simulations and games are supported by current research on the nature of intelligence and cognitive processes. The new generation of participants demands interactive strategies in the classroom. In the workplace, training games provide the optimum environment for exploring teamwork, globalization, increasing diversity, rapid change, and other such trends. This book features a variety of field-tested activities from an authoritative author who has been researching, designing, and facilitating training games and activities around the world for the past four decades.

What can you achieve with this book?

In a single sentence, you will increase both the motivational and the instructional effectiveness of your training sessions. More specifically, you will confidently use tested training games and activities that appeal to participants at different levels in the organization and provide hands-on experiences with principles and procedures related to the workplace. The activities (which are based on proven laws of learning and principles of cognitive science) will challenge and intrigue your participants at an optimum level and ensure the application of the new skills and knowledge to the workplace environment.

How is this book organized?

The book is organized into eleven convenient sections that deal with frequently taught corporate training topics such as communication, teamwork, leadership, diversity, and critical thinking. Each section contains several ready-to-use games and activities. Instructions for each activity are presented in a consistent, easy-to-use format that specifies the purpose, number of participants, time requirement, supplies, preparation, step-by-step instructions for conducting the activity, and debriefing suggestions. Reproducible masters for handouts and play materials are provided immediately after the description of each activity.

About Pfeiffer

Pfeiffer serves the professional development and hands-on resource needs of training and human resource practitioners and gives them products to do their jobs better. We deliver proven ideas and solutions from experts in HR development and HR management, and we offer effective and customizable tools to improve workplace performance. From novice to seasoned professional, Pfeiffer is the source you can trust to make yourself and your organization more successful.

Essential Knowledge Pfeiffer produces insightful, practical, and comprehensive materials on topics that matter the most to training and HR professionals. Our Essential Knowledge resources translate the expertise of seasoned professionals into practical, how-to guidance on critical workplace issues and problems. These resources are supported by case studies, worksheets, and job aids and are frequently supplemented with CD-ROMs, websites, and other means of making the content easier to read, understand, and use.

Essential Tools Pfeiffer's Essential Tools resources save time and expense by offering proven, ready-to-use materials—including exercises, activities, games, instruments, and assessments—for use during a training or team-learning event. These resources are frequently offered in looseleaf or CD-ROM format to facilitate copying and customization of the material.

Pfeiffer also recognizes the remarkable power of new technologies in expanding the reach and effectiveness of training. While e-hype has often created whizbang solutions in search of a problem, we are dedicated to bringing convenience and enhancements to proven training solutions. All our e-tools comply with rigorous functionality standards. The most appropriate technology wrapped around essential content yields the perfect solution for today's on-the-go trainers and human resource professionals.

Essential resources for training and HR professionals

www.pfeiffer.com

To the memory of
P. Kandaswamy
My student, my friend, and my accomplice

THIAGI'S

Favorite
Games

Sivasailam "Thiagi" Thiagarajan

Pfeiffer

A Wiley Imprint

www.pfeiffer.com

Published by Pfeiffer
A Wiley Imprint
989 Market Street, San Francisco, CA 94103-1741 www.pfeiffer.com

For additional copies/bulk purchases of this book in the U.S. please contact 800-274-4434.

Pfeiffer books and products are available through most bookstores. To contact Pfeiffer directly call our Customer Care Department within the U.S. at 800-274-4434, outside the U.S. at 317-572-3985, fax 317-572-4002, or visit www.pfeiffer.com.

Pfeiffer also publishes its books in a variety of electronic formats. Some content that appears in print may not be available in electronic books.

Library of Congress Cataloging-in-Publication Data
Thiagarajan, Sivasailam.
  Thiagi's 100 favorite games / Sivasailam Thiagarajan.
    p. cm.
  ISBN-13: 978-0-7879-8199-0 (pbk.)
  ISBN-10: 0-7879-8199-0 (pbk.)
  1. Employees-Training of-Problems, exercises, etc. 2. Management games. 3. Educational games. I. Title: Thiagi's one hundred favorite games. II. Title.
  HF5549.5.T7T448 2006
  658.3'124—dc22   2006008661

Acquiring Editor: Martin Delahoussaye
Director of Development: Kathleen Dolan Davies
Developmental Editor: Arlette Ballew

Production Editor: Dawn Kilgore
Editor: Rebecca Taff
Manufacturing Supervisor: Becky Carreño

Printed in the United States of America
Printing   10 9 8 7 6 5 4 3

Contents

PART XI CLOSERS

Acknowledgments

I want to thank several people whose positive reactions have been reinforcing my neurotic behavior of designing one new training activity every day:

- Facilitators, trainers, and designers around the world who keep spreading my games:

    Marie Jasinski, Australia

    Samuel van der Bergh, Switzerland

    David Gouthro, Canada

    V. Thanikachalam, India

    Willy Kriz, Austria

    Pieter van der Hijden, The Netherlands

    Fred Percival, the United Kingdom

    Bruno Hourst, France

    Frances Seaw, Malaysia

    Nina Nemicheva, Russia

    Frances Kemmerer, my playmate, patron, and role model (wherever she is)

- More than six thousand people who regularly read my online newsletter
- Tens of thousands of visitors who made *www.thiagi.com* the top website for training games
- Raja Thiagarajan, for being my computer programmer and web master ever since he was seven years old
- Matthew Richter, for generating enough revenue so I can write books without worrying about mortgage payments
- My special friends at Jossey-Bass/Pfeiffer: Kathleen Dolan Davis, Martin Delahoussaye, and Dawn Kilgore
- My sweetheart, Lucy
- Other members of my wonderful family: Julie, Jason, Matt, Kat, and Lia

Introduction

Since I consider my life to be a game, it is only appropriate that I begin this book with a condensed story of my life.

The Story of My Life

Like any other Tamil child, I grew up playing all sorts of folk games (except I was not permitted to play marbles with the street children). My favorite game was Goats and the Tiger. Whenever I chose to handle the goats, all my fifteen goats were soon devoured by the single opposing tiger. Whenever I chose to be the tiger, I was quickly trapped by the opponent's goats. I managed to keep losing several other games also. Things came to a crisis when I was seven years old and my uncle taught me how to play Checkers. Losing this game repeatedly gave me an inferiority complex. In sheer desperation, I suggested changes to the rules of the game. With these rule changes, I was able to win more than half of the time. This is when I realized that it is better to be a game designer than a game player.

Twelve years later, I made the important connection between playing and learning. At that time I was trying to teach physics to a high-school classroom of fifty adolescents who were not too excited about the four-stroke cycle of the internal combustion engine. In desperation, I organized the students into teams and announced a contest to see which team brought a carburetor to the next class.

One of the students asked, "Hey teach, what's a carburetor?"

I advised him to check out the physics textbook. All students scrambled through the textbook, reviewed the content, and studied the diagrams with avid interest. Sure enough, three teams brought carburetors to the class next day, one from a repair shop, one from his family's abandoned car, and one from some mysterious source. I designed a game that involved taking the carburetor apart, identifying each part, and putting everything back. Players earned score points for their physical skill and cognitive talents. I kept simplifying my elaborate scoring system, rewarding student-players for higher-order thinking skills. Most players cheated, but everyone spent a lot of time learning lessons in physics.

Fast forward three decades: On March 21, 1998, I began designing one new training game every day (making sure that each day's game was of a different type from the ones I designed during the past three days). Through this exercise, I learned about different types of interactive training activities and started publishing a monthly online newsletter about training games.

I now conduct public and in-house workshops on how to design training games. All my participation in professional conferences involves conducting interactive sessions. I design games and simulations for corporate clients and nonprofit organizations. I have branched off into online games and e-learning courses integrated with games and simulations.

Prediction about the next segment of the life-game: My epitaph says, "He never worked a single day in his life."

1

The Origin of This Book

Let me rewind the autobiography to the current time. Recently, when my friend Martin Delahoussaye, an editor at Pfeiffer, suggested that we should publish a collection of my favorite games, I tried to discourage him by claiming that I had hundreds of favorites. But Martin persisted and I had the unpleasant job of choosing among my children. With inputs from my more objective friends, I eventually came up with the 100 training games that are included in this book.

What Are Games and Activities?

Technically, this book does not contain 100 games. It contains 100 training activities.

A game has four defining features: conflict, control, closure, and contrivance.

Conflict arises when players have a goal to achieve and various obstacles that prevent them from achieving the goal. Conflict frequently occurs in the form of competition among players or teams. But you can also have cooperative games in which the conflict is represented by previous records, tight time limits, and limited resources.

Control refers to the rules of the game that specify how you take your turn, make your move, and earn score points. Some rules may be explicit (example: *you must not change your symbol from "X" to "O" in the middle of the game*), while others may be implicit (example: *you must never deliberately throw a game*).

Closure refers to a special rule (called the *termination rule*) that specifies when and how the game ends. Termination rules involve time limits, target scores, or elimination. They determine who wins the game.

Contrivance refers to the characteristic of a game that makes people say, "After all, it was only a game." This term refers to the built-in inefficiencies in a game.

An *activity* is an event in which a person participates. Training activities refer to both physical behaviors and covert mental processes that are related to the achievement of learning objectives. According to this definition, all games are activities. However, different types of training activities are not games. This book contains 100 training activities, some of which are games, while the others are not.

The Book Is Organized into Sections

The training games and activities in this book are organized into eleven convenient sections. Three of the sections are related to the positioning and the function of the activities during a training session:

Openers

The book begins, appropriately, with a section that contains opening activities (sometimes referred to as *icebreakers*). The criterion that I use in designing, selecting, and conducting these opening activities is that the activity should be related to the training objective and content. Like most participants, I hate irrelevant icebreakers that provide "fun" and end up wasting time. The eight activities in the opening section of the book explore topics and help participants achieve goals related to establishing expectations, identifying current levels of participants' experience, exploring potential areas of application, defining the training topics, identifying participants' attitudes toward the topic, encouraging collaboration, getting acquainted with fellow participants, providing a preview of the training session, and encouraging interaction among participants.

Closers

Equally appropriately, the book ends with a section that contains closing activities. The five activities in the final section of the book explore topics and help participants achieve goals related to enhancing participants' self-image, visualizing successful application of the new skills and their potential impact, planning for application, and identifying personal highlights in the session.

Review

A special type of closing activities involves reviewing the training content. These review activities can also be applied before and during the training session to reinforce reading assignments and lecture presentations. The nine activities in this section (which precedes the final *closers* section) deal with goals that are related to demonstrating the mastery of the training content by answering questions.

The other sections in this book are organized according to popular topical areas in corporate training.

Communication

Skills and knowledge associated with communication provide the foundation for all workplace performance. The eleven activities in this section explore topics and help participants achieve goals related to identifying and using different modes of communication, solving communication problems, applying best practices in presentations and storytelling, identifying humor in everyday situations, making personal statements, increasing communication flexibility, increasing meaningfulness, summarizing messages, collaborating spontaneously, taking appropriate risks, and using plain language.

Sales and Marketing

Everyone is a salesperson who sells different things, ranging from merchandise to services to ideas. The six activities in this section explore topics and help participants achieve goals related to creating mission statements, applying effective sales practices, improving relationships among suppliers, employees, and customers, influencing and persuading others, answering hostile questions with honesty, and focusing attention on end-users and customers.

Teamwork

Most corporate work is being increasingly conducted in teams. The fifteen activities in this section explore topics and help participants achieve goals related to recognizing stages in team development, applying teamwork principles, ensuring effective participation by all members of a team, handling changes in the team, clarifying team-member roles and responsibilities, increasing trust, behaving in a socially responsible fashion, mediating and managing conflicts, negotiating effectively, encouraging win-win solutions, increasing the effectiveness of virtual teams, and tapping into the wisdom of crowds.

Leadership

The concept of leadership is undergoing critical changes and become more flexible. The nine activities in this section explore topics and help participants achieve goals related to identifying leadership concepts through a survey, analyzing leadership advice, identifying characteristics of effective leaders and facilitators, exploring everyday applications of leadership principles, taking charge when appropriate, specifying performance goals, and delegating roles and responsibilities.

Diversity

The increasing diversity in the corporate workplace is presenting interesting challenges and opportunities. The six activities in this section help participants achieve goals related to identifying and integrating concepts related to diversity, leveraging diversity in work groups, encouraging mindful examination of differences, exploring the causes and consequences of stereotyping, and experiencing the pain of being excluded.

Problem Solving

All jobs involve solving problems and making decisions. The eleven activities in this section help participants achieve goals related to improving brainstorming, generating and integrating ideas, identifying future impact of present decisions, appealing to different stakeholders, planning in a proactive fashion, critically examining assumptions, and avoiding the complacency due to initial success.

Critical Thinking

One of the main goals of this book is to require and reward participants to think critically. The ten activities in this section help participants to achieve goals related to recognizing mindless behaviors, reducing negative self-talk, increasing recall, predicting the impact of business strategies, recognizing critical (but hidden) components of the total system, applying principles of experimental research, making logical inferences, and avoiding overestimation or underestimation.

Corporate Training Topics

This section contains a miscellaneous set of frequently taught topics. They include prioritizing tasks in a to-do list, maximizing the value of time, identifying frequent time wasters and reducing their impact, understanding and applying paradoxical principles related to training, selecting interactive training strategies, experiencing the power of job aids, exploring facts and opinions related to outsourcing, planning for change management, coping with constant change, and preventing workplace violence.

How Each Activity Is Organized

During the last couple of decades, I have been developing, testing, and revising a structured-text format for communicating step-by-step instructions for conducting training games and activities. I have used this approach to effectively explain game rules and instructions to thousands of facilitators, trainers, and players. Each activity in this book is described using this validated format.

Each activity begins with a short introduction to provide background information. Then the description of the activity is organized under the following functional sections:

Purpose

This section identifies the learning outcome in terms of what the participants will be able to do at the end of the activity. Although I am capable of writing precise behaviorally stated training objectives, I prefer to specify the learning outcome in simple, plain language.

Participants

In this section, I identify the minimum and maximum numbers of participants for the activity and give a range of numbers that produces the best play outcomes. This section also indicates whether (and how) participants are divided into teams. In general, the best size for a group of participants is between twelve and thirty, preferably twenty-four. The best size for a team is between three and seven, preferably five. Most games in this book permit play with a wide range of group sizes.

Time

This section specifies a range of time for conducting the activity. In general, I prefer briefer games and conduct them at a fairly fast pace. The time requirements for the activities in this book range from ninety-nine seconds to a couple of hours.

Supplies

This section lists the supplies and equipment required for conducting the game. Generally, I tend to be a minimalist and use easily available materials. This section also lists handouts that are used during the game. Reproducible masters for these handouts are found at the end of each activity.

Whenever I conduct games, I always use a count-down timer (for implementing time limits) and a whistle (to announce the beginning and the ending of an activity and to get participants' attention in the middle). Inexpensive electronic timers are readily available in kitchen-supply stores. I use a software program with a countdown timer that can be projected on a screen through an LCD projector. After testing several noise-makers for getting participants' attention, I have selected a wooden train whistle because it produces the least jarring and the most pleasant sound.

Preparation

This section gives instructions for preliminary activities before conducting the training activity. Examples of preparation activities include photocopying sufficient copies of handouts, constructing appropriate survey questions, and collecting the latest information from the library.

Flow

This key section provides step-by-step instructions for facilitating the activity. In this section, each step is pre-viewed by a short sentence in bold letters. Some steps are followed by examples printed in italics.

Debriefing

Reflection and sharing of insights after a simulation game is a critical component in the learning process. The debriefing section after an activity provides suggestions on how to conduct this type of discussion and what key learning point to emphasize. In some cases, this section includes a set of suggested questions.

Handouts

Whenever appropriate, reproducible masters for handouts, forms, and other documents related to the activity are included immediately after the description of the activity.

Additional Sections

In addition to the preceding list of standard sections, you may see one or more of these additional sections in some activities:

Set-Up

This section contains preparatory instructions for arranging the furniture in the room and for distributing supplies ahead of time.

Caution

This section identifies things that can go wrong and explains how to avoid or handle them.

Adjustments

This section explains how to compress or expand the time requirement and modify the game to suit different group sizes.

Participant Allocation Table

These tables indicate how different numbers of participants are distributed among different teams and how participants should pair up to work with a partner.

The Best Way

I have organized the book and structured each activity to make it easy for you to understand and conduct your training sessions. The best way to master these activities, however, is to walk through each of them with a group of colleagues and friends—and actually conduct them with real participants. At the end of each session, debrief yourself by reflecting on what went right and what can be improved. Feel free to modify the activities to suit your skill, your needs, and your resources.

Remember, a good facilitator plays within the rules of a game, while a great facilitator plays with the rules of the games.

PART I
Openers

1
Hello

Hello is an opener that is directly related to the workshop topic. This strategy is in contrast to the typical icebreakers that are just fun without any relevance to the training topic.

Purpose

To establish expectations, baseline of experiences, application areas, and alternative definitions related to the workshop topic

Participants

Minimum: 8
Maximum: 52
Best: 12 to 32
(Participants are divided into 4 teams.)

Time

20 to 40 minutes

Supplies

- A deck of playing cards
- Sheets of flip-chart paper
- Felt-tipped markers
- Timer
- Whistle

Preparation

Assemble a packet of playing cards. Estimate the number of participants. Divide this number by 4, round up the answer if necessary. From a deck of cards, remove this many cards of each suit. Shuffle this packet of cards and use them for allocating participants to the four different teams.

Example: *You have 29 participants. Dividing this by 4, you get 7.25. You round this up to 8. From the deck of cards, you remove Ace, 2, 3 . . . 8 from each of the 4 suits. You shuffle this packet.*

Flow

Brief the participants. Explain that you are going to conduct an activity called Hello. This activity involves all participants collecting and sharing some useful information about ourselves.

Introduce the four topics. Explain that you are interested in these four topics:

- **Expectations.** What are you looking forward to in this training session?
- **Experience.** How much and what type of experience do you have that is related to the workshop topic?
- **Current project.** What are you currently doing in your job to which you plan to apply your new skills and knowledge?
- **Definition.** How would you define the workshop topic?

Explain the activity. Tell participants that you are going to organize them into four teams. Each team will be assigned one of the four topics. Instruct the teams to collect information from all participants—including members of their own teams—related to the topic assigned to them.

Set the agenda. Explain the following schedule:

3 minutes for planning how to collect the information from everyone
3 minutes for collecting information from everyone in the room
3 minutes for analyzing all the information that teams collected
1 minute (for each team) to make a summary presentation of the information

Make team allocations. Shuffle the packet of playing cards and ask each participants to take a card. Ask participants to find other members of their teams who have cards of the same suit. Invite each team to gather around in a convenient corner. Assign the topics to the teams in this order:

Clubs: Expectations
Hearts: Experience
Spades: Current project
Diamonds: Definition (of the workshop topic)

Coordinate the planning activity. Ask each team to begin planning how to collect information from everyone in the room (including members of their own teams). Announce a 3-minute time limit and start the timer.

After 2 minutes, announce a 1-minute warning. After 3 minutes, announce the end of the planning period.

Coordinate the information-collection activity. Announce that each team now has 3 minutes to collect information on the topic assigned to it. Get out of the way as everyone tries to talk to as many others as possible. Announce a 3-minute time limit and start the timer.

After 2 minutes, announce a 1-minute warning. After 3 minutes, announce the end of the planning period.

Coordinate the analysis activity. Ask members of teams to return to their teams. Invite team members to share and tabulate all the information they collected. Distribute sheets of flip-chart paper and ask teams to summarize their information on this sheet. Announce a 3-minute time limit and start the timer.

After 2 minutes, announce a 1-minute warning. After 3 minutes, announce the end of the analysis period.

Coordinate the reporting activity. Randomly select a team and ask it to display its flip-chart poster. Ask a representative from this team to present its results and conclusions. Start the timer and announce the end of the reporting period at the end of 1 minute.

Repeat the procedure until all teams have given their reports.

Debriefing

Discuss the findings with participants. Present your training objectives and an outline of the workshop format. Relate these items to participants' expectations, experience, and current projects. Give your definition of the workshop topic and explain how it relates to their definitions.

2
Taking the Pulse

It's a good idea to get a feel for the participants' attitudes toward the training topic, especially if it is a potentially controversial one. This opener enables you to obtain useful attitude data without forcing anyone to reveal personal feelings.

Purpose

To collect and share personal attitudes toward the workshop topic, while maintaining total anonymity of the data

Participants

Minimum: 5
Maximum: 50
Best: 10 to 30

Time

10 to 15 minutes

Supplies

- Flip chart
- Felt-tipped markers
- Worksheet (for computing the average reaction scale value)
- Pens or pencils
- Blank paper for participants

Preparation

Construct an attitude scale. This scale consists of a single item and nine sequenced alternatives. The item can be the name of the topic (examples: *affirmative action, casual Fridays, or harassment policy*) or a statement (examples: *The proposed health-insurance plan protects the rights of the employees* or *We should celebrate our workplace diversity by including different types of ethnic food in our cafeteria menu*).

The alternatives progress from the most negative response to the most positive.

Example:
1—very strongly disagree
2—strongly disagree
3—disagree
4—slightly disagree
5—neutral
6—slightly agree
7—agree
8—strongly agree
9—very strongly agree

Prepare the display. Transfer your item and the alternatives to a sheet of flip-chart paper. However, do not display this scale until later.

Construct a worksheet. Draw the table on another sheet of flip-chart paper or transparency sheet.

Flow

Introduce the topic. Welcome the participants and identify the training topic. Because of the potentially controversial nature of the issue, get the group's permission to begin with an anonymous pulse-taking activity.

Display the scale. Exhibit the flip-chart page.

Collect data. Ask each participant to think about the issue and select 1 of the 9 alternatives that best reflects her personal reaction. Instruct participants to write the appropriate number (between 1 and 9) on a small piece of paper to indicate their responses. The participants should all fold their pieces of paper and pass them on to you.

Compute the statistics. Collect the pieces of paper and ask one or two participants to tabulate the data on the worksheet. Briefly explain to the volunteer statisticians how to record the number of participants, selecting each alternative and how to calculate the average reaction score.

Ask for predictions. Give these instructions (in your own words) to the participants:
Think about the training topic and your fellow participants. Estimate the range of reactions toward the topic among all the participants in the room. Write down your estimated range, from the lowest to the highest choices.

Estimate the average reaction score. Write down your estimate, correct to two decimal places.

Identify the best estimate for the range. Ask the participants to report their estimated ranges. Announce the actual range. Identify the people with the closest estimates and congratulate them.

Identify the best estimate for the average. Build up suspense by asking people whose predictions are within ever-narrowing ranges.

Example: *If the average were 2.73, ask participants whose estimates were between 1 and 4 to stand up. Then ask participants whose estimates were between 2 and 3 to remain standing while the others sit down. Then estimates between 2.5 and 3, and so on.*

Repeat the process until you have identified the participants with the correct (or the closest) estimates. Congratulate these participants for their psychic ability.

Use the opener as a springboard for the training session. For example, you may begin by asking the participants to discuss why different people react differently to the topic.

Worksheet for Computing the Average Reaction Scale Value

Reaction Scale Value	Number of Participants	Scale Value x Number of Participants
1		
2		
3		
4		
5		
6		
7		
8		
9		
Totals: Average = (Total of last column)/(Total of middle column)		

3
Placards

Participants come to the training session with specific expectations. It is a good idea to let them share these expectations at the beginning of the workshop. Placards encourages the participants to do exactly that.

Purpose

To identify and discuss participant expectations for the workshop

Participants

Minimum: 5
Maximum: Any number
Best: 10 to 30

Time

20 to 30 minutes

Supplies

- Blank sheets of paper
- Felt-tipped markers
- Timer
- Whistle

Flow

Prepare a wish list. Ask participants to independently prepare "wish lists" of features of their ideal training sessions. Although the participants work alone, they should think of positive features that would appeal to most of the other participants.

    Prepare a placard. Distribute a blank sheet of paper and a felt-tipped marker to each participant. Ask each participant to write the most desirable feature of an ideal training session on the sheet of paper using big, bold letters.

    Take a walk. Ask the participants to hold up their placards (the sheets of paper with the desirable training session feature) and silently walk around. Participants should read each other's placards without any comments.

Persuade each other. After a few minutes of the walk-around, blow a whistle and ask participants to stop wherever they are. Give these instructions (in your own words) to the participants:

Pair up with the participant standing nearest to you.

Read and discuss your placards. Try to persuade the other person that your placard contains a more desirable training session feature.

Jointly decide which placard contains the more desirable feature. Keep this placard and drop the other on the floor.

Walk around with your partner. After a suitable pause, blow the whistle and ask each pair to make their final choice. If any pair has not chosen a placard, ask them to flip a coin to force a choice. Now ask both partners to hold the selected placard by the opposite ends and silently walk around the room, studying other placards.

Form a team. After a suitable pause, blow the whistle and ask everyone to stop. Give these instructions (in your own words) to the pairs of participants:

Join another pair of participants and discuss the two different placards. As before, try to persuade the other pair that your placard contains a more desirable training session feature.

Jointly decide which of the two placards to keep. Drop the other placard on the floor.

Persuade other teams. Blow the whistle after a suitable pause. Give these instructions (in your own words) to the teams:

Locate other teams with the same training session feature (or a similar one) as yours on their placards. Invite them to join you. Persuade other teams to join you by explaining why your placard contains a superior feature.

You have 2 minutes to persuade the other teams to join your team.

Prepare a commercial. At the end of 2 minutes, blow the whistle and ask the expanded teams to move to convenient corners of the room. Ask each team to prepare a 30-second public-service announcement to persuade the other participants to agree to their choice of the most desirable training session feature. Announce a time limit of 3 minutes.

Persuade the masses. Blow the whistle at the end of 3 minutes. Ask each team to come to the front of the room and make its 30-second presentation. At the end of all presentations, ask participants to indicate their personal choices among the different presentations through a show of hands.

Respond to the inputs. Thank the participants for sharing their desired expectations and wish lists for the training session. Briefly describe the training format and discuss how it matches the participants' wishes. Negotiate appropriate changes.

4
Balancing Act

I t's a good idea to get the participants to stand up and move around at the beginning of the workshop. Balancing Act gets the participants energized in a fun way.

Purpose

To create a metaphor for interactivity and collaboration among the participants

Participants

Minimum: 5
Maximum: 30
Best: 10 to 20

Time

10 to 20 minutes

Supplies

- Training manual (or a set of handouts)
- Masking tape

Preparation

Create the track. Find a clear space that is approximately 10 feet wide and 20 feet long. If necessary, temporarily create such a space by rearranging the furniture in the room. Mark the *start* and the *finish* lines with masking tape on the floor.

Flow

Assemble the participants. Ask them to bring their workshop manuals or collections of handouts and stand at the *start* line.

Give instructions. Explain that the participants will race from the *start* line to the *finish* line. Give these additional details (in your own words):

You should balance your workshop manual on your head as you race from the start line to the finish line.

Once you have left the start line, you should not touch the manual with your hand.

Don't pick up the manual if it falls down. Ask someone else to help you by picking up the manual and replacing it on your head.

You may help the others whenever you want to. But you cannot touch anyone else's manual as long as it is on that person's head.

The object of this activity is to get everyone across the finish line as quickly as possible.

Once you have crossed the finish line, you may drop your manual. But you cannot return to help the others.

Conduct the activity. Blow the whistle, start the timer, and step out of the way. Let participants race toward the *finish* line. Make sure that everyone observes the rules.

Conclude the activity. Blow the whistle when everyone has crossed the finish line. Announce the time taken and congratulate the group for the great job they did.

Debriefing

Conduct a brief discussion about how the participants feel about their success and what they learned from the activity.

Draw the analogies. Explain (in your own words) how this activity reflects your guidelines for the session:

We succeed only if everyone succeeds.

We should help each other.

When we cannot do certain things by ourselves, we should ask others to help us.

We should help others whenever we can.

We cannot succeed unless everyone succeeds.

We don't succeed by being the first ones to finish.

We should work and learn as fast as we can, but without losing our grip.

We should try to achieve a balance between our heads (thinking) and our hands (acting).

Collect more analogies. Invite participants to add more analogies that relate the opening activity to the training session.

5
Intro

At the beginning of my training workshops, I have been trying to avoid the usual routine of everyone standing up and introducing him- or herself. However, participants have resisted this innovation and demanded the traditional introductions. As a compromise, I have added an ending to the usual ritual to let participants have it their way while I stay faithful to my principle of interactivity in everything I do. This opening activity rewards participants who pay attention to other people's introductions instead of rehearsing what they are going to say.

Purpose

To encourage careful listening and accurate recall of information about people

Participants

Minimum: 6
Maximum: 30
Best: 10 to 20

Time

10 to 20 minutes, depending on the number of participants

Supplies

Paper and pencils

Flow

Briefing. Announce that you are going to start the session in the usual fashion by asking everyone to take turns as they stand up and briefly introduce themselves. Explain that most participants do not pay too much attention to these introductions. For a change, ask participants to listen carefully to what other participants say about themselves. Instruct participants not to take any notes but to focus on different participants' introductions.

   Facilitate introductions. Ask the first person to stand up, clearly state her name and briefly introduce herself. Ask other participants to continue the activity by repeating this procedure. Once again, remind participants to pay careful attention to the others.

Prepare quiz questions. Listen carefully and jot down a list of questions related to content of participants' introductions. This is for your benefit only, so you don't have to practice your best penmanship. (But make sure that you can read your writing later.) Each question should have a single correct answer. (Be sure to jot down the answer also.) Here are some samples:

Who is currently working as a creative director for a law firm?

What is Leeva's last name?

Which participant claims to have learned a lot of leadership skills by working with her horse?

Who has been a manager for more than fifteen years?

You don't have to write down a question related to each participant. However, you may want to write more than one question about the same participant, just to keep participants wide awake. You may have to edit some of the earlier questions during later introductions to ensure that there is only one correct answer.

Example: *Who has been a manager for more than fifteen years and recently visited Shanghai?*

Announce a contest. Ask participants to hide their name tags and any other personal identification. Announce that you are going to conduct a quiz contest. Ask everyone to grab a piece of paper and a pen. Read your questions, one by one, and ask participants to write down the answers. After a suitable pause following each question, give the correct answer. Ask each participant to show her written answer to her neighbor to get credit.

Determine the winner. After about a dozen questions, identify the participant with the most correct answers. Use self-reporting on the honor system. If there is more than one participant with the highest score, ask a few more tie-breaker questions until you have singled out a winner. Lead a round of applause for this participant.

6
Postcard from a Friend

I enjoy generative training sessions in which participants create new content that can be used by future groups. This opening activity is based on a closing activity (see game number 99, Postcard to a Friend) that involves participants writing notes to friends, identifying highlights for the workshop. This activity involves distributing postcards from previous participants with their highlights and advice for a new group of participants.

Purpose

To provide a preview to a training session and some advice on how to get the most out of it

Participants

Minimum: 6
Maximum: Any number
Best: 10 to 20
(Participants are organized into teams of 3 to 7.)

Time

15 to 30 minutes

Supplies

- Postcards written by participants from a previous session. If necessary, copy some postcards (in your own handwriting) to make sure there is one for each participant.
- Blank pieces of paper
- Pens or pencils
- Sheets of flip-chart paper
- Felt-tipped markers
- Masking tape

Flow

Brief participants. Present the following scenario in your own words:

Let's pretend that one of your friends has gone through this training session earlier. You send her an e-mail note asking for her comments on the session and advice on how to get the most out of it. She sends you a postcard.

Conduct the card reading session. Distribute one postcard to each participant. Explain that it was written under the scenario that you presented earlier. Ask participants to read their postcards and review the information. Tell them that you will be taking the postcards back in a few minutes.

Ask participants to compare notes. After about 3 minutes, retrieve the postcards from the participants and organize them into teams of three to seven. Ask each team to compare the advice from the postcards and to select the three most useful pieces of advice.

Prepare posters. Ask participants to display the three most useful pieces of advice on sheets of flip-chart paper. After a suitable pause, ask teams to tape their posters to the wall. Encourage participants to review the posters from the other teams.

Conduct a Q&A session. Ask the participants to return to their locations. Invite them to ask you questions about any of the items from the postcards they received. Give brief responses.

7
Little-Known Facts

Did you know that I once talked to Mahatma Gandhi (when I was seven years old)? Do you know that I am addicted to murder mysteries? People enjoy sharing little-known facts (LKFs) about themselves—perhaps because it makes them feel like celebrities.

Purpose

To increase the level of personal disclosure

Participants

Minimum: 10
Maximum: Any number
Best: 10 to 30
(Participants are divided into 2 groups.)

Time

10 to 20 minutes

Supplies

- Index cards
- Pens or pencils

Flow

Ask participants to write little-known facts about themselves. Give an index card to each participant. Ask participants to write a little-known fact about themselves and keep it hidden from the others.

Divide the participants into two groups. Collect the cards from one group (called the *confessors*) and give them to the other group (called the *interrogators*), one card per participant, with the written side down. Warn the interrogators not to read the statements on the cards they received.

Display the cards. Ask all interrogators to stand up and hold their index cards against their foreheads with the written side showing. Make sure that the interrogator does not read the card, but everyone else is able to.

Locate the confessor. Ask the interrogators to walk around the room, asking different confessors whether the card belongs to them. If a confessor sees her card, she has to say "Yes."

Figure out the LKF. Once an interrogator has tracked down the confessor, she asks a series of *Yes/No* questions to discover the exact nature of the LKF. The confessor responds truthfully but limits her responses to "Yes" or "No."

Verify the LKF. The question-and-answer session continues until the confessor concedes that the interrogator has discovered the LKF. The interrogator verifies her guess by reading the statement on the card.

Switch roles. Conclude the first round of the icebreaker after a suitable period of time. Repeat the activity by giving the LKF cards from the interrogators to the confessors. Switch the roles and ask participants to replay the game.

Debriefing

Usually, openers do not require any debriefing. However, since there is something intriguing about what facts people choose to reveal about themselves, I conduct a quick debriefing using these questions. Although the questions are about people in general, they encourage participants to reflect on their own behaviors:

What facts do people reveal about themselves?

Would some people make up interesting facts about themselves? Why would they do it?

8
Working the Room

A major purpose of an opening activity is to help participants get acquainted with each other. Here's an opener that identifies and rewards participants who would make good politicians.

Purpose

To energize participants and to encourage interaction among them

Participants

Minimum: 10
Maximum: Any number
Best: 10 to 30
(Participants work individually.)

Time

15 to 20 minutes

Supplies

- Working-the-Room Contest Instruction Sheet. Change the start time to suit your session schedule.
- Pens or pencils

Flow

Briefing. As participants come in, greet them at the door and give them copies of the instruction sheet. If anyone asks you questions about the contest, repeat the information from the instruction sheet.

   Keeping time. Keep an eye on the clock. One minute before the ending time of the "mingle-and-chat" activity, give an appropriate warning.

   Start the contest. At the exact time, blow the whistle. Tell participants to stop talking with each other. Ask participants to hide their name tags and any other personal identification.

   Conduct the popularity contest. Explain that the first phase of the contest involves *visibility*. Ask participants to stand up if they believe that their names will be remembered by many people in the room. Bring the group of standing participants to the front of the room. Point to the first contestant and ask the other participants in the room to write his full name on a piece of paper. Announce the name of the participant and ask each participant to check the name written by his neighbor. Ask those who wrote the correct name to stand up, and count the number. Repeat the process with each of the other contestants. Identify the winner (or the winners) whose name was correctly written by the most other participants.

Begin the memory contest. Explain that the second phase of the contest involves memory. Ask participants to look around the room and estimate how many others they can name. Start an auction, asking participants to bid the number of full names that they recall correctly. Identify the highest bidder (or bidders).

Conduct the memory contest. Ask the highest bidder to go around the room, whispering (to prevent the others from hearing) the full names of each participant. Ask all participants who have been correctly named to stand up. If the highest bidder has succeeded in correctly naming the number of participants he bid (or exceeded the number), he wins. Otherwise, repeat the activity with the second-highest bidder.

Working-the-Room Contest Instruction Sheet

We want you to meet and interact with as many other participants as possible.

This is a do-it-yourself icebreaker. You have approximately 7 minutes to mingle and chat with the other participants. Collect information from different people and share information about yourself. Use this contest as an excuse to behave like an intrusive extrovert.

You will not receive any other instructions until the time is up.

In exactly 7 minutes, we will conduct a contest that will reward your ability to work the room. You will have 2 chances to win!

PART II
Communication

9
Communication Modes

When you were a child, did you ever play a game called Telephone in which the first player whispers a message to the second player, who in turn whispers it to the third player, and so on? By the time the message reaches the last player it has become totally garbled! The other day, I was thinking about what would happen if each player converted the message into a different mode of communication before whispering it to the next player. Also, what if, instead of whispering, we actually wrote down the messages so we could figure out how it got distorted?

Purpose

To flexibly switch from direct and indirect modes of communication and to identify distortions in the message

Participants

Minimum: 5
Maximum: Any number
Best: 5 to 30

Time

10 to 20 minutes

Supplies

- Handout, Direct and Indirect Communication, one copy for each participant
- Copies of the Telephone Message Form, one for each participant
- Pens or pencils

Flow

Explain the difference between direct and indirect communication. Distribute copies of the handout, Direct and Indirect Communication, one copy for each participant. Ask participants to read the handout. After a suitable pause, respond to any questions.

   Give paper-folding instructions. Distribute the Telephone Message Forms. Demonstrate how to fold the forms. First fold the paper horizontally in half on the line. Fold it twice more on the rules. When you open the paper, they will see creases separating the paper into 8 strips. Have them do the same thing with their own forms.

Get the game started. Ask each player to secretly select either the indirect or the direct mode of communication and write a message in Strip 1, using that mode. After completing the message, ask players to pass the paper to the next person. (The message from the last player is given to the first player.)

Convert the message. Ask each player to read the message and figure out whether it is in the direct or indirect mode. Instruct players to convert the message into the other mode and write it in Strip 2. Then ask everyone to carefully fold the bottom strip of the paper upward so the first message is hidden and the second message is visible. Ask players to pass the message to the next person as before.

Continue the game. During each subsequent round of the game, ask the players to:

- Read only the latest version of the message
- Determine in what mode the message is written
- Convert the message into the other mode
- Write the converted version in the next strip
- Fold the paper upward so that only the latest strip (with their own message) is visible
- Pass it to the next player

Conclude the game. Stop the game at the end of the sixth round (or, if you have fewer than six players, after everyone has had a turn). Ask participants to open the papers and trace the alteration of the message from the first to the last strip.

Debriefing

Real-world examples. Ask participants to share real-world examples of how a message was distorted when transmitted from one person to another.

Other communication modes. Ask participants for examples of other types of communication polarities (such as logical and intuitive, impulsive and reflective, liberal and conservative, masculine and feminine, individualistic and communitarian, democratic and authoritarian, academic and practical, challenging and submissive, jargon and plain language, inclusive and exclusive, and assertive and meek). Select any of these pairs of communication modes and replay the game using that mode.

Telephone Message Form

7	
6	
5	
4	
3	
2	
XXXXXXXXXXXXX	
1	

Direct and Indirect Communication

Direct communication makes everything explicit. People using this mode of communication tell you exactly what they mean in a direct and assertive fashion.

Indirect communication assumes that people understand the meaning without being told everything. This mode tones down unpleasant aspects of a message by using convoluted language, abstract words, and metaphors.

An Example

Direct: *You're stupid!*

Indirect: *There are many factors that make one person different from another. In the factor of difference, you are beautiful. In the factor of strength, you are strong. In the factor of intelligence, you are somewhere among typical people, slightly below the statistical average. Of course, that does not mean that you are not a wonderful human being.*

The next player sees the message in the indirect mode and converts it into the direct mode. This alternating conversion continues and at the end we can compare different versions of the same message in two different modes.

An Extended Example

Here's what may happen when a message is repeatedly translated between direct and indirect modes.

Direct: *I love you.*

Indirect: *I hand-knitted this poncho for you. I thought you would like it.*

Direct: *Do you want to buy this hand-made poncho for $15?*

Indirect: *This is really a very good offer, high quality, nice price. Would you be able to spare $15 for this superb product?*

Direct: *No bargaining. Fifteen dollars. Do you want to buy it or not?*

10
Communication Problems

Coming up with a solution is fairly easy. Analyzing the solution and improving it is not so easy. This activity deals with several authentic communication problems and encourages participants to apply everything they know to solve each one.

Purpose

To solve communication problems—and to improve the solutions

Participants

Minimum: 6
Maximum: Any number
Best: 10 to 30
(Participants are divided into 6 teams of approximately equal size.)

Time

30 minutes to 2 hours

Supplies

- Handout with samples: Problem, Solution, Critique, Testimonial, Improved Solution, and Scores (at the end of this activity)
- Blank sheets of paper (at least 6 per team)
- Pens or pencils
- Paper clips

Flow

Brief players. Explain that the game will consist of six rounds and announce time allocation for each round. Indicate that players will specify a communication problem in the first round and let go of it during the subsequent rounds while they are busy dealing with other problems and solutions.

Ask for problems. Instruct each team to come up with a real or fictional communication problem in the workplace. Ask each team to describe the problem by briefly answering the following questions:

- Who owns the problem?
- What is the context for the problem?
- Who are the key people involved in the problem?
- What is the gap between the desired goal and the current state?

Announce a time limit for completing this task.

Distribute the handout. Give a copy of the handout to each participant. Draw everyone's attention to the first section that presents a sample problem. Ask teams to use this as an example of what is required of them. Tell the teams to ignore the other sections of the handout.

Ask for solutions. At the end of the time limit, ask each team to give its problem description to the next team. (The last team gives its problem to the first team to complete the sequence. Tell teams that they will play the role of communications consultants during this round. Explain the task by asking teams to review the problem descriptions they received and write suitable solutions. Encourage teams to keep the suggested solution brief and specific. Discourage them from using such delaying tactics as asking for additional data or suggesting further analysis of the problem. Refer to the *Solution* section of the handout. Announce a time limit for completing this task.

Ask for critiques. At the end of the time limit, ask each team to rotate its solution and the earlier problem description to the next team, as before. Tell teams that they will play the roles of cynical critics during this round. As a critic, each team reviews the problem and the suggested solution. The team identifies the weaknesses, limitations, and negative consequences of the solution and records them in a short critique. Encourage players to ignore all positive aspects of the solution and to accentuate the negative. Refer to the *Critique* section of the handout. Announce a time limit for completing this task.

Ask for testimonials. At the end of the time limit, ask each team to rotate the packet of three items (problem, solution, and critique) to the next team, as before. Tell the teams that they will play the roles of boosters during this round. As a booster, each team reviews the problem, the solution, and the critique. Each team identifies the strengths, virtues, and positive consequences of the suggestion and records them in the form of a short testimonial. The booster teams are asked to overlook all negative aspects of the solution. Refer to the *Critique* section of the handout. Announce a time limit for completing the task.

Ask for improved solutions. At the end of the time limit, each team rotates the packet of four items (problem, solution, critique, and testimonial) to the next team, as before. Tell each team that it will play the role of an enhancer. In this role, they will review the problem, solution, critique, and testimonial and suggest an improved solution to the original problem. Refer to the *Improved Solution* section of the handout. Announce a time limit for completing this task.

Ask for comparative scores. At the end of the time limit, instruct each team to rotate these three items to the next team: problem, original suggestion, and improved solution. The two solutions should be shuffled a few times before being handed over to the next player so that there is no indication which one is the original and which one is the enhanced version. Tell each team that it will play the role of an evaluator. In this role, team members will jointly compare the two solutions and distribute 200 points between them to reflect their relative effectiveness. Refer to the *Scores* section of the handout. Announce a time limit for completing this task.

Conclude the activity. Tabulate the scores from different players by recording the scores for the original solution and for the enhanced solution. Give each pair of solutions to the team that wrote the original problem description. Invite teams to review the two solutions to their original problems and use them as the basis for arriving at their own solutions. Also ask participants to reflect on the six different roles (problem owner, consultant, critic, booster, enhancer, and evaluator) they played during the game and think about what they learned by playing each role. Suggest that they should be able to objectively play all six roles the next time they solve their own problems.

Sample Communication Problem

Problem

My name is Russ Powell, and I am the director of customer service at a financial services organization. Sam, one of the four team leaders who work for me, presents a performance problem. When we recently collected feedback data using a 360-degree questionnaire, 6 out of 10 members of Sam's team rated his communication style as unacceptable. These six employees are all women. The four male members of the team rated Sam's communication style as acceptable. I have also heard complaints about Sam's rude behavior from women employees on other teams. My performance goal for Sam is that all members of his team, irrespective of the member's gender, rate his communication style as acceptable.

Solution

Send Sam to a training workshop on cross-gender communication that focuses on skills related to communicating with women. Also ask Sam to read popular books on gender differences.

Critique

The suggested solution assumes that Sam is lacking skills and knowledge. It is more likely that Sam's problem is primarily attitudinal, arising out of a need to maintain a macho image. Sam will perceive the training workshop as a punishment and a challenge. In Sam's perception, he probably wants to treat all employees the same, irrespective of their gender. So he may treat the suggestion as an example of politically correct management behavior. Anyhow, most workshops on this topic merely increase players' awareness levels and don't provide any useful skills. These workshops are of a generic nature and examples used in them are likely to be irrelevant to the specific needs of Sam's organization. Combining the workshop with reading assignments is likely to add to Sam's frustration and irritation. Some pop-psychology books in this field are written by authors who lack expertise and an empirical basis. Principles and procedures presented in these books are likely to contradict each other and contradict what is taught in the training workshop.

Testimonial

I like the double-barreled approach: a training workshop and popular books. There are many effective performance-based workshops that can increase Sam's level of awareness about the impact of his communication style on women. Such a workshop will also provide useful knowledge about differences in communication styles between men and women. Most importantly, the workshop will provide skills practice though low-risk role playing. There are many popular books that are both research-based and practical. Some of these books have been on best-seller lists, suggesting high perceived value.

Improved Solution

Have a coaching conversation with Sam, presenting a business case and a personal case for reducing complaints from women employees. Establish a mutual and measurable goal related to cross-gender communication skills. Let Sam work out details of how he will reach the goal and demonstrate his achievement. Offer a menu of several appropriate strategies, including training workshops, books, counseling from the Employee Assistance Program, and discussion with his team members. Assure Sam of your support, but explain negative consequences of continued complaints from women employees.

Scores

60 points for the original solution (training workshop plus books)

140 points for enhanced solution (coaching and other support)

(These scores are just examples.)

11
Presentation Skills

Most adults have lots of experience in being inspired by good presentations and bored by bad ones. This activity taps into the collective wisdom of participants in figuring out what to do—and what not to do—when giving presentations.

Purpose

To share best practices related to making presentations

Participants

Minimum: 3
Maximum: Any number
Best: 12 to 24
(Participants are divided into groups of 3.)

Time

30 to 45 minutes

Supplies

- **Question cards.** 21 cards, each containing an open-ended question related to presentation skills. (See the list of sample questions at the end of this activity.)
- Blank pieces of paper
- Pens or pencils
- Timer
- Whistle

Suggestion to Trainer

Although this activity involving scoring and "winning," conduct it in a playful manner, stressing the importance of thinking quickly and acting spontaneously. Some people may worry about the second player cheating by not completely covering his or her ears. In hundreds of field tests, this has not been a problem because the questions are open-ended and players prefer to show off their creative thinking.

Flow

Give a preview of the game. Explain that the game involves groups of three participants working through several open-ended questions. Give an example of the question ("How many times should I rehearse?"). Announce that two participants will independently answer each question and the third participant will act as the judge and decide which answer was the better one. Participants will take turns playing the role of the judge.

Explain how the game will end. Announce a 20-minute time period for the play of the game. After 20 minutes, the game will come to an end. The participant whose answers were judged to be the better ones most frequently wins the game.

Form triads. Organize participants into groups of three. Distribute a set of question cards to each triad.

Select a judge for the first round. In each triad, ask the shortest person to be the judge for the first round. Ask the judge to turn the cards with the question side down, shuffle the packet, and place it in the middle of the table.

Conduct the first round. Ask the judge to take the top question card, place it question side up on the table, and read the question aloud. Ask the judge to pause for about 10 seconds, during which time the other two players think of a suitable answer. The judge points to one of the players. The other player covers his or her ears immediately.

Listen to the answers. The selected player gives her answer, focusing on a few selected key items, because there is a 60-second limit on the length of the answer. The judge now points to the other player, who gives his answer, working within the same 60-second limit. (There is no need for the first player to cover his or her ears.) After hearing the second answer, the judge briefly summarizes the first answer.

Cast a secret vote. The judge compares the two answers and decides which answer was the better one. (This is a forced choice, which prohibits any ties.) The judge secretly writes the name of the person who gave the better answer on a piece of paper, folds the paper to hide the name, and places this vote in the middle of the table next to the question cards.

Reassign the judge's role. The participant seated to the judge's left becomes the new judge for the next round.

Repeat the procedure. The next round is conducted the same way as the previous round (with the judge reading a question from the card, listening to the two answers, and secretly voting for the better answer).

Conclude the activity. Repeat the same procedure during the subsequent rounds of the game. At the end of 20 minutes, blow the whistle to signal the end of the round. Ask participants in each triad to mix up all the pieces of paper with the judges' votes, open them, and count the number of times each participant's name appears. Identify the participant whose name appears most frequently and congratulate the person for winning the game.

Adjustments

If you cannot divide participants into groups of three, have one or two groups with four members. After the judge reads the question, the two participants seated to the judge's left prepare and give their answers, as in the three-person version. The fourth participant listens to the answers, acts as an additional judge, and secretly votes for the better answer.

21 Questions About Presentations

1. How should I make a presentation to an international audience?

2. How many times should I rehearse?

3. How can I increase audience interaction without wasting people's time?

4. How can I create an attention-getting title for my presentation?

5. What is the one best way to handle someone who keeps interrupting my presentation with irrelevant questions?

6. What is the worst mistake made by presenters?

7. How should I handle people who leave before my presentation is finished?

8. When should I invite questions from the audience?

9. What type of handouts is most effective?

10. What is the best way to present statistical data?

11. If I am a member of a panel of three experts, what should we do to ensure that all of us don't duplicate, contradict, or attack each other?

12. How should I handle hostile questions?

13. What is the best length for a presentation?

14. What is the best way to tell a joke?

15. How do I get the attention of audience members?

16. What is the best room arrangement for a group of thirty people?

17. What special precautions should I observe if I am the last presenter at a conference and the participants are eager to go home?

18. What is the best way to get useful feedback from audience members?

19. What is the best way to close my presentation?

20. What is the best way to open my presentation?

21. How do I ensure that my visual aids are effective?

12
Storytelling

Observing and analyzing the performance of experts is a good way to master presentation skills. With the powerful and lightweight camcorder technology now available, it has become easier to record and replay quality videos. With four different recordings, Storytelling avoids excessive copying of the style of a single master performer.

Purpose

To discover, discuss, and apply best practices in corporate storytelling

Participants

Minimum: 8
Maximum: Any number
Best: 12 to 20
(Participants are organized [and reorganized] into teams.)

Time

40 to 60 minutes

Supplies

- Four sets of video equipment and monitors
- Blank paper
- Pens or pencils

Preparation

Make video recordings. Select four excellent storytellers and have each of them select a story that can be told in about 7 minutes. Videotape each of these people telling a story to a small group. Make sure that the storytellers, the stories they tell, the audiences, and the purposes of the story are all different from one another.

Flow

Round 1. Analyzing
Brief the participants. Explain that storytelling is a powerful communication tool and that all jobs involves telling stories—to customers, co-workers, team members, and managers.

Set up four video stations. Set up a video player and a monitor in each of four different rooms if possible. If not, set them up in four different corners of the room to minimize interference.

Divide participants into four teams of approximately equal size. It is not critical if a team has one more or one fewer participant than the other teams. Assign each team to one of the four video stations.

Ask each team to watch the video at its station. Instruct the team members to take notes on the storyteller's actions and identify what worked and what did not work.

Ask teams to analyze the storyteller's techniques. After the video segment ends, encourage team members to consolidate their notes and come up with a list of *Do's and Don'ts for Storytelling*. Also ask teams to identify best practices that they observed.

Round 2. Sharing

Reorganize participants into new teams. Each new team should have a member from each video station. If you have extra participants (because some video stations had one more participant than the others), add them to one or more of the new teams. You will end up with some teams having two people from the same video station, but this should not present any problem.

Ask the new teams to share their storytelling guidelines. Begin by asking each team member to share the best practice he observed in the video. Encourage team members to continue by sharing and consolidating their lists of *Do's and Don'ts*. Invite participants to discuss apparent contradictions, recalling situations in which specific behaviors were used.

Debriefing

Invite participants to select a workplace situation for which storytelling would be a useful skill. Ask them to prepare for a storytelling session that incorporates the *Do's and Don'ts*.

13
Your Funny Life

When people ask me for the secret behind my ability to make everyone laugh, I honestly cannot figure out the answer. However, here's a short activity to increase your ability to find humor in ordinary, everyday events. Perhaps this is the secret.

Purpose

To see the funny side of everything and everybody (including yourself)

Participants

Minimum: 1
Maximum: Any number
Best: 10 to 20
(Participants work individually.)

Time

7 to 15 minutes

Flow

Ask participants to find circular objects. Say something like this:

Quickly! Look around and find all circular objects. Work silently and individually. Find as many as you can within the next 20 seconds.

Explain the point. Pause for 20 seconds. Get participants' attention and tell them that the exact number of circular objects does not matter. Point out that the participants did not create these circular objects. They already existed in the environment and people just found them. They simply chose to notice them and focus their attention on them.

Conduct a quick debriefing. Ask and discuss these types of questions:

- *Did you "cheat" by including parts of noncircular objects?*
- *Did you count the same object twice, as in the case of a round CD and a round hole in the middle of the CD?*
- *Did you treat an oval as a circle, as in the case of the buttons on your cell phone?*
- *Did you count multiple occurrences of the same object, as in the case of all of the periods in a printed handout or all the watches in the room?*

Reassure participants that these behaviors are not cheating. They were just operating at a higher level of vigilance.

Ask participants to find funny events. Say something like this:

Let's now move on to the second part of the exercise. The circle exercise involved scanning your present landscape for a tangible physical element. The next exercise involves scanning your past timescape for an intangible conceptual element.

*Here's how you do it. Close your eyes and think of everything that happened last week. Recall all **funny** things that happened. Choose to find funny things that already happened last week. Be creative in coming up with laughable events. Pretend that you have a remarkable sense of humor and look at your life for comedy materials. Do some creative cheating and put a comic spin on your recent reality. Spend 30 seconds doing this.*

Give additional instructions. After 30 seconds, ask each participant to focus on one of the funniest episodes he or she recalled. Ask the person to make it funnier, if necessary, through creative distortion and exaggeration. Encourage participants to keep working on their funny incidents until they have to burst out laughing. Announce another 30 seconds for this exercise.

Share the humor. After another 30 seconds, ask participants to pair up and share their funny stories with their partners. Recommend that everyone laugh uproariously at the partner's story. Pause for 2 to 4 minutes. Roam around the room eavesdropping on different conversations.

Conduct another debriefing. Share a couple of funnier stories that you overheard. Then ask and discuss these types of questions:

- *Was it easy for you to discover humorous elements in everyday incidents?*

- *How do you think that the ability to laugh at yourself reduces tension?*

- *Think back on this activity. What are some of the humorous elements in the process?*

- *Who are the people you usually share your funny experiences with? What happens when you do this?*

- *Do you have a favorite comedian? How does this person find humor in everyday incidents?*

14
Light, Medium, or Heavy

To people from other cultures, Americans from the United States make too many self-disclosure statements to total strangers. However, I have met people from all around the world who could benefit from the ability to make these types of statements.

Purpose

To encourage participants to make personal statements

Participants

Minimum: 5
Maximum: Any number
Best: 10 to 50
(Participants are divided into teams of 4 to 6 members each.)

Time

15 to 30 minutes

Supplies

- **Stimulus cards.** These cards contain words or phrases that the participants talk about. Create your own packet of about 20 cards to suit your participants and your topic.

  Example: Here are some of the stimulus cards that we used in a workshop on team building: *lemonade, followers, income tax, freeloaders, role, ground rules, goal, waste of time, computers, budget, beeper, midnight, window, money, short people,* and *leadership.* Note that some words are related to the topic and some are irrelevant; some are bland and some are potentially embarrassing.

- Blank paper
- Pens or pencils

Flow

Distribute the game materials. Shuffle the stimulus cards and place them face down in the middle of the table.

Start the game. Ask the first player to pick up the top card and read the stimulus word aloud. This person now has to make a personal statement related to the word that reveals something about herself. This statement should not take more than a minute.

Example:

Greg picks up the card with the stimulus word lemonade *and says: When I was about nine years old, my mother always asked me to get lemonade for my grandfather. I used to spit in the glass before giving him the lemonade because I guess I didn't like my grandfather. When he died recently, he left me a lot of money. I feel very guilty about what I did during those lemonade days.*

Indicate the score. After the statement, each of the other players holds up one, two, or three fingers to indicate how personally revealing the statement was. A light statement receives 1 point. A heavy, emotional, embarrassing statement receives 3 points. Other statements belong to the medium category and receive 2 points. Different players may hold up different numbers of fingers. The speaker counts the total number of fingers and writes it down on her scorecard.

Example:

The four other players find Greg's statement schmaltzy. They each gave him 3 points, for a total of 12.

Permit skipping a word. If a player does not want to talk about a particular stimulus word, he can pass, getting no points for the round. The next participant may then use the skipped card or pick a new card.

Continue the game. Ask the next player to pick up a new stimulus card. Remind all players to keep track of their total scores.

Conclude the game. Depending on the available time, conclude the activity after the third, fourth, or fifth round. Make sure that everyone has an equal number of turns.

Debriefing

Ask participants about their feelings of discomfort in making self-disclosure statements and listening to other people's statements. Use these questions to structure the discussion:

- *How uncomfortable did you feel in making heavy statements?*
- *How uncomfortable did you feel in listening to heavy statements from others?*
- *Did it become easier for you to make (and listen to) heavy statements during the later rounds of the game?*
- *When you were growing up, did your family members make self-disclosure statements or avoid them?*
- *Do your community and workplace encourage self-disclosure statements?*
- *What encourages people to make self-disclosure statements? What discourages people?*
- *When do you think that self-disclosure statements are appropriate and useful? When are they inappropriate and useless?*

15
Flextalk

The ability to present the same message in different ways is a valuable communication skills. Flextalk is an activity that will increase participants' communication flexibility.

Purpose

To increase your communication flexibility

Participants

Minimum: 3
Maximum: Any number
Best: 10 to 30
(Larger numbers of participants can be divided into groups of 3 to 10.)

Time

3 to 5 minutes

Supplies

One Koosh® ball (or any other soft fuzzy ball) for each group

Flow

Begin the activity. Ask participants to stand in a circle. Make a statement and toss a ball to one of the participants. This person catches the ball and immediately makes a different statement that presents the same message. The participant tosses the ball to someone else. This ball-catcher repeats the process.

Eliminate participants. After catching the ball, a participant is eliminated if he or she hesitates for a long time, repeats an earlier statement, or significantly alters the meaning of the message. The game continues until only one participant remains. This participant is the winner.

Example: *In a recent play of Flextalk, my original message was "Shut up!" Here are some of the different versions:*
Please close your mouth.
Kindly abstain from any further oral communication.
I'll choke you if you keep talking!
Have you ever considered the wisdom behind the aphorism, "Silence is golden"?

Stop talking!

You are talking too much. Please give the others an opportunity to participate in the conversation.

Shh!

It's better to keep your mouth shut and have the others wonder if you are stupid than to open your mouth and confirm their suspicions.

16
Sequencing

You can more effectively recall things that make sense to you. Integrating bits of information into meaningful sequences is an essential communication skill. This activity dramatically demonstrates the importance of meaning.

Purpose

To sequence bits of information to increase meaningfulness

Participants

Minimum: 2
Maximum: Any number
Best: 10 to 20
(Participants work individually.)

Time

5 to 7 minutes

Supplies

- The Memory Test handout in two different versions. (Both are at the end of this activity.)
- Paper
- Pencils
- Whistle

Preparation

Make an equal number of copies of the two versions of the handout and mix them up in a random order. Place the handouts printed side down.

Flow

Brief participants. Tell them that you are going to administer a simple memory test. Distribute copies of the handout to all participants and ask them to hold them printed side down until you give instructions.

Conduct the memorization exercise. Tell participants that they will have 40 seconds to memorize the stuff on the back of the page. Blow the whistle to signal the start of the test. After 40 seconds, blow the whistle again to conclude the test. Ask participants to place the test sheet with the printed side down.

Conduct the recall exercise. Distribute blank sheets of paper and a pencil to each participant. Ask them to write a list of *words,* one word per line, in any order, from the material they memorized. Announce a 1-minute time limit. While they are writing the words, take back the test sheets.

Score the recalled words. After 1 minute, blow the whistle and ask participants to exchange their word lists and score them (by giving 1 point for each correct word) as you read this list of words:

Ability
Aliens
Apples
At
By
Green
Have
Just
Sourness
Staring
Strange
Taste
The
To

Identify high-scoring participants. Count down from 14 (the maximum possible score) and locate the top 5 to 10 scores. Keep counting down to give everyone a feel for the distribution of scores.

Reveal the secret. Point out that there were two versions of the memory test sheet, one with a list of words and the other with the same words arranged in a sequence to form a sentence.

Debriefing

Conduct a discussion about why it is easier to recall the sentence than a list of words. Ask questions to help participants conclude that arranging bits of information in an appropriate sequence makes it more meaningful. Discuss the implications of this insight beyond words and sentences to paragraphs, sections, and reports.

Memory Test 1

Memorize the following sentence:

Strange aliens have the ability to taste sourness just by staring at green apples.

Memory Test 2

Memorize the following list of fourteen words:

At
By
To
The
Just
Have
Green
Taste
Aliens
Apples
Staring
Strange
Ability
Sourness

17
Half and Half

As a writer, I spend an enormous amount of time editing, cutting, and revising my articles and books. I am not sure whether all of these excruciating rewrites and alterations improve my material, but I am sure that I have a better understanding and mastery of the content. This simple insight inspired Half and Half.

Purpose

To recall and describe essential features of human performance technology

Participants

Minimum: 6
Maximum: Any number
Best: 10 to 30
(Participants are organized into teams of 2 to 7.)

Time

20 to 30 minutes

Supplies

- Blank pieces of paper
- Pens or pencils

Flow

Brief the players. Explain that you are going to facilitate an activity that will require input from all team members toward the creation of a brief definition of Human Performance Technology.

Form teams. Organize participants into three to five teams of two to seven members each.

Get started. Instruct each team to share what they know about human performance technology, identify the key features, and come up with a definition in exactly sixty-four words—no more, no less. Assign a 5-minute time limit.

Review the definitions. Collect definitions from different teams and read them aloud. Encourage everyone to listen carefully so they can borrow ideas from other people's statements for later use. After reading all definitions, ask individual participants to identify the best statement by raising their hands as you read the statements again. No participant may raise his or her hand more than once nor choose the statement from her own team.

In a recent session, here's the definition from Trish's team:

Human Performance Technology uses a results-based multidisciplinary approach for improving human performance. It takes a total-systems approach and uses a systematic process to identify the gap between the ideal state and the actual state, discover the root causes for this gap, select an appropriate intervention to remove or reduce the impact of the gap, design and develop the selected intervention, and implement it effectively.

Shrink to thirty-two words. Ask teams to rewrite their definition in exactly thirty-two words. In this process, they may borrow ideas from other statements. Suggest that teams reduce the length of their definitions by removing unimportant ideas, superfluous words, and redundant language. Assign a 3-minute time limit.

Here's the condensed definition from Trish's team:

The HPT process involves defining the problem in terms of a performance gap, selecting an intervention to remove the root cause of this gap, designing this intervention, and effectively implementing the intervention.

Reduce by 50 percent. Repeat the process of collecting and reading the thirty-two-word definitions. Select the best definition as before. Now ask teams to reduce their definitions to one-half of its current size (to exactly sixteen words), while retaining the essential features. Encourage teams to leave out secondary ideas instead of merely deleting words. Assign a 2-minute time limit.

Here's the sixteen-word definition from Trish's team:

Use a scientific approach to close the gap between what you want and what you have.

Elegant eight. Repeat the process of collecting, reading, and evaluating the definitions as before. Then ask definitions to reduce the definitions to exactly eight words by dropping all but essential ideas and by tightening up the language. Assign a 2-minute time limit.

None of the earlier definitions from Trish's team was selected as the best one. During this round, the team decided to start from scratch and incorporate ideas borrowed by other successful teams. This is what they came up with:

Improve individual, team, organizational, societal, and global performance.

Final four. After reading and polling the eight-word definitions, ask teams to reduce the definitions to four words. Assign a 1-minute time limit for this round.

Here's what Trish's team came up with:

Systematically improve human performance.

Synthesize the final definition. Invite teams to create their final definitions without any word limits. Encourage them to recall and combine essential ideas and memorable phrases from their earlier versions.

18
Spell and Count

Improv games help us become more spontaneous and teach us to pay attention to others. Several years ago, my friend Alain Rostain taught me an interesting improv activity. Here's my version of that activity.

Purpose

To increase your spontaneity, risk taking, and attending to others

Participants

Minimum: 5
Maximum: Any number
Best: 10 to 20
(Larger groups of participants are divided into groups of 5 to 7.)

Time

10 to 15 minutes

Flow

Set-up. Have each group sit around a table or stand close to each other.

Spelling. Ask group members take turns spelling the word *TEAMWORK*, each person contributing the next letter during his or her turn.

Counting. After the group completes this spelling task, ask the members to count from 1 to 10, each person saying the next number when it is his or her turn.

Counting and spelling. Now ask the group members to count from 1 to 10 and spell the word *TEAMWORK*, both at the same time. Each member should contribute *either* the next number *or* the next letter during his or her turn.

Final challenge. After the group has completed this activity, introduce the final challenge. As before, the group members have to count and spell at the same time—with these additional restrictions:

- Group members should close their eyes.

- Group members cannot say anything other than appropriate numbers and letters.

- Any member of the group can spontaneously begin the activity by saying the first number or letter.

- Members of the group should *not* take sequential turns. Anyone should feel free to jump in with the next number or letter.
- More than one person cannot say the same number or letter. If this happens, the activity has to begin from the beginning. For example, if Alan says "One" and both Barb and Chuck say "Two," the group has to start all over again.

Concluding. Wait until the group succeeds so you can end the exercise on a big cheer.

Debriefing

Conduct a discussion using appropriate questions to elicit the following guidelines for active listening:

- *Tune into the group to make your team look good.*
- *Lead and follow. Talk and listen (instead of talking and waiting to talk).*
- *Let go of the need to control.*

19
Fast Work

During recent months, I have been exploring the use of crossword puzzles in training sessions. Here's an interesting jolt that incorporates a crossword puzzle.

Purpose

- To explore our tendency to compare our performance with the performances of others
- To discuss the impact of such comparisons on our own self-esteem

Participants

Minimum: 5
Maximum: Any number
Best: 10 to 30
(Participants "play" individually.)

Time

15 to 20 minutes

Supplies

- Handout, Crossword Puzzle. For more information, see the *Preparation* section below.
- Timer
- Whistle

Preparation

Make copies of the crossword puzzle. There are two versions (not labeled as such) of the puzzle: easy and hard. Make one copy of the hard version for every fifth player. Make enough copies of the easy version for the other players. Mix these copies so that the hard version is distributed to random players.

Flow

Brief the players. Explain to them that this activity is designed to explore the impact of mindfulness on players' performance speed. Players will be racing to be the first to solve the crossword puzzle. Ask players to put themselves in a positive frame of mind and to concentrate on solving their puzzles. Also instruct players to stand up as soon as they have solved the entire puzzle.

Distribute crossword puzzles. Give everyone a copy of a puzzle. Start the timer and ask players to rapidly solve the puzzle.

Recognize fast solvers. As players stand up one by one to indicate that they have solved the puzzle, announce the time they took and congratulate them.

Stop the activity. When the majority of players have solved the puzzle, blow the whistle and ask everyone to stop working on the puzzle. Congratulate the players who are standing up and ask them to sit down.

Read the solution. Ask everyone to check their answers as you read them. Read these answers (without reading any clues):

1 across: cat
2 across: ship
5 across: three
6 across: bed
7 across: ball
8 across: run
9 across: house
11 across: green
12 across: year
1 down: cash
3 down: hamburger
4 down: meeting
5 down: tea
7 down: book
10 down: sky

Point out that there are fifteen words in the puzzle and so a perfect score will be 15 points. Ask players to count the number of correct words and write down their scores.

Debriefing

Begin a debriefing discussion. Encourage players to discuss these questions:

- *How do you think the first players to solve the puzzle feel about their performance?*

- *How do you think the players who did not solve the puzzle feel about their performance?*

- *How do you think the first players to solve the puzzle feel about those who did not solve the entire puzzle?*

- *How do you think those who did not solve the entire puzzle feel about those who did?*

- *What is the impact of other players' performance on your self-image?*

- *Some people solve crossword puzzles regularly, while others are unfamiliar with them. How do you think that this difference impacted on the differences in people's performance?*

Reveal the secret about two versions of clues. Explain that a few players received a difficult set of clues. Ask players to read the easy and difficult versions of clues for a few of the words.

Continue the debriefing. Ask questions similar to these and encourage discussion:

- *How do you think the first players to solve the puzzle now feel about their performance?*

- *How do you think the players who did not solve the entire puzzle feel about their performance?*

- *How did the knowledge of the two sets of clues affect your self-image?*

- *How do players' behaviors and feelings reflect similar behaviors and feelings in the workplace?*

- *Did your self-image suffer damage in the workplace just because you were slower than your co-workers?*

- *What is the workplace equivalent of receiving easy and difficult clues?*

- *What if the first player to solve the puzzle received a cash prize? How would that have impacted other players' feelings?*

- *What if I never revealed the secret about the two versions of the clues? How would this have affected your self-image?*

- *What if only one player received the difficult set of clues and everyone else finished solving their puzzles?*

- *What if we had teams solve the puzzle and one team had the difficult set of clues and the other teams had the easy ones? How would this have affected the unity among team members?*

Summarize major insights from the debriefing discussions. Ask players how they would apply their new insights to their workplace performance.

Crossword Puzzle

Across

1. An animal that says "Meow"

2. Ocean liner

5. Two plus one

6. Furniture used for sleeping

7. A round object that's used in different games

8. Move on your feet, faster than when you walk

9. Building in which you live

11. Color of growing grass

12. Twelve months make up a _____

Down

1. Check, charge, or _____

3. Popular fast-food item in the U.S.

4. Coming together to discuss things

5. Coffee, _____, or milk

7. Bound copy of printed pages

10. Blue region surrounding the earth

Crossword Puzzle

Across

1. Feline mammal

2. Transport commercially

5. A prime number that is greater by a unit than two

6. The ground under a body of water

7. A pitch that is not in the strike zone

8. An unbroken series of events

9. Aristocratic family line

11. Naive and easily deceived

12. Time taken by a planet in the solar system to make a complete revolution around the sun

Down

1. Money in the form of bills or coins

3. Resident of a port city in Germany

4. Coming together for business, social, or religious purposes

5. An eastern Asian evergreen shrub having fragrant glossy leaves that are dried to prepare a hot beverage

7. To arrange for tickets in advance

10. The celestial region

PART III
Sales and Marketing

20
Best Slogan

In our training sessions, one of the reasons that we seldom ask participants for creative responses is that it is difficult to select the best response. If we assume that popularity is generally related to creativity, we can use participants to take responsibility for evaluating responses and selecting the best one. When I incorporated this idea into some of my training games, I was impressed by the additional benefit of how much participants learned in the process of jointly evaluating different responses. Best Slogan uses this simple idea.

Purpose

To come up with a slogan that captures essential elements of the organization's mission

Participants

Minimum: 6
Maximum: Any number
Best: 10 to 20
(Participants work organized into teams of 4 to 7.)

Time

15 to 30 minutes

Supplies

- Index cards
- Pens or pencils
- Timer
- Whistle

Flow

Brief participants. Ask everyone to review the organization's mission statement and identify the key concepts. Pretending to be highly paid advertisement copy writers, ask each participant to write a catchy slogan that captures the essence of the organization's mission. Distribute blank index cards to each participant and announce a 3-minute time limit.

Provide additional instructions. At the end of 3 minutes, ask participants to stop writing. Ask them to write a four-digit identification number on the other side of their cards. Participants should remember this number so they can identify their cards later.

Form teams. Organize participants into teams of four to seven members each. Seat each team around a table. Ask someone at each team to collect the slogans from team members and shuffle the packet of cards.

Exchange and evaluate. Give the packet of slogan cards from the first team to the second one, from the second team to the third one, and so on, giving the cards from the last team to the first one. Ask members of each team to collaboratively review the slogans and select the best one, using whatever criteria they want. Announce a 5-minute time limit.

Conclude the evaluation activity. At the end of 5 minutes, ask each team to read the slogans, reserving the final spot for the one they rated as the best slogan. After all teams have read the slogans, ask each team to re-read the best slogan and identify the author by reading the number on the back of the card. Ask these people to stand up and lead a round of applause.

Debriefing

Conduct a debriefing discussion. Briefly comment on the slogans, identifying the key points. Discuss the following types of questions:

- *How does the process of creating a slogan contribute to better understanding the mission of our organization?*

- *What are the similarities among the slogans? What are the differences?*

- *What do these similarities and differences indicate about different elements of our mission?*

21
The World's Worst

I have been using improv games as a training tool for several years. One of my favorite improv games is The World's Worst, which involves participants acting out comical blunders of people in different professions. For a long time, I merely used this game as a fun energizer. Recently I discovered a powerful instructional application of this game for sales training.

Purpose

To identify and apply effective sales behaviors

Participants

Minimum: 10
Maximum: Any number
Best: 10 to 30
(Participants are divided into pairs.)

Time

15 to 20 minutes

Supplies

A doormat or a piece of carpet placed in front of the room. (This serves as the "platform.")

Flow

Invite actors. Explain that you need a few willing volunteers for an improv theater activity. Point out that the activity will be a lot of fun.

Position the actors. Ask them to stand behind the platform, facing the audience.

Brief the actors. Explain that the actors are to portray the world's worst salespeople. Present the following instructions, in your own words:

I will describe different sales situations.

Any actor who is ready to portray the blundering behavior of the world's worst salesperson in this situation should step on the platform and act it out. This portrayal should be brief and comical.

Actors don't have to take turns; whoever feels ready to step on the platform should do so. The same actor may take more than one turn.

After a suitable number of portrayals of this situation, I will call out another sales situation. Actors will repeat the same procedure. I will continue the game until you have explored a wide variety of sales situations.

Describe the first situation. Use a phrase or a short sentence. Remind the actors that anyone who wants to act out the behavior of the world's worst salesperson in this situation should step on the platform.

Recently, we played The World's Worst Salesperson with a group of financial-service professionals. The first situation that I called out was greeting the customer.

Model if necessary. After a reasonable time, if no actor steps on the platform, you do it. Demonstrate a suitable (but not too brilliant) portrayal. Then wait for the other actors to do their stuff. Applaud each portrayal.

With my recent group, I did not have to give a demonstration. The first couple of actors immediately stepped up on the platform and came up with obnoxious statements such as this:

Hey, let's not waste time with small talk. How about signing this order form right now?

Move on to the next situation. Describe this sales situation briefly. Wait for the actors to do their portrayals.

Continue the activity. Call out new and different sales situations from your list. For a change of pace, invite audience members (and the actors) to suggest other situations.

Conclude the activity. Stop the drama when you feel that you have covered a sufficiently diverse set of situations. Thank the actors and lead a round of applause.

Debriefing

Explain the rationale. Point out that it is more engaging to come up with portrayals of dysfunctional behaviors than desirable ones. A powerful creativity technique called *Double Reversals* is based on coming up with negative ideas and then modifying them to come up positive ones.

Convert the negative portrayals into positive guidelines. Ask participants to brainstorm a list of Do's and Don'ts based on the earlier portrayals.

22
Supply Chain

I designed this game as an introduction to U.S.-type entrepreneurship for people in countries that are newly embracing free-market capitalism.

Purpose

To explore the relationship among suppliers, employees, and customers

Participants

Minimum: 6
Maximum: 100
Best: 20 to 40
(Participants are divided into three subgroups.)

Time

20 to 30 minutes

Supplies

- Handout, Instructions for Group 1
- Handout, Instructions for Group 2
- Handout, Instructions for Group 3
- A large number of index cards (cut in half)
- Play money
- Blank pieces of paper
- Pens or pencils
- Timer
- Whistle

Set-Up

Assign Group 1 to one end of the room and Group 3 to the opposite end. Place Group 2 in the middle.

Flow

Organize three groups. Divide the participants into three approximately equal-sized groups. Send the groups to the appropriate areas of the room.

Brief the players. Present these three pieces of information:

- Each group has different instructions.

- Each participant is working independently and competing with other members of his group.

- Members of Groups 1 and 3 may not interact directly with each other.

Distribute the materials. Give $200 in play money to each member of Group 3, along with the instruction sheet. Give $5 to each member of Group 2, along with the instruction sheet. Give fifty index card halves to each member of Group 1, along with the instruction sheet.

Ask the participants to read their instructions. Visit each group and answer any questions.

Announce the beginning of the game. Blow the whistle and start the timer. Let the participants play the game for 5 minutes.

Stop the game. Blow the whistle at the end of the 5-minute period.

Identify the winners. Ask members of the first two groups to count their money. Ask the members of Group 3 to count their cards. In each group, identify the winner and congratulate him or her.

Debriefing

Link the activity to the customer-supplier chain. Relate the activity to the workplace. Use additional questions to go beyond the experience to retail sales activities in general. Ask the following types of questions to get the discussion going:

- *Members of Group 1 are wholesalers. What is the primary aim of this group in the game? What is the aim of wholesalers in the real world?*

- *Which member of Group 1 won the game? What strategies did the person use? Are these similar to real-world strategies?*

- *Did members of Group 1 try to cooperate among themselves? Is it possible to cooperate in this situation? If Group 1 members cooperated with each other, what could they have achieved?*

- *The suggested retail price was $1. Did anyone try to sell the cards at a lower (or higher price)? If so, what was the motive for this move?*

- *Do you know what happened to the cards after you sold them to members of Group 2?*

- *How have the Internet and globalization changed the way wholesalers operate?*

- *Members of Group 2 are retailers. What is the primary aim of this group in the game? What is the aim of retailers in the real world?*

- *Which member of Group 2 won the game? What strategies did this person use? Are these similar to real-world strategies?*

- *Did members of Group 2 try to cooperate among themselves? Is it possible to cooperate in this situation? If Group 2 members cooperated with each other, what could they have achieved?*

- *Did anyone try to buy or sell the cards at a lower (or higher) price than the suggested price? If so, what was the motive for this move?*

- *Do you know what happened to the cards after you sold them to members of Group 3?*

- *How have the Internet and globalization changed the way retailers operate?*

- *Members of Group 3 are customers. What is the primary aim of this group in the game? What is the aim of customers in the real world?*

- *Which member of Group 3 won the game? What strategies did this person use? Are these similar to real-world strategies?*

- *Did members of Group 3 try to cooperate among themselves? Is it possible to cooperate in this situation? If Group 3 members cooperated with each other, what could they have achieved?*

- *Did anyone try to buy cards at a lower (or higher) price than the suggested price? If so, what was the motive for this move?*

- *Do you know where members of Group 3 got their cards?*

- *How have the Internet and globalization changed the way customers behave?*

- *If you were to play the game again, what strategies would you use if you were a wholesaler? retailer? customer?*

Instruction Sheet for Group 1

All members of your group have the same instructions. The two other groups have different instructions.

Your goal is to make more money than any other member of your group.

You have a large supply of index-card halves. Sign your name on each card half.

You can sell the signed cards to any member of Group 2. You cannot sell the cards to anyone else. The suggested retail price is $1 per card.

You may sell up to five cards to a single person at any given time. You may not sell more cards to the same person until you have sold some cards to someone else.

The game will end after 5 minutes. At that time, if you have the most money in Group 1, you win the game.

Instruction Sheet for Group 2

All members of your group have the same instructions. The two other groups have different instructions.

Your goal is to make more money than any other member of your group.

You begin the activity with $5.

Your job is to buy cards from the members of Group 1, sign your name under the signature on each card, and sell the cards to the members of Group 3.

The suggested purchase price of the cards from Group 1 is $1 each. The suggested selling price to Group 3 is $2 each.

You may sell only one card at a time to any Group 3 member. You may not sell another card to the same person until you have sold a card to someone else.

The game will end after 5 minutes. At that time, if you have the most money in Group 2, you win the game.

Instruction Sheet for Group 3

All members of your group have the same instructions. The two other groups have different instructions.

Your goal is to collect more cards than any other member of your group.

You begin the activity with $200. You may use this money to buy cards from the members of Group 2.

Each card costs $2. Make sure that each card has two different signatures, one below the other.

The game will end after 5 minutes. At that time, if you have the most cards in Group 3, you win the game.

23
Influence

After talking to an obnoxious telephone salesperson, I had an interesting insight: I behave in an equally obnoxious fashion whenever I am trying to influence others. I am now going to influence you to use a brief activity based on this insight.

Purpose

To increase participants' level of self-awareness about influencing techniques they use

Participants

Minimum: 3
Maximum: 10
Best: 3 to 5
(Participants work individually.)

Time

99 seconds

Supplies

- Blank pieces of paper
- Pens or pencils

Flow

Brief participants. Explain that you are going to ask an open-ended question. Instruct participants to rapidly write down as many answers as they can within the next 25 seconds. Encourage participants to write down the answers that pop into their minds.

Ask the first question: "What techniques irritate you when other people try to influence you?" Remind them to write an immediate answer. Pause for 25 seconds while participants write their answers.

Ask participants to turn the pieces of paper over. Tell them that you are going to ask another question. As before, encourage them to rapidly write as many answers as possible within the next 25 seconds.

Ask the second question: "What techniques do you use when trying to influence other people?" Do not point out that this question is related to the first one. Pause for 25 seconds while participants write their answers.

Ask participants to compare the two answers. Point out that the questions are related to each other. Invite participants to raise their hands if they never used influencing techniques that they find personally irritating. (Usually, very few people will raise their hands.)

Reflect on the inconsistencies. Explain that most participants find an interesting similarity between what they *don't* want from others and what they give others. Using a helpful tone (rather than a righteous tone), ask participants to figure out why this inconsistency exists.

24
Persuasion

This activity is designed for use with large groups. It serves dual purposes through the content (of organizational culture change) and the process (of persuasion).

Purpose

Content focus: To explore critical factors associated with increasing organizational innovation

Process focus: To explore critical factors associated with effective facilitation

Participants

Minimum: 20
Maximum: Any number
Best: 30 to 100
(Participants are divided into pairs.)

Time

30 minutes to 1 hour

Supplies

- Questionnaire (two copies to each participant, one for pretest and another for post-test)
- Role Assignments (four different versions, each printed on paper of a different color)
- Timer
- Whistle

Flow

Administer a pretest. Tell participants that you are going to give them a 30-second questionnaire. Distribute copies of the questionnaire to the participants. Ask them to select one of the two positions for each item. Collect the completed questionnaires and give them to your co-facilitator. If you don't have a co-facilitator, set the questionnaires aside.

Assign roles. Distribute equal numbers of the four *Role Assignments* to participants so that each participant receives one assignment. Ask participants to spend a couple of minutes reading the instructions. In taking on their assigned roles, remind participants to set aside their personal positions.

Set up meeting areas. Assign four corners of the room to participants with the four different Role Assignments. For example, point to the northeast side of the room as the location for people who are assigned the structural change position. Assign the diagonally opposite (southwest) side for participants who are assigned the training position. Assign participants with the opposing positions (deterministic versus opportunistic) related to the second topic (implementation) to the other two diagonally opposite corners of the room.

Form groups. Ask participants with the same role assignment to move to their assigned areas and form informal groups of five to ten members each. All participants with the same role assignment do *not* have to form a single group.

Develop strategies. Ask participants in each group to discuss the roles assigned to them and come up with strategies for persuading others in the room to agree with their positions. Here are some suggested strategies:

- Come up with a clear and compelling message to be delivered to the others.
- Develop logical arguments in support of your position.
- Share personal anecdotes in support of your position.

Announce a 7-minute time limit for this strategy-development period.

Conversation period. At the end of 7 minutes, blow the whistle and announce the end of strategy-development period. Ask participants to hold conversations with people from the other areas of the room on a one-on-one basis and try to persuade them to accept their positions. Suggest that participants should talk to others who were working on a different topic before trying to persuade people with the opposite position on their own topics. Encourage participants to conduct a discussion rather than delivering their messages and moving away in search of the next listener. Announce a 10-minute time limit for this phase of the activity.

Administer a post-test. After 10 minutes, blow the whistle to signal the end of the conversation period. Distribute copies of the questionnaire (the same one that you used as the pretest) and ask participants to select one of the two positions for each item, as before. After a suitable pause, collect the completed questionnaires and quickly count the number of people who selected each of the four alternatives.

Debriefings

Debrief the results. Announce the pretest results related to the first topic in terms of the number of people selecting structural change and training. Ask participants to predict whether this distribution would have changed in the post-test. Encourage participants to make a guess and to share their reasoning. Announce the actual post-test results for the first topic. Conduct a discussion of the differences (or the lack of differences) between the pretest and the post-test.

Repeat the procedure with the second topic.

Debrief the process. Ask participants to think of the strategies that they used to persuade the others. Conduct a discussion on the persuasion process using these types of questions:

- *Did you use the same strategy to persuade everyone or did you modify the strategy from one person to the next? If you changed your strategy, what were the reasons for doing so?*

- *Did you stay with the original strategy developed by your group or did you change it? If you changed the strategy, why did you do that?*

- *Was your pretest choice different from the position assigned to you? How did this difference impact your persuasion strategy?*

- *If you had to convince others of a position that was different from your initial position, did you end up changing your own mind?*

- *What types of strategies did other people use to persuade you? Which strategies were effective? Which ones were ineffective?*

- *Did you ever try to persuade someone who had the opposing point of view on the same topic as yours? If so, what strategies did you use? What were the results?*

- *Did you have a real conversation with the other people you met? Did you actively listen to their messages?*

- *Did you change your choice on the other topic between the pretest and the post-test? If yes, what persuaded you?*

- *Did you meet two people who had the opposite positions on the other topic? Which of the other two did a better job of convincing you?*

Organizational Culture Change Questionnaire

Topic 1: Which of these is the more effective way to make our organization more innovative?

   Position 1: Make structural changes. Alter reporting relationships in the organization chart and modify the ways employees solve problems and resolve conflict.

   Position 2: Provide training. Help employees master new skills, knowledge, and attitudes related to organizational innovation.

Topic 2: Which of these is the more effective way to implement our design for increased organizational innovation?

   Position 1: Take a deterministic approach. Have a specific plan and stick to it.

   Position 2: Take an opportunistic approach. Be flexible and depart from the plan whenever appropriate.

Role Assignment 1

Make structural changes. Alter reporting relationships in the organizational chart and modify the ways employees solve problems and resolve conflict.

Play the role of a person who holds this position when trying to make our organization more innovative. Set aside your personal position if it is different from this position.

During the conversation period, your mission is to persuade others to accept this position.

Role Assignment 2

Provide training. Help employees master new skills, knowledge, and attitudes related to organizational innovation.

Play the role of a person who holds this position when trying to make our organization more innovative. Set aside your personal position if it is different from this position.

During the conversation period, your mission is to persuade others to accept this position.

Role Assignment 3

Take a deterministic approach. Have a specific plan and stick to it.

Play the role of a person who holds this position as the most effective way for implementing our design for increased organizational innovation. Set aside your personal position if it is different from this position.

During the conversation period, your mission is to persuade others to take this position.

Role Assignment 4

Take an opportunistic approach. Be flexible and depart from the plan whenever appropriate.

Play the role of a person who holds this position as the most effective way for implementing our design for increased organizational innovation. Set aside your personal position if it is different from this position.

During the conversation period, your mission is to persuade others to take this position.

25
Hot Seat

Recently, I had the pleasure of watching a Peace Corps volunteer calmly and non-defensively answer a bunch of provocative questions from a local crowd in a developing country: "Why are American women so loose?" "Why does every American have two cars?" Her effective performance suggested a way of training employees on how to respond to questions about their organizations.

Purpose

To provide calm and honest answers to questions about your organization

Participants

Minimum: 5
Maximum: Any number
Best: 10 to 30
(Participants are divided into teams of 5.)

Time

8 to 15 minutes

Supplies

Handout, Sample List of Questions, one copy for each participant

Flow

Organize teams. Ask participants to form themselves into teams of five members each. Distribute left-over participants to different teams so some teams have six members. Ask members in each team to place their chairs in a circular arrangement and sit facing each other.

 Brief participants. Explain that the object of the activity is to think on your feet and answer unexpected questions quickly, calmly, and truthfully. Invite participants to suggest some guidelines for doing this, but do not spend too much time in getting ready. Distribute copies of the handout and explain that these are sample questions. Point out that some questions are neutral, while others are provocative. Explain that participants can select, modify, and use any of these questions or make up their own questions that are pertinent to the organization.

Begin the activity. In each group, ask the tallest person to take the first turn to answer questions. Explain that he is in the hot seat for the next 2 minutes. Ask other participants to begin shouting out questions (making sure that they are pertinent to the organization) at him at a rapid rate. Ask the person to give accurate answers in a non-defensive manner. Tell the others that they do not have to take turns or wait for the complete answer before piling up more questions.

Repeat the activity. Blow the whistle at the end of 2 minutes. Ask another participant in each team to occupy the hot seat and ask the others to continue firing questions as before. Encourage participants to repeat the same question from time to time. Continue this round for 2 minutes. Blow the whistle and switch to the next hot-seat person. Repeat until everyone has had an opportunity to answer questions.

Debriefing

Discuss tough questions. Assemble all teams for a debriefing discussion. Invite participants to identify the toughest questions they had to face. Encourage other participants to recall and suggest suitable answers. Add your suggestions.

Discuss guidelines. Ask participants to suggest guidelines for maintaining calmness and objectivity while being bombarded with questions, including hostile ones. Encourage participants to base their suggestions on what they did, what they observed other people do, and what second thoughts they had. Add your own guidelines whenever appropriate.

Sample List of Questions

1. How do you obtain feedback from your customers?

2. Is it true that you are planning to close down your retail facilities in small towns? What is your justification for this decision?

3. Why does your testing procedure involve cruelty to animals?

4. Why are you outsourcing many of your jobs and firing your employees?

5. What type of benefits do your full-time employees receive?

6. How long have you been a publicly owned company?

7. Is it true that you are interfering with the political affairs of small Asian nations?

8. What is your policy toward outsourcing?

9. Why do you sell products manufactured in sweat shops in developing nations?

10. What are your plans for the near future?

11. What is your return policy?

12. Why are you employing undocumented aliens?

13. Why are your headquarters located in the Cayman Islands?

14. Who is your current CEO?

15. Why are you exporting your design functions overseas?

16. What community projects do you support?

17. How do you plan to handle the competition from China?

18. When was your organization founded?

19. How many employees do you have?

20. How can young people get a job in your company?

21. How do you ensure that poor people can purchase your products?

22. What was your total profit last year?

23. What percentage of your employees are from minority groups?

24. What is your profit margin?

25. What is your policy about environmental protection?

26. Why don't you have any women among your top managers?

27. Why do you discriminate against women?

28. What is your best product?

29. Why does your CEO make so much money when the employees are paid so little?

30. Why don't you have a customer hotline?

PART IV
Teamwork

26
FCC

In working with case studies, I discovered that people who write up the cases learn much more than people who analyze ready-made cases. Also, from an instructional point of view, creating fictional cases is as effective—and more fun—than creating real cases. The FCC acronym stands for Fictional Case Creation. That is exactly what you do in this activity.

Purpose

To recognize and apply the four stages in the development of a team

Participants

Minimum: 10
Maximum: 100
Best: 15 to 30.
(Participants are divided into 5 or more teams, each with 2 to 7 members.)

Time

1 to 2 hours

Supplies

- Handout, Four Stages of Team Development, one copy for each participant
- Handout, Sample Case 1: The Quality Team, one copy for each participant
- Handout, Sample Case 2: Alien Contact, one copy for each participant
- One flip chart for each team
- Felt-tipped markers
- Timer
- Whistle
- Masking tape

Flow

Distribute the handouts. Give a copy of each of the three handouts to each participant. Ask them to take a couple of minutes to scan the handouts.

Brief the participants. After a suitable pause, blow the whistle and explain how the handouts will support the performance of a task. Explain that participants will form teams and write fictional case studies about the development of different teams. The handout on the stages of team development will provide the plot for the realistic piece of fiction they will be creating. The two sample case studies provide two very different examples of the fictional case studies. Both case studies are from earlier teams of typical participants. They are not meant to be perfect examples of what is required of the teams today.

Form teams. Ask participants to create five teams of approximately equal size. It does not matter if some teams have one more member than the others. Ask team members to stand around a flip chart and introduce themselves to each other.

Ask teams to write the prologue. Tell each team to provide the context for the fictional case study by writing a prologue. Recommend that they include in this prologue answers to the what, why, where questions related to team by specifying the mandate for the team, the organizational setting, and the number and nature of its members. Invite participants to review the prologue sections of the two sample cases. Suggest a limit of one flip-chart page and announce a 7-minute time limit for this activity.

Ask teams to move to the next flip chart. After 6 minutes, blow the whistle and announce a 1-minute warning. After 7 minutes, blow the whistle to indicate the end of the activity. Ask participants to emotionally detach themselves from the prologue that they created and move to the next team's flip chart with an open mind. (The last team moves to the first team's flip chart.)

Ask teams to write Chapter 1. Suggest to the participants that they forget the earlier prologue they created and carefully study the new prologue on the flip chart they moved to. Explain that each team is going to write the first chapter of the fictional case study dealing with interesting details of the forming stage in the development of the team described in this prologue. Invite participants to review the first chapters in the two sample cases. Suggest a limit of one flip-chart page for this chapter and announce a 7-minute time limit for this activity.

Repeat the procedure for Chapter 2. After 6 minutes, blow the whistle and announce a 1-minute warning. After 7 minutes, blow the whistle to indicate the end of the activity. As before, rotate the teams to the next teams' flip charts. Explain that each team will now write the second chapter to continue the story in progress on their new flip chart. Before they begin their creative procedure, each team has to carefully read the earlier prologue and first chapter to ensure smooth continuity. Recommend that teams review the description of the *storming* stage in the four-stages handout as well as the second chapters in the two sample cases. Announce the page limit and a new time limit of 10 minutes.

Continue the procedure. Conclude the second-chapter activity after 10 minutes. Repeat the same procedure for the third chapter (*norming*) and the fourth chapter (*performing*).

Conclude the activity. After the completion of the fourth chapter, ask each team to post all five flip-chart pages on some convenient location of the wall. Invite all teams to walk around the gallery and read the different case studies, paying particular attention to how the teams integrated the five different contributions.

Debriefing

Ask teams to examine the stages in their own development. After a suitable pause, assemble all participants back for a debriefing discussion. Briefly recap details of the four stages in team development and discuss how they are manifested in the five different cases. Now ask participants to apply these four stages to the development of their FCC team today. Ask and discuss these two questions:

- *What stage of development is your team in?*
- *What happened to your team during earlier stages of development?*

Follow up the activity. Tell participants that you will type up today's fictional case studies and post them all on a website. (Be sure to follow up on this promise.)

Four Stages of Team Development

In 1965, B.W. Tuckman, who had been studying the behavior of small groups, published a model that suggested that all teams go through four distinct stages in their development:

Forming. The first stage in a team's development is *forming*. During this stage, the team members are unsure about what they are doing. Their focus is on understanding the team's goal and their role. They worry about whether the other team members will accept them. Team members frequently look for clarification from their leader.

Storming. The second stage in a team's development is *storming*. During this stage, the team members try to get organized. This stage is marked by conflict among the members and between the members and the leader. Through this conflict, the team attempts to define itself.

Norming. The third stage in a team's development is *norming*. This stage follows storming, after the team members have succeeded in resolving their conflicts. They now feel more secure with one another and with their leader. They effectively negotiate the structure of the team and the division of labor.

Performing. The fourth stage in a team's development is *performing*. During this stage the team members behave in a mature fashion and focus on accomplishing their goals. This stage is marked by direct, two-way communication among the team members.

Sample Case 1: The Quality Team

(Created by Steve, Sara, Les, Matt, and Raja)

Prologue

The small government agency suddenly had a need to create "quality teams." A functionally diverse, yet surprisingly intelligent team was recruited from various units of the agency. The team was given a mandate to better the workflow and the *esprit de corps* of the agency.

Chapter 1. Forming

Some problems arose immediately—what does it mean to *better the work flow*? How could they improve the *esprit de corps* of the agency? One group within the team felt that *bettering the workflow* simply meant speeding up the process, so that the end results could come more quickly. Another group thought that it meant simplifying the tasks of people who do the actual work. Nobody seemed to agree on how to improve *esprit de corps*.

Chapter 2. Storming

The team's frequent bickering suggested the exact opposite of better workflow and improved *esprit de corps!* The team agreed to meet weekly, but that seemed to be all they agreed on. Arlene was appointed committee lead by the agency's director. However, her emails went unread and phone calls went unreturned. The customer service officer on the team turned his back on the fiscal officer whenever she said something. Arlene began the meeting.

"Ladies and gentlemen," she said, "we simply have to move forward. I am going to make some assignments, and I need you to be ready to report on them at next week's meetings." The computer technician muttered something to the customer service officer, who snickered.

"What was that?" Arlene asked.

"You might as well know now," he replied. "The rumor is that the only reason you are leading this team is because you're sleeping with the director. People are pretty unhappy about it."

Arlene took a deep breath. "First," she said, "those rumors are untrue. Second, I was appointed to take the lead here, and I will expect these assignments to be carried out."

She paused for a minute. The team hadn't been this quiet since it was formed. Everyone was looking intently away from anyone else.

"Since we have practiced some unhealthy behaviors," Arlene continued, "let's set some ground rules for our team behavior."

Chapter 3. Norming

Setting up ground rules, agreeing to live by them, and then living by them—these turned out to be different things. At the next meeting, Arlene decided to address this personal and highly inaccurate belief about her rise to power. She kicked off the meeting by saying flatly that the rumor was not true. Then through an open dialogue, people started to actually believe Arlene had been maligned. To close the meeting, the team reviewed its purpose and promised each other to support the goal and move forward.

Chapter 4. Performing

So it was that after getting off to a very bad start, the team actually started working on their task. Things weren't perfect—they had their share of problems and disagreements later on—but everyone respected Arlene and bought in to the importance of the task and to the importance of openness about their problems.

Sample Case 2: Alien Contact

(Created by Steve, Sara, Les, Matt, and Raja)

Prologue

Aliens have sent a radio message to Earth, announcing that their spaceship will come to Earth in seven days. You have been chosen as part of a team to brainstorm ideas and suggestions for the President of the United States. Your team is to start from the assumption that the aliens will be hostile and decide what we should be doing.

Chapter 1. Forming

Each team member is a recognized expert in a different field. The team includes a physicist, a military strategist, a medical doctor, a systems engineer, and an anthropologist. An artificial intelligence facilitator is also part of the group, as is common at this time. Almost immediately, the military strategist asked the team members themselves about their perception of the situation. Within 15 minutes two patterns of responses became apparent: *defensive first-strike* versus *dialogue*. The military strategist then asked the group to appoint the anthropologist as leader.

Chapter 2. Storming

The military strategist's suggestion prompted an immediate debate.

"Why are you suggesting we let Arthur, the anthropologist, be our leader?" asked John Richter, MD. "Leadership should be based on qualifications, not appointment."

"Wait a minute," interjected the Ken Caulton, the physicist. "Certainly we need a more thorough decision-making process that includes more than just qualifications. I have twenty-five years of experience, and I am highly regarded in the field of theoretical astrophysics."

"Hold on, hold on," Arthur Johnson, the anthropologist, shouted, "We have only two hours to submit our recommendations to the President. We can't waste valuable time with this type of bickering."

Chapter 3. Norming

"Arthur's right," the systems engineer said softly. "We should prioritize our tasks. Do we all agree that submitting a recommendation is our highest priority? Good. How can we select a leader quickly, then, given the differences in our opinions that we've just witnessed?"

The discussion was short: the team selected the artificial intelligence facilitator to guide the meeting.

Chapter 4. Performing

With the guidance of this facilitative robot, team members were able to maneuver around each other's egos and see the contributions different people were making. The anthropologist demonstrated a keen understanding of interracial communications and helped the team decide what actions might appear hostile, and which might appear friendly, to a culture with no common references to planet Earth. The MD added some speculation about biological functions that the aliens might have in common with humans. General Richter was firm in his first-strike conviction.

"Are you all willing to gamble the life of everyone on Earth that these alien creatures are not hostile? We have to assume they have been watching us for some time now, with their superior technology. Bloody their noses now and they'll respect our strength when we contact them."

Eventually, a funny thing happened. History, normally doomed to repeat itself, became the guiding principle for the group's decision. Arthur suggested that the team look at past conflicts. At no point in history had a first strike in the name of potential self-defense led to anything good.

The physicist suggested that the President's group must attempt communication first. "If we don't hear from them, then perhaps a first strike is suggested. But how can we in good conscience attack a group of people without fully understanding their motives? What makes us right in that case? What makes us good? First blood goes against the values of our planet."

The military strategist harrumphed. "Is it better to go against a stupid value and stay alive, or to live by a set of values and die?"

The physicist said, "Of course, it is better to be alive, but we are more than drones set to survive at all cost. We have a morality that we have claimed makes us more than just another species of mammal."

And the debate continued for several hours, culminating in a high-level strategy that all on the team could support. And the military strategist and physicist became best friends.

27
Teamwork Concepts

Your brain remembers pictures more clearly and for a longer period of time than it remembers words. Teamwork Concepts makes you draw pictures and interpret them. The game also requires an interesting combination of cooperation and competition among the players.

Purpose

To review and integrate teamwork concepts and principles

Participants

Minimum: 4
Maximum: Any number
Best: 10 to 20
(Participants are divided into groups of 4 to 7.)

Time

15 minutes to 1 hour

Supplies

- 20 to 30 game cards related to teamwork. Each card has a word, a phrase, **or** a sentence.

  Sample game cards:

  Word: Facilitator

  Phrase: Stages of development

  Sentence: There is no "I" in teamwork.
- Paper and pencils
- Timer

Flow

Artist. Select one player to be the first "artist." Ask this artist to pick a game card, read it silently, and keep it hidden from the other players.

Timer. Ask a player to set the timer for 1 minute and start it.

Task. Ask the artist to draw a series of pictures on blank sheets of paper to convey the message. The artist must not use any text or numbers.

Guessing. While the artist is rapidly sketching the pictures, ask the other players to try to guess the message and shout out their guesses.

Concluding. If a player shouts out the correct message, the artist says, "Done!" and shows the message on the card.

Scoring. The artist *and* the player who guessed the message correctly each earn a point as their reward.

Timing. If the players run out of time before anyone guesses the message, no one receives a reward. In this situation, the artist shows the card to everyone and puts it in a discard pile.

Repeating. Select another player to be the artist. The same procedure is repeated until the players run out of time or game cards. The player with the most points wins the game.

28
Secret Coaches

As a facilitator, one of my goals is to put myself out of business by letting the team members take on the responsibility for conducting effective and inclusive meetings. Secret Coaches is an add-on activity that can be attached to any regular meeting to ensure distributed facilitation.

Purpose

To ensure equal and effective participation by all team members

Participants

Minimum: 5
Maximum: 15
Best: 5 to 10
(Participants work individually.)

Time

Add 10 minutes to the scheduled meeting time

Supplies

- Index cards
- Pens or pencils

Flow

Assign protégés. At the beginning of the meeting, ask each participant to write his or her name on an index card. Collect these cards, turn them face down, shuffle them, and pass them around. Everyone takes a card, making sure it doesn't have his or her own name. The name on the card (which is kept hidden from everyone else) is the person's secret protégé.

Monitor participation. During the meeting, ask everybody to contribute to the discussion. In addition, each participant monitors his or her protégé and makes sure that he or she participates appropriately. They do this working subtly without letting anybody figure out who their protégés are.

Example: *If your protégé, John, is withdrawn, you may encourage him by saying, "What do you think of Mary's idea, John?" On the other hand, if John dominates the discussion, you may ask Mary, "What do you think of John's idea, Mary?"*

Explain: *Remember, the idea is for you not to get caught. So distribute your comments to several different people throughout the meeting. Also, work indirectly through someone else to coach your protégé.*

Conclude the meeting. Set aside 5 minutes at the end of the meeting. Ask the participants to identify their secret coaches. Then ask each person to reveal his or her secret protégé. Identify the person who did his or her job without getting caught as the *Most Flexible Facilitator* (or the *Sneakiest Manipulator*).

29
Switch

I become irritated whenever a client removes members from a team that has been assigned to work with me. Perhaps I could cope with this situation much more calmly and effectively if I had played Switch.

Purpose

To effectively handle the removal (or addition) of team members in the middle of a project or discussion

Participants

Minimum: 16
Maximum: Any number
Best: 20 to 40
(Participants are divided into 4 teams.)

Time

30 to 45 minutes

Supplies

- Flip charts (one for each team)
- Felt-tipped markers
- Timer
- Whistle

Flow

Organize teams. Divide participants into an *even* number of teams, each with four to seven members. It does not matter if some teams have one more member than the others. Seat the teams as far away from each other as possible.

Example: *You have twenty-two participants and you divide them into four teams. Two of the teams have five members and the other two have six members. You send the four teams to four separate breakout rooms.*

Assign topics for brainstorming. Ask one half of the teams to discuss this topic:

How can we handle problems associated with losing some members of a team in the midst of a project?

Ask the other half of the teams to discuss this topic:

How can we handle problems associated with new members being assigned to a team in the midst of a project?

Tell teams that they will have 10 minutes to complete their discussion and to record their ideas on flip charts.

Example: *The first two teams are assigned the "losing" topic (how to handle losing some team members). The other two teams are assigned the "gaining" topic (how to handle new members).*

Switch team members. After the teams have been brainstorming for about 5 minutes, randomly select one or two members from each "losing" team and ask them to join a "gaining" team. Do this switch without attracting too much attention.

Example: *You go to the first team that is discussing the "losing" topic and ask two of its members to follow you. You take them to the room where a team is discussing the "gaining" topic. You ask the two members to join this team and to work on the "gaining" topic. You now return to the original team and inform them that two of its members have been given another important assignment. You repeat the same procedure with the other pair of teams.*

Conclude the brainstorming activity. At the end of 10 minutes, assemble all teams at the same location. Explain that two of the teams lost members and the other two gained some members in the midst of the activity. Point out that the team working on the "losing" topic lost some members, while the team working on the "gaining" topic gained some members.

Debriefing

Conduct a reflective debriefing. Ask each team to reflect on how it reacted to losing or gaining members. Give sufficient time for this discussion. Follow up by asking each team to review its list of brainstormed ideas. After a suitable pause, invite each team to discuss these questions:

- *When your team lost or gained some members, did you use the ideas that you had generated? If you did not use the ideas, what prevented you from using them? If you did use the ideas, what was the effect?*

- *What are the disadvantages of losing some team members in the middle of the project? What are the disadvantages of gaining new team members in the middle of a project?*

- *Which is worse: losing team members or gaining new members?*

- *In your workplace, have you ever been on a project team that lost some members? Have you been on a team that gained new members? Why did these changes occur? What was the impact of these changes?*

- *Are there any advantages to losing team members in the middle of a project? What are they? What are the advantages of gaining new members?*

- *Which of your brainstormed ideas has the greatest application for improving the teamwork in your organization?*

30
Equal Air Time

Members of effective teams take turns to talk and listen so that everyone participates on an equal basis. Equal Air Time encourages this type of behavior by increasing team members' awareness of excessive talking.

Purpose

To increase the awareness of dominating behaviors during meetings and to suggest some guidelines for reducing them

Participants

Minimum: 6
Maximum: Any number
Best: 10 to 30
(Participants are divided into teams.)

Time

7 to 12 minutes

Supplies

- Flip charts (one for each team)
- Felt-tipped pens
- Timer
- Whistle

Flow

Organize teams. Divide participants into equal-sized teams of six to ten members each. Ask each team to stand around a flip chart.

Give instructions to teams. Explain that teams have only 4 minutes to complete the task. Within that time, each team should brainstorm guidelines for ensuring that everyone participates equally during team discussions. They should record these guidelines on a flip chart and select the top three guidelines.

Begin the activity. Ask teams to get started and start the timer. Walk around the room and observe the level of equal participation in each team.

Conclude the activity. At the end of 3 minutes, give a 1-minute warning. After 4 minutes, blow the whistle again and stop the activity.

Debriefing

Explain your focus. Announce that you are more interested in the ability of teams to walk the talk rather than come up with a list of brilliant guidelines. Tell participants that you are going to let each team decide how effectively it provided equal air time to all its members.

Specify the task. Ask each team to go through its list of guidelines and see how many of them they applied to the task of preparing equal-participation guidelines. Encourage teams to critically evaluate whether they were able to apply the guidelines that they are listing to their own behavior. Announce a time limit of 2 minutes for this activity.

Encourage action planning. Assemble all teams and ask them to share their self-assessments and insights. Suggest that each participant select one of the guidelines and be accountable for implementing it during future team activities.

31
Want and Give

T his is one of those activities that appears to be more complicated in its written form than in reality. Just to give you an advance organizer, here is a brief summary of the activity:

1. Team members agree on a common goal.

2. Each team member writes down three items that he or she expects ("wants") from each of the other team members.

3. Without discussing the wants, each team member now writes down three items that he or she will give ("gives") to each of the other members.

4. Team members organize these items into a *Want and Give Matrix* and negotiate their roles and responsibilities to achieve an improved score.

Purpose

To clarify roles and responsibilities of each team member in their joint effort to achieve a common goal

Participants

Minimum: 3
Maximum: 10
Best: 3 to 5
(Participants work individually.)

Time

30 minutes to 3 hours. Actual time requirement depends on the number of team members and on how well they understand each other's roles and responsibilities.

Supplies

- Pads of Post-it® Notes in two different colors
- Pens or pencils

- Flip chart
- Felt-tipped pens
- Calculator (to compute scores and percentages)

Flow

To illustrate each step in this activity, I have included (in italics) extensive details from a recent meeting of a conference planning team that met in Zurich.

Specify a common goal. Ask team members to discuss their goal to ensure that they have a shared mental picture. Encourage team members to specify the quality standards related to this goal.

Eric, Heidi, Peter, Sam, and Thiagi meet to play Want and Give. They begin the activity by reminding themselves that the team's goal is to design a brochure for next year's international conference in Zurich. They discuss the criteria for ensuring that the brochure will be professional looking, easy to read, and convenient to use.

Introduce *Want List*. Give each team member a pad of green-colored Post-its. Explain that they are going to create a *Want List* that specifies what each team member wants from each of the other team members to help achieve the goal. Ask each participant to write her name on top of the notepaper, followed by the phrase "wants from ____," filling in the name of another team member.

Each of the five members of the team prepares four Want Lists, one for each of the other members. For example, Eric prepares these four lists:

Eric wants from Heidi . . .
Eric wants from Peter . . .
Eric wants from Sam . . .
Eric wants from Thiagi . . .

Prepare *Want Lists*. Ask each team member to list three items that he wants from each of the other team members in order to ensure that the team achieves its goal. Ask each person to work independently, without talking to the others.

Here are some examples of Eric's Want Lists:
Eric wants from Sam

- *A list of items to be included on the front cover of the brochure*
- *Edited descriptions of eight different workshops*
- *Final list of items to be included in the registration form.*

Eric wants from Heidi

- *Short biographies of the conference speakers*
- *Suggestions for the design of the brochure cover*
- *Timely approval of the layout for the brochure*

Collect the *Want Lists*. After a suitable pause, gather the *Want Lists* from each team member, making sure that there is a list for every other team member. Put these lists aside without reading them.

Since there were five members in the team and since each person wrote four Want Lists, the team produces a total of twenty Want Lists.

Introduce *Give Lists*. Give each team member a pad of yellow-colored Post-its. Explain that they are going to create *Give Lists* that are the opposites of the *Want Lists*. The *Give List* specifies what each team member will give to each of the other team members to help achieve the common goal. Ask each person to write his or her name on top followed by the phrase "gives to ____," filling in the name of another team member.

Each of the five members of the team creates four Give Lists, one for each of the other members. For example, Eric prepared these four lists:

Eric gives to Heidi . . .
Eric gives to Peter . . .
Eric gives to Sam . . .
Eric gives to Thiagi . . .

Prepare *Give Lists*. Ask each team member to write a list of three items that she will give to each of the other team members in order to help the team achieve its goal. As before, ask each person to work independently, without talking to the others.

Here are some examples:
Eric gives to Sam

- *Specifications for the brochure*
- *Sample layout of a typical workshop description*
- *Three alternative formats for the Conference Registration Form*

Eric gives to Heidi

- *A blank form for listing information about the hotel*
- *Three sample cover designs*
- *Copy of the outline, along with specific requests for feedback*

Prepare the *Give and Want Matrix*. While team members are busy writing their *Give Lists*, draw a matrix on the flip chart and label each column and each row with the names of the team members, in the same order. Ignore the diagonal cells with the name of the same person as the label for both the column and the row. Notice that each of the other cells of the matrix is identified with a name for the column and a different name for the row.

Here is the matrix for the Zurich conference planning team:

SAMPLE MATRIX

	Eric	Heidi	Peter	Sam	Thiagi
Eric					
Heidi					
Peter					
Sam					
Thiagi					

Post the *Want Lists* on the matrix. Organize the *Want Lists* that you collected earlier by the name of the person that appears as the first word in each list. Work through each column of the matrix and stick each list (with its three items) on the top half of each cell.

Here's how the matrix looked with the Want Lists placed on the correct cells. Notice that the diagonal cells (with the same person's name for both the column and the row) are blank:

MATRIX WITH THE *WANT LISTS*

	Eric	Heidi	Peter	Sam	Thiagi
Eric		Heidi wants from Eric …	Peter wants from Eric …	Sam wants from Eric …	Thiagi wants from Eric …
Heidi	Eric wants from Heidi …		Peter takes from Heidi …	Sam takes from Heidi …	Thiagi takes from Heidi …
Peter	Eric takes from Peter …	Heidi takes from Peter …		Sam wants from Peter …	Thiagi wants from Peter …
Sam	Eric wants from Sam …	Heidi wants from Sam …	Peter wants from Sam …		Thiagi wants from Sam …
Thiagi	Eric wants from Thiagi …	Heidi wants from Thiagi …	Peter wants from Thiagi …	Sam wants from Thiagi …	

Collect and organize *Give Lists*. After a suitable pause, gather the *Give Lists* from each team member, making sure that there is a list for every other team member. Work through each *row* of the matrix and stick each note (with its three items) on the lower half of the appropriate cell.

This is what the matrix looks like at this juncture:

MATRIX WITH THE *WANT* AND *GIVE LISTS*

	Eric	Heidi	Peter	Sam	Thiagi
Eric		Heidi wants from Eric ... —Eric gives Heidi ...	Peter wants from Eric ... —Eric gives Peter ...	Sam wants from Eric ... —Eric gives Sam ...	Thiagi wants from Eric ... —Eric gives Thiagi ...
Heidi	Eric wants from Heidi ... —Heidi gives Eric ...		Peter wants from Heidi ... —Heidi gives Peter ...	Sam wants from Heidi ... —Heidi gives Sam ...	Thiagi wants from Heidi ... —Heidi gives Thiagi ...
Peter	Eric wants from Peter ... —Peter gives Eric ...	Heidi wants from Peter ... —Peter gives Heidi ...		Sam wants from Peter ... —Peter gives Sam ...	Thiagi wants from Peter ... —Peter gives Thiagi ...
Sam	Eric wants from Sam ... —Sam gives Eric ...	Heidi wants from Sam ... —Sam gives Heidi ...	Peter wants from Sam ... —Sam gives Peter ...		Thiagi wants from Sam ... —Sam gives Thiagi ...
Thiagi	Eric wants from Thiagi ... —Thiagi gives Eric ...	Heidi wants from Thiagi ... —Thiagi gives Heidi ...	Peter wants from Thiagi ... —Thiagi gives Peter ...	Sam wants from Thiagi ... —Thiagi gives Sam ...	

Score the matrix. Inform participants that you are going to analyze the matrix and discuss ways to improve the teamwork. Explain that each cell in the matrix can earn a maximum score of 3 points if the items in the *Want List* are the same as the items in the *Give List*. If the actual score for the matrix is the same as the maximum possible score, all team members share the same mental map of how they should interact with each other. With the help of participants, go through each cell in the matrix and write down the scores. Add the scores and compare this total with the maximum possible total score. Discuss the differences.

Eric wants from Heidi short biographies of the conference speakers, suggestions for the design of the brochure cover, and timely approval of the layout of the brochure. Heidi gives Eric the conference logo, names of the speakers, and constructive feedback. There is no match between the "wants" and "gives," and so this cell of the matrix gets a 0!

When the Zurich conference team completes scoring all the cells in the matrix, they obtain a total score of 27.

Since there were twenty cells in the matrix (ignoring the five blank cells), the maximum total score is 60. The actual total score of 27 is 45 percent of the maximum, indicating there is plenty of room for improvement!

Compute and discuss empathy scores of individual team members. Work through each row and add the scores of all cells in that row. This total indicates the correlation between what the team member is willing to give the others and what the others want from him or her. If the total score for a row is the same as the maximum possible score, this team member has a high level of empathy, since the person is giving to the other team members exactly what they want from him or her.

In the Zurich conference team matrix, Heidi received the highest empathy score of 5. Since the maximum score for the row is 12, Heidi's level of empathy was slightly less than 50 percent. The other team members scored lower, with Sam scoring a dismal 16 percent.

Discuss ways to move toward a perfect score. Work through each cell in the matrix. Ask the two members associated with the cell to explain what they want from each other and what they are willing to give each other. Invite other team members to facilitate this discussion. Emphasize the fact that all team members should focus on achieving the common goal. Based on these discussions, revise the *Want* and *Give* items on each cell to achieve a perfect score for the matrix.

The Zurich team needed more than an hour of intense discussion before each team member's expectations and commitments were aligned to each other's. Although the discussion was exhausting, everyone ended up feeling positive about the shared understanding.

Debriefing

The immediate effect of Want and Give is effective clarification of team members' roles. In addition, there is a long-term outcome in terms of better teamwork and communication. To focus on these outcomes, conduct a debriefing discussion using the following types of questions:

- *What is the best time to negotiate and renegotiate roles and responsibilities of team members?*
- *How frequently should we discuss and negotiate roles and responsibilities—without wasting productive time?*
- *How can we effectively negotiate what we want from each other and what we are willing to give to each other?*
- *In case of differences of opinion about roles and responsibilities, what is the best way to resolve these conflicts?*
- *What is the appropriate level of detail at which we should negotiate and plan?*

32
Easy Money

The use of actual cash is particularly effective in exploring such concepts as trust and risk taking. It may cost you about $20 to conduct Easy Money, but the impact is worth it.

Purpose

To explore trust among team members

Participants

Minimum: 7
Maximum: 50
Best: 12 to 25

Time

15 to 45 minutes

Supplies

- 5 blank envelopes
- 5 $20 bills
- Calculator
- Timer
- Whistle

Flow

Distribute the five blank envelopes randomly among the players. Explain that the players who received the envelopes are *investors* who will directly participate in the game. The other players are advisors and spectators.

Specify communication constraints. Investors cannot talk to each other. Advisors and spectators may talk to each other and to the investors, but they should not transmit information from one investor to another.

Explain the investment procedure. Each investor should place some money inside his or her envelope. The investment amount may vary from nothing to $900.

Explain the consequences. You (the facilitator) will count the money inside the five envelopes and keep it. The investment money will not be returned. However, you will give each investor $20 if the total amount of investment in the five envelopes adds up to at least $79.79. You are not interested in individual investments, so even those who gave you empty envelopes will receive $20. However, if the total investment is less than $79.79, none of the investors will receive any money. You will not even return their investment amounts.

Pause while the players reflect on the rules. Answer any questions by repeating the information from the previous paragraph.

Give final instructions. Explain that the investors will have 3 minutes to make their individual decisions, secretly place the investment amount inside the envelope, seal it, and write their initials on the face of the envelope. Remind the investors that they can hold discussions with the advisors and spectators, but they should not communicate with the other investors.

Collect the envelopes. After 3 minutes, blow the whistle and collect the envelopes. Make sure that the investors' initials are written on the envelopes.

Conduct an audit. Promote one of the Advisors to an Auditor. Give the envelopes to this person and ask him or her to count the money inside each envelope, record the amount on the face of the envelope, put the money back in the envelope, and compute the total.

Ask for predictions. While the auditor is counting and computing, ask players to predict the total amount (and explain the basis for their predictions).

Announce the results. Ask the auditor to report the total amount of investment in the envelopes.

If this amount is more than (or equal to) $79.79, give each investor $20. Keep the envelopes with the money.

If the amount is less than $79.79, keep the envelopes with the money. Explain that no one receives $20 because the investors did not meet the minimum requirement.

Ask the auditor to read the investment amounts in each envelope, without identifying the investor.

Debriefing

Conduct a debriefing discussion by asking the following types of questions:

- *What did you learn from this activity?*
- *What did you learn about trust?*
- *What did you learn about risk taking?*
- *How do you react to these generalizations:*

  Some people are greedy and some people are generous.

  Some people don't trust other people's motivations.

  It is possible for an investor to make a profit of $20.

  It is easier to give advice than to make your own decision.

  Lack of communication increases distrust among the team members.

- *In what ways does Easy Money remind you of workplace events?*

- *What do you think would have happened if the investors were permitted to talk to each other, but they still had to place the money secretly inside the envelopes?*
- *What do you think would have happened if each investor could receive $50 instead of $20 (but the minimum total investment stayed the same)?*

Follow-Up

If the participants did not meet the minimum investment requirement and, therefore, did not win any money, return the envelope to each investor with the amount of money he or she invested. However, do this after the debriefing.

Also, if the investors met the requirement and one or more investors had contributed disproportionately large amounts of money, return their investments minus the $20 you gave them.

General principle in conducting cash games: Always pay out the money the participants win and return any money from the participants—but do this after the debriefing.

33
Survivor

I enjoy incorporating instructional puzzles into simulation games to act as metaphors for the realities of the workplace. Survivor incorporates cryptograms to reflect team-based problem solving. But the main focus of this game is the impact of downsizing.

Purpose

To explore causes and consequences of downsizing

Participants

Minimum: 5
Maximum: Any number
Best: 20 to 30
(Participants are divided into teams of 5 to 7.)

Time

30 to 45 minutes

Supplies

- Copies of How to Decode Cryptograms
- Copies of the Sample Cryptogram
- Copies of six different cryptogram puzzles
- Blank pieces of paper
- Pens or pencils
- Whistle
- Timer

Flow

Form groups. Organize participants into groups of five to seven participants each. Ask members of each group to sit around a table.

Appoint Game Wardens. Select the tallest member of each group to play the role of a "Game Warden." Explain that the other members of the group will work as a team to decode a series of cryptograms, but the "Game Warden" will not participate in this activity. Instead, the Game Warden will ensure that the team members follow the rules of the game.

Explain how to decode a cryptogram. Distribute copies of the instructions for decoding and copies of the sample cryptogram to each team. Explain that all cryptograms used during this session will deal with laws of learning. Demonstrate how to decode the cryptogram by walking the participants through the process. (Note that the solutions are on a sheet following this activity.)

Begin decoding the first cryptogram. Distribute a copy of the first cryptogram to each team. Ask team members to collaboratively decode the cryptogram. Ask the Game Warden to let you know when the team has decoded the entire cryptogram.

Conclude the decoding activity. After all teams have decoded the cryptogram or after 3 minutes, blow a whistle to indicate the conclusion of the first round. Announce the correct solution. Identify the team that decoded the cryptogram first (or the team that decoded the most words in the cryptogram) and congratulate its members.

Explain the downsizing move. Announce that as a downsizing move, each team has to eliminate one of its members. Ask the Game Wardens to distribute pieces of paper to each team member. Ask team members to think back about the contributions of different people during the decoding, secretly write the name of the person who contributed the *least*, and fold the piece of paper to hide this name. Emphasize that team members should write the name of the person who should be eliminated from the team.

Eliminate a team member. Ask the Game Wardens to collect the pieces of paper and place them on the middle of table, exposing the names. The person whose name appears on the most pieces of paper is eliminated from that team. In case of a tie, ask the Game Warden to choose one of the tied names to be eliminated. Ask the eliminated team members to come and join you at the front of the room.

Process the second cryptogram. Distribute copies of the next cryptogram to each team. Also create a new team consisting of the downsized team members. Repeat the process of asking teams to decode the cryptogram, concluding the session after 3 minutes, announcing the correct solution, and identifying the winning team.

Eliminate a second player. Ask the Game Wardens to repeat the process of distributing pieces of paper and eliminating the least-contributing member of each team. You conduct the same process with your team of previously downsized participants.

Repeat the activity. Continue with additional cryptograms and elimination of more players, one player per round. Create new teams with the additional participants eliminated during each round.

Conduct the final elimination round. When the original teams are reduced to just two players, announce a modification in the elimination process: During this round, the Game Wardens (playing the role of an external consultant) decides who is to be downsized.

Congratulate the survivor. Identify the person who was not eliminated during this round. This person is the winner.

Debriefing

To ensure maximum learning from this activity, conduct a debriefing discussion. Encourage everyone to think back on their experience, come up with insights about teamwork, and share them with each other. Begin by asking the survivors how they feel about their current situation. Follow up with these types of questions:

- *How do the people who were eliminated during the first round feel? How do the people who were eliminated during the final round feel?*
- *How did the team members feel about selecting someone to be downsized?*
- *What criteria did you use for deciding which team member was to be eliminated?*
- *What dilemmas did you face in naming a person to be downsized?*
- *Which was easier: to select the first person to be eliminated or the last person?*
- *What did you learn from this activity?*
- *How does the activity reflect what happens in the workplace?*
- *What if the final survivor received a cash prize? How would that have changed players' behaviors?*
- *What if you were the Game Warden? How would you have behaved?*
- *What advice do you have for a person who is about to play this game for the first time?*

How to Decode Cryptograms

In a cryptogram, each letter in a message is replaced by another letter of the alphabet. For example, LET THE GAMES BEGIN may become this cryptogram:

YZF FOZ JUKZH CZJVQ.

In the cryptogram Y replaces L, Z replaces E, F replaces T, and so on. Notice that the same letter substitutions are used throughout this cryptogram: Every E in the sentence is replaced by a Z, and every T is replaced by an F.

Here are some hints for decoding a cryptogram:

Letter Frequency

The most commonly used letters of the English language are e, t, a, i, o, n, s, h, and r. The letters that are most commonly found at the beginning of words are t, a, o, d, and w. The letters that are most commonly found at the end of words are e, s, d, and t.

Word Frequency

One-letter words are either a or I. The most common two-letter words are to, of, in, it, is, as, at, be, we, he, so, on, an, or, do, if, up, by, and my. The most common three-letter words are the, and, are, for, not, but, had, has, was, all, any, one, man, out, you, his, her, and can. The most common four-letter words are that, with, have, this, will, your, from, they, want, been, good, much, some, and very.

Word Endings

The most common word endings are -ed, -ing, -ion, -ist, -ous, -ent, -able, -ment, -tion, -ight, and -ance.

Doubled Letters

The most frequent double-letter combinations are ee, ll, ss, oo, tt, ff, rr, nn, pp, and cc. The double letters that occur most commonly at the end of words are ee, ll, ss, and ff.

Punctuation

A comma is often followed by but, and, or who. It is usually preceded by however. A question often begins with why, how, who, was, did, what, where, or which. Two words that often precede quotation marks are said and says. Two letters that usually follow an apostrophe are t and s.

Sample Cryptogram

EMB WX CLGAXWCDLJLAU:

___ __ _____:

YMCUGDGYMAUV ELMCA UW CLYLMU

_____ _____ __ _____

KLPMRGWCV UPMU MCL CLBMCSLS.

_____ ____ ___ _____.

WUI EL DSEARETUW WDUVTRTJ:

DXDTAB AOUA UVD UKKESFUTRDH

CN RTADTBD DSEARETB VDBYWA RT

WETJ-WUBARTJ WDUVTRTJ.

Cryptogram 2

SVN WG VUZHFK SKVJTHTL:

VUZHFK JKCXWTMHTL XJWMPUKC

OWJK KGGKUZHFK SKVJTHTL ZAVT

XVCCHFK SHCZKTHTL WJ JKVMHTL.

IMX FA JKMVSNVD MHT ADDTRMVQ:

IDMKHDKE VMHHFS WMESDK

EQNIIE XNSOFGS KDJDMSDT

JKMVSNVD MHT ADDTRMVQ.

FQP JW AGKZVJYX KDAKGVKTNK:

TKP FKQGTVTO XCJYFU RK FVTLKU

EJ (QTU RYVFU JT) ECK

KDAKGVKTNK JW ECK FKQGTKG.

MFY UQ AGRAZARIFM

RAQQVLVGDVK:

RAQQVLVGW OVUOMV MVFLG AG

RAQQVLVGW YFJK.

SVN WG JKSKFVTUK:

KGGKUZHFK SKVJTHTL HC

JKSKFVTZ ZW ZAK SKVJTKJ'C SHGK

VTM NWJD.

Solutions (for Facilitator's eyes only)

Sample Cryptogram

Law of reinforcement: Participants learn to repeat behaviors that are rewarded.

Cryptogram 1

Law of emotional learning: Events that are accompanied by intense emotions result in long-lasting learning.

Cryptogram 2

Law of active learning: Active responding produces more effective learning than passive listening or reading.

Cryptogram 3

Law of practice and feedback: Learners cannot master skills without repeated practice and feedback.

Cryptogram 4

Law of previous experience: New learning should be linked to (and build on) the experience of the learner.

Cryptogram 5

Law of individual differences: Different people learn in different ways.

Cryptogram 6

Law of relevance: Effective learning is relevant to the learner's life and work.

34
Garbage

There is a major clash between corporate competitiveness and environmental concern. Garbage reflects this dilemma.

Purpose

To explore the clash between environmental protection and industrial competition

Participants

Minimum: 3
Maximum: Any number
Best: 10 to 20
(3 to 5 players are assigned to a table. Any number of table groups can play the game simultaneously.)

Time

10 to 20 minutes

Supplies

One regular deck of cards per table

Flow

Organize participants. Assign three to five players to each team. Ask the players to sort their decks into the four different suits.

   Explain the significance of the suits. In this game, the values of the cards do not matter. All red cards—whether hearts or diamonds—are regular garbage. Spades are hazardous garbage. Clubs are monitor cards that force people to reveal what they are dumping.

   Deal the cards. Ask the first dealer at each table to give each player any five red cards (diamonds or hearts), any two spades, and any one club.

   Explain the object of the game. Tell players that the first person to get rid of all the garbage cards (regular and hazardous) in his or her hand wins the game. Players need not (and *cannot*) get rid of the monitor card (club).

Explain how each round of the game is played. During the round, each player secretly selects a card from his or her hand and places it face down in front of him- or herself.

Explain what happens if no club is played. If nobody played a club, all face-down cards are collected, shuffled, and placed face-up in the middle of the table ("garbage heap"). Players can now see what types of garbage have been discarded—but not who discarded what.

Explain what happens if one or more clubs are played. If one or more people played a club, then all players turn their cards face up. Regular garbage (red) cards are thrown into the heap. Hazardous garbage cards (spades) and monitor cards (clubs) are taken back by the players. Then *each* club player gives a red card from his or her hand to each spade player.

Alan, Barbara, Cathy, and David are playing at a table. During Round 1, Alan and Barbara play it safe and get rid of a red card each. Cathy tries to get a head start by playing a spade. David anticipates this move and plays his club. When the cards are turned face up, Alan and Barbara throw their cards into the garbage heap in the middle of the table. Cathy takes back her spade and David takes back his club. David gets rid of a red card by giving it to Cathy as a punishment.

Explain what happens when additional red cards are needed. A club player may not have enough red cards to give to spade players. In this case, after passing out the red cards from his or her hand, the club player distributes as many red cards from the garbage heap as needed.

During the seventh round of the game, Alan, Barbara, and David play spades. Cathy plays a club. Cathy gets to punish the other three players. But she has only one red card, which she gives to Alan. She then digs up two other red cards from the garbage heap and hands them to Barbara and David.

Explain how to process hazardous garbage. At any time during the game, a player can exchange a hazardous garbage (spade) card for four red cards from the garbage heap. This exchange can only take place if there are enough red cards in the heap.

Start the game. After explaining the rules, answer any questions from players. Ask them to begin playing their first game. Move around the room, clarifying rules if needed.

End the game. When a player has disposed of all garbage cards and is left with only the club, the game at that table comes to an end. This player wins the game.

Debriefing

Help players process their experience and derive generalizations about what people do when confronted with a clash between competing with others and caring for the environment. Have them relate the metaphoric behavior from the game to real-life events. Here are some generalizations that the players came up with during recent plays of Garbage:

- *People wait and see how others behave before deciding what they want to do.*
- *You feel foolish when you play a club and discover that no one has dumped any hazardous garbage.*
- *Excessive dumping of hazardous waste is usually followed by a zealous play of clubs.*

- *Different people react differently to getting caught—and to getting away with hazardous dumping.*

- *People focus so much on winning that they do not pay attention to the significance of the spades.*

- *You fall behind if you spend your resources monitoring other people. Most attempts at collaborative monitoring (e.g., taking turns to play a club) are futile.*

- *People say one thing and do something else in competitive situations.*

- *It is difficult to follow rules and regulations when you know that the others are not following them.*

35
Fight Right

Conflict management is the foundation for peace on earth. At the workplace, it is an essential interpersonal skill that can contribute every day to effective personal and professional life. Fight Right is a collection of three role plays that help participants acquire conflict management skills. All these role plays are conducted in triads. Participants progress from natural behaviors through external mediation to self-mediation.

Purpose

To explore factors associated with conflict management, to effectively mediate in a conflict, and to use self-mediation techniques to resolve a conflict

Participants

Minimum: 3
Maximum: Any number
Best: 10 to 30
(Participants are divided into triads.)

Time

45 to 90 minutes

Supplies

- The following six role play scenarios:
    Project Management: Alan's Story
    Project Management: Barbara's Story
    Customer Service: Bob's Story
    Customer Service: Cathy's Story
    Deadlines: Chuck's Story
    Deadlines: Angela's Story
- Observation Checklist (for use during the *Project Management* role play)
- Mediation Checklist (for use during the *Customer Service* role play)
- Mediation Guidelines (for use during the *Customer Service* role play)
- Observation Checklist (for use during the *Deadlines* role play)
- Timer
- Whistle

- Flip chart
- Felt-tipped markers

Flow

Role Play 1: Project Management

Organize participants. Divide participants into triads. If there are one or two additional participants, ask them to come to the front of the room and help you conduct the activity by distributing handouts, keeping time, and observing participants. In each triad, ask participants to assign themselves the identification letters A, B, and C.

    Distribute copies of the *Project Management Role Play Scenarios*. In each triad, A receive Alan's story and B receives Barbara's story. Ask participants to read the scenarios and get ready for the role play.

    Brief the observers. Call the C's to the front of the room and give them copies of the *Observation Checklist*. Go through each item in the checklist and answer any questions. Emphasize that C's task is to observe the role play and note any interesting behaviors and statements.

    Start the role play. Set your timer for 5 minutes. Ask Alan and Barbara in each triad to act out the confrontation.

    Conclude the role play. At the end of 5 minutes, announce the conclusion of the role play. Ask the role players to take a few moments to snap out of their roles and to return to the current reality. Encourage participants to talk to each other about their experience.

Debriefing

Debrief the role play. Gather all participants for a debriefing discussion. Discuss the following types of questions:

- *If you were playing the role of Alan, did you believe Barbara's story? What was the reason for your belief or disbelief?*
- *If you were playing the role of Barbara, did you believe Alan's story? What was the reason for your belief or disbelief?*
- *As a role player, how did you feel before the role play? During the role play? After the role play?*
- *What two adjectives would you use to describe the other person's behavior? What two adjectives would you use to describe your own behavior?*
- *What would have happened if you had more time for the role play?*
- *If you were an observer, what do you think was the crux of the confrontation between Alan and Barbara?*
- *Many people believe that this conflict was due to a difference in perceptions rather than a fundamental difference in values or beliefs. Do you agree or disagree with this statement? Why?*

    Debrief the observers. Read each item from the observation checklist and ask the observers to report their observations during the role play. Be sure to include the extra participants who are assisting you. Invite others to comment on these observations.

Transition

Introduce the concept of mediation. Explain that many people believe that the presence of a neutral mediator could help resolve conflicts more effectively. Ask participants whether they agree with this opinion. Also ask them to explain the reasons for their agreement or disagreement.

Role Play 2: Customer Satisfaction

Distribute copies of the *Customer Satisfaction Role Play Scenarios*. Within each triad, B receives Bob's story and C receives Cathy's story. Ask these participants to read their stories, think about it, and get ready to act out the confrontation.

    Brief the mediators. Call all A's to the front of the room. Give them copies of the *Mediation Checklist* and the *Mediation Guidelines*. Explain that they will be mediating the dispute during the next role play. Walk the mediators through the items on the checklist. Also ask the mediators to read the guidelines. Answer questions to clarify the guideline items.

    Start the role play. Set your timer for 8 minutes. Ask the mediators to make their opening statements and get the discussion started.

    Monitor the role play. Walk among the triads, eavesdropping on the conversations, and taking notes about interesting mediation activities.

    Conclude the role play. After 8 minutes, announce the end of the role play. Ask role players to take a few minutes to leave their roles and to return to the current reality. Encourage participants to talk to each other about the experience.

Debriefing

Debrief the role play. Ask participants to discuss questions such as the following:

- *If you were playing the role of Bob or Cathy, did you believe the other person's story? What is the reason for your belief or disbelief?*

- *If you were playing the role of Bob or Cathy, what was your reaction to the mediator? Was the mediator neutral or did he or she take sides? Did the mediator help you to resolve the conflict more effectively?*

- *What two adjectives would you use to describe the mediator's behavior? What two adjectives would you use to describe your own behavior? What two adjectives would you use to describe the other person's behavior?*

- *What would have happened if you had more time for the role play?*

- *If you were the mediator, what do you think was the crux of the confrontation?*

- *What were the major differences between the previous role play and this one?*

    Discuss the job aids. Distribute copies of the *Mediation Checklist* and *Mediation Guidelines* to B's and C's. Explain that the mediators used these job aids during the role play. Go through each item in the checklist and invite participants to discuss these three questions:

- *How effectively did the mediator implement this step?*

- *How did this mediation step affect the disputants? How did it contribute to the resolution of the conflict?*

- *How could the mediator have done a better job?*

Transition

Introduce the concept of self-mediation. Explain that it is not feasible to have a mediator to help resolve all conflicts. In some situations, the two parties to the conflict should act as their own mediators, monitoring their behaviors, and making suitable suggestions to each other. Go through the items and guidelines. Explain that some guidelines (such as "Ask disputants to talk to you, not to each other") can be used only by a third-party mediator, but most guidelines can be adapted for self-mediation. Discuss how each guideline can be suitably modified.

Role Play 3: Deadlines
Distribute copies of the *Deadlines Role Play Scenarios*. Within each triad, C receives Chuck's story and A receives Angela's story. Ask these participants to read the story, think about it, and get ready to act out the confrontation.

　　Brief the observers. Call all B's to the front of the room and distribute copies of the *Observation Checklist*. Emphasize that they will not be mediating the conflict, but silently observing the behaviors of the two disputants and noting the use of self-mediation techniques.

　　Start the role play. Set your timer for 8 minutes. Ask the people playing Chuck and Angela to begin their conversation.

　　Monitor the role play. Walk among the triads, eavesdropping on the conversations, and take notes about interesting self-mediation activities.

　　Conclude the role play. After 8 minutes, announce the end of the role play. Ask the role players to take a few minutes to leave their roles and to return to the current reality. Encourage participants to talk to each other about the experience.

Debriefing

Debrief the role play. Ask participants to discuss questions such as the following:

- *If you were playing the role of Chuck or Angela, did you believe the other person's story? What is the reason for your belief or disbelief?*

- *What two adjectives would you use to describe the other person's behavior? What two adjectives would you use to describe your own behavior?*

- *What would have happened if you had more time for the role play?*

- *What were the differences between this role play and the first one? In what ways did the self-mediation principles and procedures help you?*

- *What were the differences between this role play and the preceding one? How easy or difficult was it for you to recall and use self-mediation techniques?*

- *What suggestions do you have for improving the use of self-mediation techniques?*

　　Conclude the session. Thank participants for their contributions. Encourage everyone to apply the self-mediation technique to manage future conflicts.

Role Play Scenario

Project Management: Alan's Story

You are Alan and this is your story:

I thought that my manager Barbara was a nice person, but she turns out to be a jerk. For the past six months she has been praising my project management skills, but I understand that last week she stabbed me in the back. Someone told me that at the executive management meeting, another manager asked Barbara whether I could lead a major product-development initiative. Apparently Barbara told everyone that I am too inexperienced for such a big responsibility. I know that I can manage the project and Barbara knows that too. Maybe she is planning to keep me enslaved to her department. I have asked for a meeting with her, and I am going to ask her point-blank why she is holding me back.

Role Play Scenario

Project Management: Barbara's Story

You are Barbara, and this is your story:

Alan is a very competent person and he is advancing rapidly in his career. During the past six months he handled two different projects and completed both of them ahead of schedule and under budget. But Alan is naive about company politics and I have to act as a mentor to protect him. Many of the other managers are jealous of him and they are trying to get rid of him. For example, Peter, one of the other managers, asked me innocently if Alan would make a good manager for the Model 17 product-development initiative. Everyone knows that project is going to fail miserably and the previous manager quit her job because of that. Peter's looking for a scapegoat and I don't want Alan to be blamed for the failure of this doomed project. So I told Peter to find someone else with more experience.

Role Play Scenario

Customer Service: Bob's Story

You are Bob, and this is your story:

I work at the hotline desk and I think that my supervisor Cathy is a control freak. She won't let go of her authority and enjoys bossing people around. Last month the company started emphasizing customer satisfaction, but Cathy thinks that it's all a fad. If I take extra time to talk to a customer, she yells at me and reminds me that my quota is handling ten calls every 15 minutes. But if we really want to delight our customers, I have to spend more time, especially those people who are clueless about computers. Cathy is threatening to get me fired. I am not going to put up with all this harassment, so I sent a complaint letter to the president of the company.

Role Play Scenario

Customer Service: Cathy's Story

You are Cathy, and this is your story:

We hired Bob because he had a very friendly personality, but I don't think that he will make a good hotline employee unless he changes his attitude. He thinks that all callers don't know anything about computers and wastes a lot of time coaching them on the fundamentals, which they already know. Also, he wastes time socializing with the customers instead of solving their technical problems. We all know that customers get hostile if they are put on hold for long periods of time. That's why we have this quota of handling ten calls every 15 minutes. That way, customers are happily surprised on how quickly their calls are answered. Actually, we are rated number 1 in this area. I told Bob yesterday that with his personality he'd make a great sales person. Today I understand that he sent an anonymous complaint about me to the president of our company. I am having a meeting with Bob to straighten him up.

Role Play Scenario

Deadlines: Chuck's Story

You are Chuck, and this is your story:

I always try to finish my work on time, but last week I had the flu and I was worried it could be that anthrax thing because I opened a junk mail envelope from Florida. With all this terrorist business, I could not focus on my work and had to get some counseling. And then Angela yelled at me for not finishing the tables for the monthly report. That woman is obsessed with trivial details. Nobody reads those reports anyhow, and who cares if it is late by a couple of days?

Role Play Scenario

Deadlines: Angela's Story

You are Angela, and this is your story:

Chuck never finishes anything before the deadline. We both agree when his part of the task is to be completed, but he is always late and always with a handy excuse. Last month his kid was sick. This month he had the flu. He has my sympathy, but I expect my co-workers to behave in a professional manner. He also complains that nobody reads the monthly reports anyhow, but it's not our job to make policy, is it?

Observation Checklist for Use During the *Project Management* Role Play

1. From your perspective, what was the crux of this conflict?

2. Did Alan and Barbara seem more eager to talk or to listen?

3. What types of active-listening behaviors did you notice?

4. Did you see any attempt at goal setting and planning for the future?

5. Most conflicts are accompanied by negative behaviors and emotions. What are some examples of negative behaviors and emotions (such as accusations, betrayal, domination, hostility, anger, frustration, and sarcasm) that you observed in the conversation between Alan and Barbara?

6. Some conflict-management conversations are accompanied by positive behavior and emotions. What are some examples of positive behaviors and emotions (such as understanding, apologizing, empathy, support, and hope) that you observed in the conversation between Alan and Barbara?

Mediation Checklist

1. Frame the session:

   - Explain that conflicts are inevitable results of healthy diversity.
   - Explain that a well-managed conflict provides an opportunity for future growth.
   - Stress the importance of listening to one another.

2. Gather information and analyze the conflict:

   - Focus the conversation on the current dispute.
   - Ask the disputants to take turns telling their stories.
   - Maintain neutrality. Don't take sides.

3. Help disputants to establish mutual goals:

   - Establish task-related goals.
   - Establish relationship goals.

4. Brainstorm strategies for achieving the goals:

   - Focus on win-win strategies.
   - Use a variety of brainstorming techniques.

5. Select the best strategy:

   - Ensure that the strategy is fair and equitable for both disputants.
   - Set up an action plan for implementing the strategy.
   - Identify the first small step for immediate implementation.

6. Debrief the participants:

   - Encourage disputants to reflect on what happened.
   - Encourage disputants to share their insights for preventing and resolving future conflicts.

Mediation Guidelines

1. Be fair but firm.

2. Maintain control through appropriate use of body language, hand gestures, and tone of voice.

3. Talk to both disputants at the same time.

4. Arrange furniture to facilitate conversation, such as not having a desk between disputants.

5. Ask disputants to talk to you, not to each other.

6. Be absolutely impartial.

7. Don't respond to disputants' questions about your opinions, perceptions, or reactions.

8. Ask disputants to take turns telling you their stories.

9. Listen actively.

10. Focus on the dispute. Focus on a single dispute. Focus on the current dispute.

11. Ask for specific and objective facts. Discourage inferences and evaluations.

12. Encourage appropriate sharing of feelings.

13. Neutralize provocative language.

14. Repeat statements that require clarification.

15. Avoid closed questions and leading questions.

16. Ask questions that begin with *what, when, where, who, in what way,* and *how*? Never ask questions that begin with why.

17. Don't make suggestions.

Observation Checklist for Use During the *Deadlines* Role Play

1. From your perspective, what was the crux of this conflict?

2. Did Chuck and Angela seem more eager to talk or to listen?

3. What types of active-listening behaviors did you notice?

4. What are some examples of negative behaviors and emotions (such as accusations, betrayal, domination, hostility, anger, frustration, and sarcasm) that you observed in the conversation between Chuck and Angela?

5. What are some examples of positive behaviors and emotions (such as understanding, apologizing, empathy, support, and hope) that you observed in the conversation between Chuck and Angela?

6. How did Chuck and Angela demonstrate their ability to use self-mediation techniques related to these checklist items?

   - Frame the session
   - Gather information and analyze the conflict
   - Establish mutual goals
   - Brainstorm strategies for achieving the goals
   - Select the best strategy
   - Debrief

36
Newton

Newton's third law says that, for every action, there is an equal and opposite reaction. This law is illustrated by this activity (which was inspired by Deidre Lakein and Alan Schneider), even though it has nothing to do with physics.

Purpose

To negotiate a win-win solution

Participants

Minimum: 2
Maximum: Any number
Best: 10 to 40
(Participants are divided into pairs.)

Time

2 to 5 minutes

Supplies

- Timer
- Whistle

Flow

Give initial instructions. Ask participants to pair up and stand facing each other. Ask them to plant their feet firmly on the ground, raise both their hands, and place them palm to palm.

Explain how to win. Tell participants that they win if they can make the other person move his or her feet within 17 seconds after you blow your whistle. Repeat this rule one more time.

Begin the activity. Blow a whistle and start a timer. Most participants will use brute force to push each other. A few martial-arts practitioners may suddenly stop pushing and let the other person's momentum topple him or her forward.

Stop the activity. After a suitable pause, blow the whistle and stop the activity.

Debriefing

Ask participants to think back on the experience and compare different strategies used for winning.

Ask for a volunteer for a quick demonstration. Assume the initial face-to-face, palm-to-palm position. Blow the whistle and move your feet immediately. Tell the other person, "You've won! We still have 11 more seconds. Would you mind moving your feet so I can win also?"

After the demonstration, participants may complain that you cheated. Point out that the rule merely required you to make the other person move his or her feet within 17 seconds. There was no prohibition against moving your own feet. Continue with the debriefing, bringing out learning points related to making assumptions, creating win-win solutions, modeling appropriate behaviors, solving conflicts, and the futility of meeting force with force.

37
Hidden Agenda

Most negotiation games are designed for two players or for two teams. I was always intrigued by what happens when three people negotiate, each with a different agenda. In Hidden Agenda, three players bring their sets of playing cards and hidden agendas. They assemble a card set using selected cards from individual players. Since some agenda items clash with each other, while others complement each other, there is plenty of scope for negotiation. After assembling the joint card set, the three players reveal their hidden agendas and compute the scores. This scoring round gives an additional opportunity for three-party negotiations.

Purpose

To explore how three people negotiate with one another

Participants

Minimum: 3
Maximum: Any number
Best: 10 to 30
(Participants are organized into triads.)

Time

30 to 45 minutes

Supplies

- Envelopes
- Five playing cards for each player
- Handout, Card Sets Instructions (three different versions for three different players)
- Timer
- Whistle

Preparation

Assemble three envelopes for each group of three players. Mark these envelopes A, B, and C.

Inside Envelope A, place any *four* playing cards and a copy of Card Sets Instructions for Player A.

Inside Envelope B, place any *five* playing cards and a copy of Card Sets Instruction for Player B.

Inside Envelope C, place any *six* playing cards and a copy of Card Sets Instructions for Player C.

Flow

Distribute the envelopes. Distribute them in the A-B-C sequence so that equal numbers of players receive each of the three envelopes.

Brief the players. Explain that the game involves players working in groups of three to assemble and arrange a set of cards. Each envelope contains a few playing cards, a set of instructions, and a hidden agenda. A player's score depends on how closely the joint card set matches the hidden agenda. Players should not show their agendas to each other or talk about them.

Ask the players to review the content of their envelopes. Ask them to read the instruction sheets and the hidden agenda silently, paying special attention to the number of points assigned to each item on the agenda. Also ask them to count and inspect the playing cards in their individual sets.

Organize the players into groups. After a suitable pause, blow the whistle and ask the players to form themselves into groups of three. Each group should have one player with each of the three envelopes. Invite the players in each group to introduce themselves to each other.

If you have an extra player with Envelope A, give this player the option of joining a group (and making it a four-player group) or acting as an observer. If you have two extra players (with Envelopes A and B), ask them to play the game as a two-person group.

Explain the play procedure. Blow the whistle to get the players' attention. Re-emphasize that no player may show (or tell) the hidden agenda to the others. Each player should now show his or her playing cards to the others and work on the joint card set. They should decide how many cards this set should contain, select appropriate cards from players' individual sets, and arrange them in a suitable display. This project should be completed in 10 minutes.

Explain the role of the hidden agenda. Announce that after 10 minutes, the joint card set created by each group will be compared with the items in each player's hidden agenda. The score for each player will be computed by adding the points assigned to the agenda items reached by the player. While the players may not directly reveal their hidden agendas, they can negotiate the selection of cards and their display.

Monitor the activity. Start the timer and blow the whistle to signal the beginning of the project. Watch the players in action, making note of interesting items to be shared during the debriefing session. If any group claims to have completed the project before the 10 minutes are up, ask them to see whether they want to renegotiate and modify the joint card set. Announce a 1-minute warning at the end of 9 minutes. After 10 minutes, blow the whistle to signal the conclusion of the project. Tell the groups not to change their joint card set in any fashion.

Get set for the scoring round. Ask the players to reveal their hidden agendas. Announce that all three players will jointly compare the individual items in each agenda with the final card set and award suitable points to each player. Players should interpret all agenda items and settle any disputes about how many points each player should receive. Announce a 5-minute time limit for this activity.

Conduct the scoring round. Blow the whistle to start the scoring round. Leave the players alone as they negotiate with each other. If any group wants you to settle scoring disputes, politely decline the invitation. Eavesdrop on different conversations, making note of interesting items for use during the debriefing session. At the end of 5 minutes, blow the whistle to signal the conclusion of the scoring round.

Debriefing

Conduct a discussion of different insights gained by the players. Here are some suggested questions:

- *Who won the game? How do the other two players feel toward this player?*
- *When did you feel most frustrated during the game? Why?*
- *Who made the first suggestion during the joint set project? What was the suggestion? How did the others react to this suggestion?*
- *Did you try to guess the hidden agendas of the other players? Why did you want to do this? How successful were you in guessing other people's agendas?*
- *Some items in the hidden agenda were in conflict. For example, all of you tried to contribute the card with the highest value. What strategies did you use in this situation?*
- *Some items in the hidden agenda were complementary. For example, all of you wanted the joint card set to contain five cards. What strategies did you use in this situation?*
- *Sometimes there were conflicts within your agenda items. For example, Player C wanted five cards and equal numbers of black and red cards. What strategies did you use in this situation?*
- *Sometimes group members come up with creative ideas. For example, the joint card set may have five cards with one of the cards turned face down. This enables you to meet three different agenda items (the set should have five cards, one card should be placed in a way that is very different from the way the other cards are placed, and the card set should display equal numbers of red and black cards). Did you come up with any such creative ideas? If you did not, what prevented you from thinking creatively?*
- *Did either of the other players support you during the project? What was your reaction to this?*
- *During the project, did the other two players team up against you? When did this happen? Why do you think this happened?*
- *What were some of the interesting compromises during the scoring round?*
- *What was the most important learning point for you?*
- *What insights did you gain about three-person negotiations?*
- *What did you learn about forming temporary alliances?*
- *What did you learn about your strengths and weaknesses in negotiating?*
- *What real-world processes does this game relate to?*
- *When was the last time you were involved in a three-party negotiation? How did that situation compare to the situation in this game?*
- *What advice would you give a participant who is about to play this game for the first time?*
- *Considering what you learned from this card game, how would you behave differently in your workplace?*

Card Sets Instructions for Player A

Your envelope contains a few playing cards, a set of instructions, and a hidden agenda.

You will work with two other players who have different cards and different hidden agendas.

As a group, you will create a joint card set using cards from your individual sets.

Your hidden agenda contains five items. It also specifies the number of points that you would score by achieving each item.

Do NOT show your agenda to any other player. Do not tell them your agenda items.

During the joint project, make suggestions that would help achieve the items on your hidden agenda. Negotiate with the other two players to increase your score.

Decide how many cards the joint card set should contain. Select appropriate cards from your three individual sets. Arrange the cards in the joint set in a suitable display.

Your joint card set should be completed in 10 minutes.

At the end of the 10 minutes, the joint card set will be compared with the items in your hidden agenda. Your score is the total of the points assigned to the agenda items achieved by you.

Hidden Agenda

1. The joint card set should contain five cards. (You score 10 points for achieving this agenda item.)

2. The card with the lowest value in the joint card set should be from you. (You score 8 points for achieving this agenda item.)

3. The joint card set should have more red cards (hearts or diamonds) than black ones (spades or clubs). (You score 10 points for achieving this agenda item.)

4. One card in the joint card set should be placed in a way that is very different from the way the other cards are placed. (You score 6 points for achieving this agenda item.)

5. One of the cards in the joint card set should be a club. (You score 1 point for achieving this agenda item.)

Card Sets Instructions for Player B

Your envelope contains a few playing cards, a set of instructions, and a hidden agenda.

You will work with two other players who have different cards and different hidden agendas.

As a group, you will create a joint card set using cards from your individual sets.

Your hidden agenda contains five items. It also specifies the number of points that you would score by achieving each item.

Do NOT show your agenda to any other player. Do not tell them your agenda items.

During the joint project, make suggestions that would help achieve the items in your hidden agenda. Negotiate with the other two players to increase your score.

Decide how many cards the joint card set should contain. Select appropriate cards from your three individual sets. Arrange the cards in the joint set in a suitable display.

Your joint card set should be completed in 10 minutes.

At the end of the 10 minutes, the joint card set will be compared with the items in your hidden agenda. Your score is the total of the points assigned to the agenda items achieved by you.

Hidden Agenda

1. The joint card set should contain five cards. (You score 10 points for achieving this agenda item.)

2. The card with the highest value in the joint card set should be from you. (You score 8 points for achieving this agenda item.)

3. The joint card set should have more red cards (hearts or diamonds) than black ones (spades or clubs). (You score 10 points for achieving this agenda item.)

4. One card in the joint card set should be placed in a way that is very different from the way the other cards are placed. (You score 6 points for achieving this agenda item.)

5. One of the cards in the joint card set should be a spade. (You score 1 point for achieving this agenda item.)

Card Sets Instructions for Player C

Your envelope contains a few playing cards, a set of instructions, and a hidden agenda.

You will work with two other players who have different cards and different hidden agendas.

As a group, you will create a joint card set using cards from your individual sets.

Your hidden agenda contains five items. It also specifies the number of points that you would score by achieving each item.

Do NOT show your agenda to any other player. Do not tell them your agenda items.

During the joint project, make suggestions that would help achieve the items in your hidden agenda. Negotiate with the other two players to increase your score.

Decide how many cards the joint card set should contain. Select appropriate cards from your three individual sets. Arrange the cards in the joint set in a suitable display.

Your joint card set should be completed in 10 minutes.

At the end of the 10 minutes, the joint card set will be compared with the items in your hidden agenda. Your score is the total of the points assigned to the agenda items achieved by you.

Hidden Agenda

1. The joint card set should contain five cards. (You score 10 points for achieving this agenda item.)

2. The card with the lowest value in the joint card set should be from you. (You score 8 points for achieving this agenda item.)

3. The joint card set should have an equal number of red cards (hearts or diamonds) and black cards (spades or clubs). (You score 10 points for achieving this agenda item.)

4. One card in the joint card set should be placed in a way that is very different from the way the other cards are placed. (You score 6 points for achieving this agenda item.)

5. None of the cards in the joint card set should be a club. (You score 1 point for achieving this agenda item.)

38
Three-Way Sudoku

Many simulation games deal with cooperation *and* competition. Three-Way Sudoku gives a new twist to the play of games.

Purpose

To explore factors associated with collaboration and competition among three people

Participants

Minimum: 3
Maximum: Any number
Best: 12 to 30
(Participants are divided into triads.)

Time

30 to 40 minutes

Supplies

- Handout, Rows, Columns, and Blocks
- Handout, Puzzle 1
- Handout, Solution 1
- Handout, Puzzle 2
- Handout, Solution 2
- Pens or pencils

Flow

Form triads. Organize participants into groups of three people. If one or two people are left over, ask them to act as observers.

    Assign three different roles. Within each triad, ask participants to distribute the roles of Row Controller, Column Controller, and Block controller among themselves.

    Distribute copies of the first puzzle grid. Also distribute copies of the handout, Rows, Columns, and Block. Point out that the puzzle grid consists of nine columns and nine rows. In addition, each grid contains nine 3 by 3 square blocks with thick lines indicating their boundaries.

Explain the play procedure. Draw attention to the fact that the puzzle grid has various boxes filled with numbers and some blank boxes. Tell participants that they will take turns to place any single-digit number (1 through 9) in any blank box. Since there are thirty blank boxes in the grid, each participant will get to place ten numbers.

Explain how Role Controllers score points. Ask participants to study the grid in the Rows, Columns, and Blocks handout. Rows go horizontally from left to right. Explain that Row 1 is a correct row because it contains all nine numbers (from 1 to 9) and no number is repeated. Explain that Row 5 is an incorrect row and ask participants to figure out why it is an incorrect row. After a pause, confirm that it is incorrect because the 5 is repeated (and the 6 is missing).

Every correct *row* gives a point to the Row Controller (and only to him or her). So when it is his or her turn, the Row Controller should place a number in the grid so that he or she can form correct rows.

Explain how Column Controllers score points. Columns go vertically from top to bottom. Explain that Column A is a correct column because it contains all nine numbers (from 1 to 9) and no number is repeated. Explain that Column E is an incorrect column and ask participants to figure out why it is incorrect. After a pause, confirm that it is incorrect because the 9 is repeated twice (and the 1 is missing).

Every correct *column* gives 1 point to the Column Controller (and only to him or her). So when it is his or her turn, the Column Controller should place a number in the grid so that he or she can form correct columns.

Explain how Block Controllers score points. Blocks are 3 by 3 squares marked by thicker lines. Explain that the block in the center of the grid is a correct block because it contains all nine numbers (from 1 to 9) and no number is repeated. Explain that the block at the lower right corner is an incorrect one and ask participants to figure out why it is incorrect. After a pause, confirm that it is incorrect because the 7 is repeated (and the 6 is missing).

Every correct block gives a point to the Block Controller (and only to him or her). So when it is his or her turn, the Block Controller should place a number in the grid so that he or she can form correct blocks.

Conduct the activity. Answer questions from the participants about playing the game. Explain that you are going to start the game and have everyone play the game for 5 minutes. At the end of that time, or when all thirty blank boxes in the grid are filled, the person with the highest score will win the game. Remind participants that the three people in each triad will take turns placing any single-digit number in a blank box. When a row, column, or a block is correctly filled, the appropriate controller will score a point.

Conclude the activity. At the end of 5 minutes, blow the whistle to signal the end of play time. Ask each participant to count the number of correctly filled rows, columns, or blocks and compute scores. Identify the participant with the highest score in each triad and congratulate this person.

Distribute the first solution. Ask participants to compute the scores for the Row, Column, and Block controller in this handout. Pause for an appropriate period of time and confirm that every blank is correctly filled and each controller scores 9 points, which is the maximum possible score. Point out that collaboration among players is essential to achieve these maximum scores for all players.

Distribute the second puzzle. Explain that you are going to give the participants an opportunity to play in a collaborative mode. Explain that this grid contains thirty blank squares, as in the previous puzzle.

Conduct the cooperative puzzle-solving activity. Ask members of the triad to play the game as before, but this time carefully collaborating with one another to ensure the maximum scores of 9 points. Announce a 10-minute time limit.

Conclude the activity. Whenever any triad completes its grid, ask them to compute the scores and verify that everyone has 9 points. At the end of 10 minutes, blow the whistle and ask the remaining players to stop. Distribute copies of Solution 2 to everyone and have them verify their solutions later.

Debriefing

Explain that you are going to facilitate a debriefing discussion so that everyone can share their insights from the activity. Be sure to include the observers in this process. Offer each of these general principles and invite participants to provide examples from the activity—and from the workplace—to support or challenge it:

- *Collaboration results in greater gains.*
- *Competition is contagious. Once you spoil other people's chances, they are likely to spoil your chances.*
- *Collaboration among three people is more difficult than collaborating between two people.*
- *It is more difficult to come up with a collaborative strategy than with a competing strategy.*
- *Time limits and deadlines increase the tendency to compete.*
- *Collaboration is more boring than competition.*

Rows, Columns, and Blocks

		Columns							
	A	B	C	D	E	F	G	H	I
1	6	5	8	7	4	2	1	9	3
2	1				9				
3	3				5				
4	5			4	7	1			
5	7	4	5	2	3	8	9	5	1
6	2			5	6	9			
7	9				2		4	3	8
8	8				9		5	7	2
9	4				8		7	1	9

Rows

Puzzle 1

	A	B	C	D	E	F	G	H	I
1	2	5	4	3	1		9	8	6
2				4		2			
3	7	9	3			6	4	2	1
4	5	3	1			9	6	4	7
5	4	6	7	1	3	5			
6				7			1	5	3
7		7	9		2	8	5	1	
8		1	2			3	8	7	
9		4	5		7	1	3	6	

Columns / Rows

Solution 1

Columns

	A	B	C	D	E	F	G	H	I
1	2	5	4	3	1	7	9	8	6
2	1	8	6	4	9	2	7	3	5
3	7	9	3	8	5	6	4	2	1
4	5	3	1	2	8	9	6	4	7
5	4	6	7	1	3	5	2	9	8
6	9	2	8	7	6	4	1	5	3
7	3	7	9	6	2	8	5	1	4
8	6	1	2	5	4	3	8	7	9
9	8	4	5	9	7	1	3	6	2

(Rows)

Puzzle 2

	A	B	C	D	E	F	G	H	I
Columns									

Rows	A	B	C	D	E	F	G	H	I
1	5	6		8	9	1	4	3	
2	7	9		4		3	6		8
3	8	3						1	2
4	3	2	6		1				
5				2	4		3	6	9
6	9	4	5		6	8	2	7	1
7	4		3		8				6
8	6		7	9	3	4		2	5
9	2		9			6	1	4	3

Solution 2

Columns

	A	B	C	D	E	F	G	H	I
1	5	6	2	8	9	1	4	3	7
2	7	9	1	4	2	3	6	5	8
3	8	3	4	6	5	7	9	1	2
4	3	2	6	7	1	9	5	8	4
5	1	7	8	2	4	5	3	6	9
6	9	4	5	3	6	8	2	7	1
7	4	5	3	1	8	2	7	9	6
8	6	1	7	9	3	4	8	2	5
9	2	8	9	5	7	6	1	4	3

Rows

39
Virtual Team Tips

Comparing, contrasting, and selecting ideas is a good way to master a training topic. In this activity, you begin with a list of ten tips for effectively participating as a member of a virtual team. Once every 2 minutes, participants remove the least-preferred tip from the list until they are left with a single item. The real purpose is not to identify the best item but to learn more about virtual teamwork.

Purpose

To explore practices that contribute to effective virtual teamwork

Participants

Minimum: 10
Maximum: Any number
Best: 10 to 30
(Participants work in constantly changing pairs.)

Time

30 to 45 minutes

Supplies

- Handout, Virtual Team Tips
- Timer
- Whistle

Flow

Distribute the handout. Give each participant a copy of Virtual Team Tips. You need seven to ten items related to the topic that you want to explore.

Preview the play procedure. Explain that participants will reflect on the relative importance of the items on the list. They will also discuss the items with each other. Once every 2 minutes, they will gradually eliminate the tips, one by one, beginning with the least important one. Eventually, they will end up with the most important single tip.

Begin the first round. Ask participants to spend a couple of minutes silently reviewing the list of tips and mentally arranging them in order of importance. After 2 minutes, ask participants to stand up, move around, and talk to each other. Explain that participants can discuss the items with only one other person at a time. During the discussion, participants share their opinions about different items, trying to persuade others to vote against a particular item. Alternatively, participants may also lobby for retaining an item that they think is important. These discussions may be of any duration; encourage participants to keep moving around and talking to as many others as possible. Move among the participants and listen to different conversations.

Conduct the first poll. After 2 minutes, blow the whistle and ask each participant to write a number on a small piece of paper, fold it, and give it to you. Emphasize that each participant should write the number of the *least* preferred item on the list. Explain that you will get rid of the item that received the most rejection votes. Collect the slips of paper from participants.

Begin the second round. Invite participants to continue lobbying each other for the removal of the next item from the list (or for the retention of an important item). While they are doing this, quickly identify the most frequently listed number among the rejection slips.

Announce results of the first poll. Announce the number of the least preferred tip and ask participants to change this number to "10." Ask participants to continue their lobbying efforts without wasting their time in talking against this least-preferred tip. Encourage participants to switch partners frequently.

Conduct the second poll. After 2 more minutes blow the whistle again, and ask participants to vote for the next tip to be removed. Collect the slips of paper and ask participants to continue their discussion for eliminating the next item.

Repeat the process. Quickly determine the tips receiving the most rejection votes and announce it. Ask participants to change the number of this tip to 9. At the end of 2 more minutes, conduct the poll for removing the third tip. Then repeat the procedure, removing one item at a time.

And then there was one. At the end of the ninth round, you will end up with a single tip. Ask participants to write 1 in front of it and point out that this tip was determined to be the most important one. Invite everyone to study the order of relative importance of all ten tips.

Debriefing

Conduct a follow-up discussion. Invite participants to express any dissenting opinions and to justify them. Make a few brief comments, presenting your personal opinion and results from previous play of the game with the same list of tips. Remove any misconceptions that you detected while overhearing earlier discussions.

Virtual Team Tips

Here are ten tips from a recent play of this game. The last three tips are from three of the participants, Anio Kis, Roberta Berg, and Nancy Bragard.

1. **Make use of diversity.** Encourage team members to use their unique cultural and individual backgrounds to contribute to the team. Do not ignore or attack ideas from others just because they are different from your way of thinking.

2. **Forget myths and misconceptions.** Don't handicap yourself by believing (and spreading) such statements as "Teams need face-to-face meetings to solve tough problems." Field research during the past five years clearly demonstrates that virtual teams have frequently outperformed teams whose members work side-by-side.

3. **Instant trust building.** In virtual teams, you have to earn your trust right away during the first couple of meetings. You do this by completing all your homework, getting to virtual meetings on time, and delivering on your promises.

4. **Select the appropriate technology.** If team members are separated by only one or two time zones, use synchronous tools (that permit same-time discussions) such as the telephone, audio- and video-teleconferencing, and electronic chat rooms. If team members are separated by more than three time zones (*example: people in Canada and in Germany*), make use of asynchronous tools (that permit responses at different times), such as the Internet, voice mail, e-mail, fax, and regular mail.

5. **Voice mail etiquette.** If you frequently use telephones and voice mail messages, change your voice mail greeting every day. When you leave a message on a team member's answering machine, make sure that is brief, clear, and to the point.

6. **Pay attention to both sides.** Effective virtual teams must utilize the best technology and the best people. Team members should spend time in learning skills related to the use of technological tools. They should also spend time in learning teamwork skills such goal setting, brainstorming, active listening, and giving feedback.

7. **Get used to asynchronous meetings.** If virtual team members are in different locations that are separated by five or more time zones, asynchronous meetings are critical. This type of meeting occurs over several days, and different team members attend the same meeting at different times. Most asynchronous meetings use a combination of e-mails and websites. Some meetings use voice mail, electronic bulletin boards, and electronic meeting systems.

8. **What is urgent?** Agree with the team about what should be considered as an urgent e-mail and how fast the answer is expected.

9. **Answer in an appropriate channel.** If, for example, you receive an e-mail that reveals that the sender has misunderstood you or is angry, in some cases it might be best to answer by phone.

10. **The meaning of silence.** Talk up-front about silence and what it implies for team members. Silence doesn't necessarily imply lack of commitment or preparation or that people aren't onboard. If members have shared their perception of silence, there's less likelihood of ill-founded assumptions.

40
Crowd Wisdom

What common phrase is hidden in this word puzzle?

FRIENDS STANDING FRIENDS
MIS

The answer is *misunderstanding between friends.* Get it? The prefix *mis* is printed *under* the word *standing.* This gives us *misunderstanding.* This is found between the two appearances of the word *friends.* So the hidden phrase is *misunderstanding between friends.*

People like solving this type of word puzzles. I have incorporated a series of these puzzles in an activity to illustrate that a "crowd" as a whole can perform better than any of its individual members.

Purpose

To demonstrate the fact that a group of people can outperform individuals

Participants

Minimum: 5
Maximum: Any number
Best: 20 to 50
(Participants work independently.)

Time

10 to 20 minutes

Supplies

- Handout, Puzzle Sheet, one copy for each participant
- Handout, Solution Sheet, one copy for each participant
- Blank pieces of paper
- Pens or pencils
- Timer
- Whistle

Preparation

Try your hand at solving the puzzles. Make a copy of the Puzzle Sheet and attempt to solve the word puzzles. Resist the temptation to peek at the solutions. Only after you have given the task your best shot, look at the Solution Sheet. Make sure that you understand each solution. Identify the difficult puzzles. Pay particular attention to Item 12 (*listed in alphabetical order*). Our field testing with hundreds of participants indicates that this is the most difficult puzzle.

Organize your accomplices. Long before the session, meet with one or more accomplices and show them the Puzzle Sheet. Let them solve a few of the puzzles. Give the correct solution to Item 12 and explain the logic of the solution. Share solutions to other difficult items and urge your accomplices to remember them.

Flow

Brief the participants. Distribute copies of the puzzle sheet to all participants. Explain how to solve word puzzles. Demonstrate the solution to the first item. Instruct participants to work independently and write down their solutions for each item. Announce a 3-minute time limit.

Stop the puzzle-solving activity. After 3 minutes, blow the whistle. Ask participants to take a break from their hard mental labor.

Ask participants to score their responses. Distribute copies of the Solution Sheet to all participants. Ask each participant to count the number of correct solutions. Find out how participants solved all puzzles. It is unlikely that anyone would have a perfect score. However, if someone has correctly solved all the puzzles, congratulate this participant.

Walk through each puzzle. Go through one puzzle at a time and ask those who solved it to stand up (or raise their hands). Emphasize that at least one participant has correctly solved each item. Your accomplices guarantee that someone knows the solution even to the most difficult items.

Debriefing

Present the concept of the wisdom of crowds. Explain that in a group, different people have different skills, perceptions, experiences, and knowledge. This suggests that large crowds are more capable of providing correct answers than any individual. Re-emphasize that the total group did much better than the most brilliant individual in the puzzle-solving activity. In his book, *The Wisdom of Crowds*, James Surowiecki claims that crowds are very effective at solving problems, fostering innovation, coming to wise decisions, and predicting the future.

Discuss the concept. Ask participants to give examples of how the general public and customer groups frequently outperform individual experts and pundits. Use these types of questions to structure additional discussions:

- *What are the advantages and limitations of crowd wisdom?*
- *What causes the superiority of the wisdom of crowds?*
- *How can we use the wisdom of crowds for achieving useful results?*
- *How can we increase the positive impact of the wisdom of crowds and decrease the negative aspects of groupthink?*

Puzzle Sheet

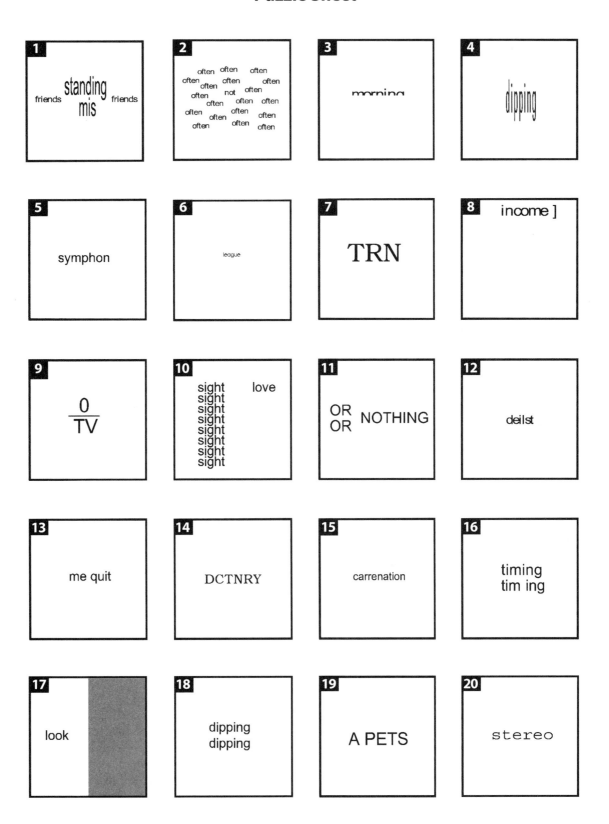

1 friends standing mis friends

2 often often often often often often often often not often often often often often often often often often often

3 morning

4 dipping

5 symphon

6 league

7 TRN

8 income]

9 0/TV

10 sight sight sight sight sight sight sight sight love

11 OR OR NOTHING

12 deilst

13 me quit

14 DCTNRY

15 carrenation

16 timing tim ing

17 look

18 dipping dipping

19 A PETS

20 stereo

Solution Sheet

1. Misunderstanding between friends

2. More often than not

3. Top of the morning

4. Skinny dipping

5. Unfinished symphony

6. Little league

7. No U turn

8. Upper income bracket

9. Nothing on TV

10. Love at first sight

11. Double or nothing

12. Listed on alphabetical order

13. Quit following me

14. Abridged dictionary

15. Reincarnation

16. Split second timing

17. Look at the bright side

18. Double dipping

19. A backward step

20. Stereotyped

PART V
Leadership

41
Leadership Survey

Everyone hates icebreakers that are trivial and irrelevant. Leadership Survey is an icebreaker that we use as an opener for our workshop on leadership. This activity focuses participants' attention on the content of the workshop.

Purpose

To prime participants with an informal survey related to leadership

Participants

Minimum: 6
Maximum: 30
Best: 12 to 24
(Participants are divided into teams of 2 to 6 members each.)

Time

15 to 45 minutes

Supplies

- Index cards
- Pens or pencils

Preparation

Estimate the number of teams. For this activity, you will organize your workshop participants into three to five teams, each with two to six members. It does not matter if some of the teams have one more member than the others. Determine how many participants will attend your workshop. Use this estimate to figure out how many teams you will have.

Example: *If you anticipate nineteen participants, organize them into three teams of five and one team of four.*

Construct survey questions. You need one question for each team. Write each question on an index card. Here are some specifications for preparing these survey questions:

- They should relate to the content that you plan to cover in the workshop.
- They should be open-ended and permit a variety of appropriate responses.
- They should require short answers.

171

Example: *Here are the four survey questions that I prepared for a recent workshop on leadership:*

1. *What is the most important quality of a leader?*
2. *Which 20th century leader best exemplifies courage?*
3. *What is one of the major complaints about political leaders?*
4. *What types of situations call for a no-nonsense, command-and-control leadership?*

Flow

Introduce the survey. Explain that you are going to conduct an informal survey related to leadership. Give these additional details (in your own words):

- *This is not a test; there are no correct or incorrect answers.*
- *I will ask a few open-ended questions.*
- *Each participant will write a short answer (a word or a phrase) on an index card.*
- *Do not write your name on your answer card.*
- *I will collect the answer cards after each question.*

Ask the first question. Distribute index cards to each participant. Read your first question. Pause briefly while the participants write their answers. Collect the answer cards and place them in a pile with your question card on top.

Continue with the survey. Repeat the same procedure with each of the other questions. Be sure not to mix up the answer cards you collect.

Process the answers. Divide participants into as many teams as there are questions. Give a set of answer cards (with the appropriate question card on top) to each team. Ask the team members to sort the cards according to the answers. They should arrange the cards with the same (or similar) answers in a pile and arrange these piles in order of frequency.

Conduct the prediction exercise. Select a team and ask one of its members to read the question it processed. Ask the other teams to predict the highest-frequency answer. Members of the other teams should discuss various alternatives and write down their final choices.

Identify the best prediction. Ask each team to read its prediction. Ask the team that processed the answers to announce the different answers and their frequencies. Congratulate the team (or teams) that made the best prediction.

Repeat the process. Conduct the prediction exercise with each of the other questions.

Debriefing

Link the workshop to the survey. Present an outline of the workshop content. Describe how it is related to the survey activity.

Re-Use

LEADERSHIP SURVEY IS A FRAMEGAME: You can use its structure to create a suitable opening activity for workshops on different training topics. All you have to do is to prepare a set of survey questions that are relevant to the training topic.

42
Leadership Advice

Today, when I searched Amazon online for books on leadership, I had to deal with a potential list of 15,483 items. I am sure that this number will swell tomorrow because writing and publishing books with leadership advice is a growth industry.

Leadership Advice provides a faster, cheaper, and better alternative to buying and reading a lot of books: You tap into the wisdom of the group—and of their role models.

Purpose

To identify and analyze participants' advice on leadership styles, characteristics, attitudes, behaviors, and skills

Participants

Minimum: 5
Maximum: Any number
Best: 10 to 30

Time

20 to 50 minutes, depending on the number of participants and the depth of discussions

Supplies

- Index cards
- Pens or pencils

Flow

Select a role model. Everyone has one or more ideal leaders whom they have personally met or read about. Ask participants to individually select role models who have inspired them. This role model could be a family member, a school teacher, a boss at work, a captain of the industry, a political leader, a sports coach, a military genius, a spiritual mentor, an inspiring writer, a fictional hero, or a prophetic guide. Ask each participant to have a clear mental picture of this leader.

Name the role model. Distribute index cards to each participant. Have them write the names of the role models (*example: Mother Teresa*) if other participants would recognize this leader. Otherwise, ask participants to write a brief description of this role model (*example: my third-grade teacher*). Pause while participants independently complete this task.

Advice from the role model. Ask participants to take on the role of the role models they selected. Ask them to imagine that a young person is asking this role model for leadership advice. Ask participants to write on their index cards one important piece of advice they would give (in their assumed role) to this young person. The advice may be about leadership styles, characteristics, attitudes, behaviors, or skills. Encourage participants to limit themselves to one or two short sentences. Pause while participants complete this task.

Exchange the advice cards. Ask participants to turn their cards with the written side down and exchange them with someone else. Repeat this procedure until all cards have been completely mixed. Blow a whistle to get participants' attention and ask them to stop the process.

Read the piece of advice. Ask participants to read the advice on the cards that they received. Invite them to think about this advice and how it would help them personally to become a better leader. Encourage them to think about applying this advice to their personal and professional lives. Pause while participants do this.

Read aloud. Select a participant at random. Ask this person to stand up and read the piece of advice from the card, without revealing the role model. Ask everyone else to listen carefully. If necessary, ask the participant to read this piece of advice again.

Guess the role model. Ask everyone to think about the piece of advice for a minute. Then ask them to guess who could be the role model (leader) who gave this piece of advice. Invite participants to call out their guesses. Point out that most leaders have similar traits, perceptions, behaviors, and ideas. Ask the participant who read this card to identify the role model specified.

Read similar pieces of advice. Invite other participants whose cards contain similar pieces of advice to read them aloud. Identify minor differences among these ideas. Discuss the potential impact of these differences.

Read opposing pieces of advice. Ask participants to review the advice on their own cards and see if it contradicts the advice read earlier. Invite any participant with such an opposing piece of advice to read it aloud from his or her card.

Reconcile the differences. Point out that even though these pieces of advice contradict each other, it is not as if one of them is correct and the other one is incorrect. This is because effective leadership requires a variety of flexible styles, depending on the nature of the situation, the type of the followers, and the personality of the leader. Discuss the context in which each of the opposing pieces of advice would be effective.

Continue the process. Select another random participant (who has not yet read from a card) and ask him or her to read aloud the advice from the card. Follow this by guessing the role model, and then reading and discussing cards with similar and opposing points of view.

Select a piece of advice. After the discussions, ask participants to think about the variety of advice from different role models and select the one that they want to implement in their personal and professional life. Remind participants not to count the number of pieces of advice they have received but make the one selected piece of advice count. Encourage them to begin implementing this piece of advice immediately.

Adjustments

Don't have enough time? You do not have to read and discuss all the cards. Conclude the activity whenever you want by moving to the final step (of personal selection and implementation). After the session, collect all the cards, type up the pieces of advice, and send them to the participants.

Not enough participants? Ask each participant to write two separate pieces of leadership advice, one on each card. During the card exchange step, ask participants to give away both cards, each to a different person.

43
Leadership Art

If beauty is in the eyes of the beholder, so are many other things associated with art. I am fascinated by the way people interpret drawings, paintings, sculptures—and inkblots. In this activity, we use alternative interpretations of graphic art to explore elements of leadership.

Purpose

To identify characteristics of effective leaders

Participants

Minimum: 2
Maximum: Any number
Best: 10 to 30
(Participants are divided into groups of 4 to 6.)

Time

20 to 45 minutes

Supplies

- Blank pieces of paper
- Boxes of crayons
- Whistle

Flow

Form teams. Divide participants into equal-sized teams of four to six members each. Seat team members around a table.

Distribute supplies. Place sheets of drawing paper and boxes of crayons in the middle of each table. Ask each participant to take a sheet of paper and to share the crayons.

Time to draw. Invite each participant to draw an abstract picture that captures the characteristics of an effective leader. Discourage participants from focusing on artistic quality and encourage them to flow with their intuitive thoughts and feelings. Prohibit the artists from using any words, letters, numbers, or symbols found on a computer keyboard. Also advise participants not to look at each other's artwork. Announce a 5-minute time limit for this activity.

Time to stop. At the end of 5 minutes, blow the whistle and ask the artists to stop their activity. Reassure them that it does not matter if their artwork is not yet complete.

Interpret other people's pictures. At each table, ask participants to take turns holding up their pictures. While doing this, ask each person to perform the difficult task of keeping his or her mouth shut. Invite other participants around the table to treat the picture as a symbolic depiction of effective leadership characteristics and report what they see in it. It is not necessary that participants take turns in presenting their interpretations. Anyone may call out insights whenever he or she feels inspired.

Interpret your own picture. After all pictures have been interpreted, ask each participant to repeat the process of holding up the pictures. This time, however, each participant should describe what leadership characteristics the picture is intended to convey.

Debriefing

Encourage a debriefing discussion at each table. Use questions similar to these to structure this discussion:

- *What leadership characteristics were the most frequently mentioned?*
- *What leadership characteristics were unexpected and unique?*
- *How accurately did the others interpret your drawing?*
- *How accurately did you interpret other people's drawings?*
- *Which leadership characteristic is your strong point? Did you include this characteristic in your drawing?*
- *Which leadership quality do you lack? Did you include this in your drawing?*

44
Leadership Envelopes

Leadership training is a major growth industry. For more than a millennium, people have been articulating basic principles of leadership. From Buddha and Confucius to Bennis and Covey, philosophers, politicians, sociologists, and management gurus have summarized the key ideas related to being an effective leader. To become a better leader, all we need to do is to translate these principles into practice. Leadership Envelopes helps participants do exactly that.

Purpose

To explore everyday applications of leadership principles

Participants

Minimum: 10
Maximum: Any number
Best: 12 to 30
(Participants are divided into 5 teams.)

Time

30 to 90 minutes

Supplies

- **Leadership principle envelopes.** Write a leadership principle on the front of each envelope.
- **Response cards.** Four index cards for each team.
- Pens or pencils
- Timer
- Whistle

Set-Up

Arrange the tables in a roughly circular format with chairs around each table.

Flow

Organize participants. Divide participants into four to six teams of three to seven members. Teams should be approximately the same size.

Brief participants. Review the leadership principles. Explain to participants that the activity requires them to translate these principles into everyday on-the-job behaviors.

Distribute the supplies. Give one leadership principle envelope and four index cards to each team.

Conduct the first round. Ask team members to discuss the leadership principle on the envelope they received and to identify how this principle can be applied to on-the-job decisions and behaviors. Tell team members to write short sentences describing these application examples on an index card. Announce a time limit of 3 minutes and encourage the teams to work rapidly. Explain that the teams' response cards will eventually be evaluated in terms of both the number and the quality of the application ideas.

Conclude the first round. After 3 minutes, blow the whistle and announce the end of the first round. Ask each team to place its response card (the index card with its application ideas) inside the envelope and pass the envelope, unsealed, to the next team. Warn the teams not to open the envelopes they receive.

Conduct the second round. Ask teams to review the leadership principle on the envelope they received, but *not* to look at the application examples on the response card inside. Tell the teams to list application ideas related to this principle on a new response card. After 3 minutes, blow the whistle and ask teams to place the response card inside the envelope and pass it to the next team.

Conduct more rounds. Conduct two more rounds of the game using the same procedure.

Conduct the evaluation round. Start the fifth round just as you did the previous rounds. However, tell teams that they do not have to write any more application ideas. Instead, teams must evaluate the four response cards inside the envelope. They do this by reviewing the individual examples on each response card and then comparing the overall merit of the cards with each other. Teams have 100 points to distribute among the four response cards to indicate each card's relative merit. Announce a suitable time limit for this evaluation activity.

Present the results. At the end of the time limit, check on the teams to ensure they have completed their task and have recorded on each response card the number of points awarded. Select a team at random to present its evaluation results. Ask the team to announce the leadership principle on the envelope and read the application examples on each card, beginning with the card that received the least number of points. The team should progress from one card to the next in an ascending order of the number of points. After reading all four cards, the team should announce how it distributed the 100 points and briefly explain the criteria used for distributing the points.

Determining the winner. Instruct teams to place all the response cards on a table at the front of the room; then call for each team to collect its cards. Ask teams to add up the points on their cards to determine their total scores. Invite the members of each team to announce their total score. Identify and congratulate the team with the highest score.

Debriefing

Conduct a debriefing discussion to add value to the activity. Here are some suggested questions:

- *What are the interesting patterns among the application examples?*
- *Can you find similarities among application examples related to different leadership principles?*
- *What leadership principle was the most difficult one for you to come up with suitable application examples? The easiest one? Why?*
- *Reflect on your workplace situation. Which leadership principle application idea could you implement immediately?*

Re-Use

LEADERSHIP ENVELOPES IS A FRAMEGAME: You can use its structure to a suitable activity for exploring different training topics. All you have to do is to prepare a set of envelopes with principles that are relevant to the chosen training topic.

45
Epigrams

I enjoy collecting, creating, and using pithy sayings. However, I want to go beyond just making static posters of these sayings. Epigrams is my attempt at incorporating interactivity into these words of wisdom. This activity provides an effective opener for a training workshop on leadership.

Purpose

To reflect on important leadership principles

Participants

Minimum: 2
Maximum: 30
Best: 5 to 15

Time

10 to 45 minutes

Supplies

- Epigram cards (see below)
- Pens or pencils
- Handout, Leadership Epigrams

Preparation

Create epigram cards. Collect or create several pithy sayings, quotes, aphorisms, adages, maxims, slogans, truisms, mottoes, proverbs, or one-liners related to leadership. Print or write each item on a separate card. Make a duplicate copy of each epigram.

Flow

Distribute epigrams. At the beginning of the session, distribute the epigram cards so that

- Each participant receives two different epigrams
- Each epigram is given to two different participants

Invite reflection. Ask the participants to reflect on each epigram, discover its deeper meaning, and identify its personal application. Warn the participants that they will be asked to make a short presentation on both of the epigrams they received.

Call for paired presentations. After a suitable pause, randomly select one of the epigrams from the list. Read this epigram or display it on the screen. Ask the two participants who received cards with that epigram to take turns and make their presentations.

Encourage discussion. After the two presentations, invite comments from the other participants. If appropriate, ask the participants to vote (by their applause) to identify the better presentation.

Continue the activity. Repeat the procedure with other randomly selected epigrams.

Conclude the activity. If you have a large group, it is not necessary that you must invite every participant to make a presentation. After a few paired presentations, invite participants who feel that they have important insights to share to make their presentations. Conclude the activity by distributing a handout that contains the complete list of leadership epigrams.

Variations

Distributed presentations. Instead of conducting all paired presentations at the end of the activity, you may distribute them throughout the workshop session. For example, you may conduct two paired presentations after each coffee break and lunch break.

Re-Use

EPIGRAMS IS A FRAMEGAME: You can use its structure to create a suitable activity for exploring different training topics. All you have to do is to collect a list of quotations related to the training topic.

Leadership Epigrams

1. Great necessities call forth great leaders. (Abigail Adams)

2. Leadership should be born out of the understanding of the needs of those who would be affected by it. (Marian Anderson)

3. No man will make a great leader who wants to do it all himself, or to get all the credit for doing it. (Andrew Carnegie)

4. You don't have to hold a position in order to be a leader. (Anthony J. D'Angelo)

5. You don't lead by hitting people over the head—that's assault, not leadership. (Dwight D. Eisenhower)

6. A sense of humor is part of the art of leadership, of getting along with people, of getting things done. (Dwight D. Eisenhower)

7. The crowd gives the leader new strength. (Evenius)

8. Whatever you do will be insignificant, but it is very important you do it. (Mahatma Gandhi)

9. Leadership is practiced not so much in words as in attitude and in actions. (Harold Geneen)

10. The leader has to be practical and a realist, yet must talk the language of the visionary and the idealist. (Eric Hoffer)

11. Leadership has a harder job to do than just choose sides. It must bring sides together. (Jesse Jackson)

12. The only real training for leadership is leadership. (Anthony Jay)

13. Leadership and learning are indispensable to each other. (John F. Kennedy)

14. The task of the leader is to get his people from where they are to where they have not been. (Henry Kissinger)

15. Because of not daring to be ahead of the world, one becomes the leader of the world. (Lao-tzu)

16. When the effective leader is finished with his work, the people say it happened naturally. (Lao-tzu)

17. I am their leader, I really ought to follow them. (Alexandre Auguste Ledru-Rollin)

18. The final test of a leader is that he leaves behind him in other men the conviction and will to carry on. (Walter J. Lippmann)

19. The function of leadership is to produce more leaders, not more followers. (Ralph Nader)

20. A leader . . . almost always acts subconsciously and then thinks of the reasons for his action. (Jawaharlal Nehru)

21. Leadership is based on inspiration, not domination; on cooperation, not intimidation. (William A. Wood)

46
Decode

The *command-and-control* style of leadership gets a bad rap in these inclusive and participatory times. However, when there is urgency and if you are the most competent person around, there's a lot to be said for taking charge.

The real name of this game is Take Charge, but if you use that name, you would be giving away the secret learning point.

Purpose

To explore factors that facilitate or inhibit a person from assuming a take-charge leadership style

Participants

Minimum: 10
Maximum: Any number
Best: 15 to 30
(Participants are divided into teams of 4 to 7.)

Time

30 to 45 minutes

Supplies

- One copy of the Instruction Sheet for each player
- Single copy of Secret Instruction Sheet
- One copy of the Cryptogram for each player
- Single copy of the Answer Key for the facilitator
- Blank pieces of paper
- Pens or pencils
- Whistle
- Timer

Flow

Organize teams. Divide participants into teams of four to seven members each. Seat each team around a table.

Brief participants. Ask how many participants have solved cryptogram puzzles before. Briefly explain what a cryptogram is (using the information from the Instruction Sheet). Explain that in this game, all teams will solve a cryptogram.

Explain time limits and the scoring system. If a team correctly and completely solves the cryptogram within 2 minutes, it will earn 200 points. If it takes more than 2 minutes but less than 3 minutes, the team will earn 50 points. If it takes more than 3 minutes, it does not earn any points.

Explain instructional support. Before receiving the cryptogram, each participant will receive an instruction sheet with hints on how to solve cryptograms. Participants can study this sheet for 2 minutes. They should not mark up the instruction sheets, but they may take notes on a blank piece of paper. The instruction sheets will be taken back from participants after 2 minutes.

Explain consultant support. Any time after receiving the cryptogram, a team can send one of its members to ask for help from the facilitator. The facilitator will decode any one of the words in the cryptogram selected by the team member.

Distribute the instruction sheet. Insert the secret instruction sheet in the middle of a pile of regular instruction sheets. Place an appropriate number of instruction sheets, face down, at each table.

Conduct the self-instruction activity. Set the timer for 2 minutes. Ask each participant to pick up one of the instruction sheets and study it independently and silently. Distribute blank sheets of paper pens or pencils to all participants for taking notes. After 2 minutes, blow the whistle, announce the end of the self-instructional period, and ask participants to place their instruction sheets in the middle of the table.

Distribute cryptograms. Place appropriate numbers of cryptograms, face down, at each table.

Begin the puzzle-solving activity. Set the timer for 2 minutes and ask teams to begin decoding the cryptogram. Remind participants that you would decode any one of the words for the benefit of each team.

Monitor the session. When team members come for decoding a word, consult the answer key and give the correct word. Also observe the behavior of the "leader" (the person who received the secret instruction sheet).

Conclude the session. If any team has completely and correctly decoded the message before 2 minutes, tell them they have earned 200 points. At the end of 2 minutes, announce the time and set the timer for another minute. At the end of 3 minutes, announce the end of the session. If the teams have not yet solved the cryptogram, read the correct solution.

Reveal the secret. Explain that one of the participants received secret instructions about the best strategy for winning the game. Explain that this technique simulated specialized competency on the part of the participant and gave him or her a leadership role.

Debriefing

To gain maximum insights from the activity and to relate it to the instructional objective, conduct a debriefing session. Use selected questions from the following list to start a discussion:

- *The special instructions given to a randomly selected participant gave this person additional knowledge. Does this guarantee that he or she will be automatically accepted as a leader? What additional skills and characteristics are required for being an effective leader?*

- *How did the selected person communicate the strategy to teammates and to the entire group? If you were the leader, how would you have done this differently?*

- *How did the selected person persuade others to follow the cooperative strategy? If you were the leader, how would you have done this differently?*

- *How did the selected person interact with other participants? If you were the leader, how would you have interacted with others?*

- *Most of the earlier groups that played this game failed to implement the strategy. What do you think were some of the reasons for the inability of the leaders of the previous groups to implement the preferred strategy?*

- *How do previous relationships and shared experiences among participants make the leader's task easier or more difficult?*

- *Did anyone else come up with the same strategy? What did this participant do?*

- *What if another participant had received the same secret instructions? How would this have changed the leader's task?*

- *How did the time limit hinder the leader from his or her task? How did the time limit help the leader? How would you have acted as a leader if you had ample time?*

- *Have you ever been in a situation in which you had an effective strategy for meeting a challenge but held back from sharing it with others? Why did this happen?*

Instruction Sheet

You are probably familiar with codes and cryptograms from your childhood days. In a cryptogram, each letter in the message is replaced by another letter of the alphabet. For example,

LET THE GAMES BEGIN!

may become this cryptogram:

YZF FOZ JUKZH CZJVQ!

In the cryptogram Y replaces L, Z replaces E, F replaces T, and so on. Notice that the same letter substitutions are used throughout this cryptogram: Every E in the sentence is replaced by a Z, and every T is replaced by an F.

Here's some information to help you solve cryptograms:

Letter Frequency

- The most commonly used letters of the English language are *e, t, a, i, o, n, s, h,* and *r.*
- The letters that are most commonly found at the beginning of words are *t, a, o, d,* and *w.*
- The letters that are most commonly found at the end of words are *e, s, d,* and *t.*

Word Frequency

- One-letter words are either *a* or *l.*
- The most common two-letter words are to, of, in, it, is, as, at, be, we, he, so, on, an, or, do, if, up, by, and my.
- The most common three-letter words are the, and, are, for, not, but, had, has, was, all, any, one, man, out, you, his, her, and can.
- The most common four-letter words are that, with, have, this, will, your, from, they, want, been, good, much, some, and very.

Secret Instruction Sheet

The other participants are learning how to solve cryptograms. But you have been specially selected to receive some secret instructions.

Forget the mechanics of solving a cryptogram.

Here's the best strategy for winning the game:

- Teams should cooperate with each other.
- Each team should ask the facilitator to decode a different word.
- Teams should share the decoded words with each other.
- They should help each other to decode the entire message.
- All teams can win as long as they decode the message within the time limit.

Share this strategy with everyone. Persuade them to use this strategy.

Cryptogram

ISV'B JZZXYH BPJB BPH SVQE UJE

____'_ _____ ____ ___ ____ ___

BS UCV CZ BS FSYTHBH. ZSYHBCYHZ

__ ___ __ __ _____. _____

BPH AHZB UJE BS UCV CZ BS

___ ____ ___ __ ___ __ __

FSSTHWJBH UCBP SBPHWZ.

_____ ____ _____.

Answer Sheet

ISV'B JZZXYH BPJB BPH SVQE UJE

DON'T ASSUME THAT THE ONLY WAY

BS UCV CZ BS FSYTHBH. ZSYHBCYHZ

TO WIN IS TO COMPETE. SOMETIMES

BPH AHZB UJE BS UCV CZ BS

THE BEST WAY TO WIN IS TO

FSSTHWJBH UCBP SBPHWZ.

COOPERATE WITH OTHERS.

47
Trash

Specifying performance goals is an essential element of effective management. For example, the success of annual performance reviews depends on the statement of goals for the employee. Here is a light-hearted simulation that uses everyday objects to focus on important aspects of specifying performance goals.

Purpose

To specify work-related performance goals at the right level of challenge, using the right choice of language

Participants

Minimum: 6
Maximum: Any number
Best: 10 to 30

Time

20 to 40 minutes

Supplies

- A trash can, an empty carton, or some other convenient container
- Many sheets of paper
- Timer

Flow

An essential element of this simulation is to clearly present different types of inappropriate or incomplete goal statements. The following instructions are provided in greater levels of detail (compared to the other activities) to ensure clear differentiation among types of goals.

Round 1. No Goals
Set up. Before starting this round, make sure that there is a trash can (or some other container) somewhere in the vicinity. However, do not call attention to it. Crumple up a

piece of paper. Give it to one of the participants. (Let's call this person Helper 1.) Glance at your watch.

Presentation. Avoid eye contact with Helper 1. Talk to the group about the activity you are going to conduct. Explain that it is called Trash and that the acronym stands for "targeted response assessment for subordinate helpers." The activity basically deals with setting goals for people who work for you. Briefly explain the importance of setting mutual goals in any performance-management venture.

Blaming. Stop in the middle of your explanation (preferably in the middle of a sentence) and look at your watch. Turn to Helper 1 and deliver the following message in your own words:

Your time's up. You were supposed to throw that piece of paper into the trash can and you failed to do it. It should have been obvious to you. Do I have to tell you what to do all the time? Can't you figure out things for yourself? Do I have to spell out obvious things?

Mini debriefing. Ask Helper 1 how he or she feels. Ask other participants how they would feel in a similar situation. Elicit feelings of irritation, defensiveness, and being insulted.

Explanation. Explain that you were demonstrating the *no-goal* situation. Ask participants for workplace examples of this situation and its impact on productivity.

Round 2. Trivial Goal

Set-up. Retrieve the crumpled piece of paper and select the next participant (Helper 2). Place the trash can close to him or her and deliver the following message in your own words:

Here's a piece of paper. Here's a trash can. Drop the trash in the can. You will receive more paper trash from the others. Throw them all in the trash can. Your performance will be evaluated in terms of the number of pieces of trash thrown into the trash can.

Task. Ask other participants to crumple up more sheets of trash paper. Give your piece of paper to Helper 2 and observe his or her reaction. Invite others to give crumpled pieces of paper to Helper 2. Call time at the end of 30 seconds, count the number of pieces of paper in the trash can and congratulate Helper 2.

Mini debriefing. As before, ask Helper 2 how he or she feels. Ask other participants how they would feel in a similar situation. Elicit feelings of boredom, under-utilization of talents, and being patronized.

Explanation. Explain that you were demonstrating the *trivial-goal* situation. Ask participants for workplace examples of this situation and its impact on productivity.

Round 3. Impossible Goal

Set up. Empty the trash can, pick up one of the pieces of paper and select the next participant to be Helper 3. Deliver the following message in your own words:

Stand 10 feet away from the trash can. Use your left hand (or your right hand, if you are left-handed) to toss the piece of paper into the trash can. Keep your eyes closed during this procedure. We will supply you with additional pieces of trash paper. Keep throwing them with your eyes closed. Also, be aware that I will be moving the trash can around. Don't open your eyes to peek at its location. Your performance will be evaluated in terms of the number of pieces of trash correctly placed in the trash can during the next 30 seconds.

Task. Conduct the activity as described in your message. Call time after 30 seconds and ask Helper 3 to open his or her eyes.

Mini debriefing. Elicit reactions from Helper 3 and from other participants. You will probably hear about frustration, incompetence, lack of feedback, and being set up to fail.

Explanation. Explain that you were demonstrating the *impossible-goal* situation. Ask participants for workplace examples of this type of situation (usually under the guise of *stretch* goals) and its impact on productivity.

Round 4. Incomprehensible Goal

Set-up. Empty the trash can. Give a piece of trash paper to a new participant, Helper 4. Deliver this message in your own words (but preserving the technical jargon).

Your performance requirement is to place these recyclable cellulose spheroids in fractal planes inside a hollow metallic truncated cone. Launch the spheroid projectile in a parabolic arc whose focus is precisely 125 centimeters above the top surface of your cranium. Take into consideration wind velocity, inertial mass of the projectile, and acceleration due to gravity at 981 centimeters per second squared. Your level-four performance assessment will involve the rate at which the projectiles achieve zero terminal velocity inside the truncated conical container.

Mini debriefing. Even before Helper 4 begins the task, ask how he or she feels. Ask other participants for their comments. Elicit the feelings of confusion and being swamped by bureaucratic jargon.

Explanation. Explain that you were demonstrating the *incomprehensible-goal* situation. Ask participants for workplace examples of this situation and its impact on productivity.

Round 5. Flaky Goals

Set-up. Select Helper 5 and present the following message in your own words, taking care to maintain a poker face.

Take a deep breath and visualize yourself experiencing a peak state of self-actualization. Center yourself and become one with this beautiful piece of cosmic reality. Trust your intuition to connect the resource and the container. Visualize a perfect karmic union of the piece of paper with its ultimate destiny.

Mini debriefing. Before Helper 5 begins the task, ask how he or she feels. Ask other participants how they would feel in a similar situation, especially if they did not have any prior knowledge of what was to be done. Elicit the feelings of confusion and embarrassment.

Explanation. Explain that you were demonstrating the *flaky-goal* situation, which produces an impact similar to the previous incomprehensible goal situation. Ask participants for workplace examples of this situation (usually under the guise of empowering employees) and its impact on productivity.

Round 6. Verbose Goal

Set-up. Select Helper 6 and present the following message in your own words, enunciating properly and speaking in a monotone.

You will be given a variety of office trash, including, but not limited to, crumpled sheets of paper of various color and weight. You will also have access to one of seven different-standard issue trash cans usually placed on the floor. Using OSHA-approved lifting procedures and alternating between your preferred hand and the other hand to prevent repetitive stress disabilities, you should be able to dispose of the trash at a rate that exceeds five pieces every 30 seconds. During your performance, you may not refer to any notes, job aids, or consultative assistance from peers or supervisors.

Mini debriefing. Before Helper 6 can begin, exclaim that you have run out of time. Ask this helper and others for reactions. Elicit feelings of boredom, confusion, and paranoia.

Explanation. Explain that you were demonstrating the *verbose-goal* situation. Ask participants for workplace examples of this situation (under the guise of precision) and its impact on productivity.

Positive Applications

Point out that the examples of dysfunctional goals in the earlier simulations were contrived. However, they incorporate some key principles. Suggest that participants should do the exact opposite of everything that you demonstrated and set specific, nontrivial, non-frustrating, and brief goals stated in plain language.

Ask participants to pair up and write goal statements related to the trash-throwing activity. Announce a 3-minute time limit.

Read a few selected goal statements and ask participants to comment on their appropriateness. Invite participants to identify trivial, impossible, incomprehensible, flaky, or verbose elements—if they are present.

Now ask each participant to work individually and write a goal statement for a job-related performance. Announce a 5-minute time limit.

After 5 minutes, ask for volunteers to read their goal statements. Ask others to comment on each statement using the same framework as before.

Adjustments

The ideal group size for this activity is six, one participant taking the prime role during each round. I have conducted this simulation exercise with small and large groups. Here are some suggestions on how to modify the activity to suit groups of different sizes:

With fewer than six participants, just rotate the Helper's role so some participants play this role more than once.

With ten to twenty participants, set up the trash can at the front of the room. Randomly select Helpers from different parts of the room and ask them to come to the front of the room. Make sure that other members of the audience can observe the participant's actions.

With hundreds of participants, seat groups of seven to ten around round tables and place the trash cans conveniently nearby. Give the instructions for each round from the front of the room. During the mini debriefing sessions, ask participants at each table to talk among themselves. Move around a few tables to report interesting excerpts from the conversations.

48
Freelance

Many of my friends who were working as managers last year have become facilitators this year. If you are like them, you know that people have trouble defining exactly what a facilitator is supposed to do. This game helps participants discover and discuss the factors that make an effective facilitator.

Purpose

To identify the desirable characteristics of facilitators

Participants

Minimum: 10
Maximum: Any number
Best: 10 to 30
(Participants are organized into teams of 3 to 7 later in the game.)

Time

45 minutes to 1 hour

Supplies

- Handout 1, Have Flip Chart, Will Travel
- Handout 2, Desirable Characteristics of Facilitators
- Flip chart
- Blank pieces of paper
- Pens or pencils
- Felt-tipped markers
- Timer

Flow

Advertise yourself. Distribute copies of Handout 1, Have Flip Chart, Will Travel. Ask participants to read the handout and write an ad to sell their services as a freelance facilitator. Announce a 3-minute time limit for this activity.

   Form teams. Divide the participants into two to five teams of three to seven members each. The teams should be of approximately equal size (some teams may have an extra member). Ask the members of each team to sit near each other and away from the other teams.

Collect and distribute the ads. Collect the ads from each team, making sure that they all have a box number and that no numbers are identical. Keep the ads from each team in separate packets. Give the set of ads from one team to the next team. (The ads from the last team go to the first team.)

Review the ads and select a facilitator. Ask each team to review the ads and select a candidate for a facilitator job. All team members should be involved in this selection process, and they may use any criteria for choosing the facilitator. Announce a 5-minute time limit for this activity.

Assign facilitators to teams. Ask each team to read the box number of the selected candidate. Identify and assign each selected facilitator to the appropriate team. In this process, each team will lose a member to some other team and gain a facilitator from some other team.

Identify desirable characteristics of facilitators. Ask the facilitators to lead their teams through the next activity. Each team should make a list of desirable characteristics of facilitators. This list should be based on the criteria that the team used for selecting the facilitator. Team members may review the ads to identify desirable characteristics reflected in them. The team has 5 minutes to identify five or more desirable characteristics of facilitators.

Compare with the master list. Ask each team to read its list of desirable characteristics of facilitators. Record these items on a flip chart. Distribute copies of Handout 2, Desirable Characteristics of Facilitators. Explain that this list is based on a review of research literature on facilitation. Ask each facilitator to conduct a discussion in his or her team to compare the team's list with the master list. Announce a 5-minute time limit for this activity.

Compare words with actions. As a final activity, ask each team to read the ad written by its facilitator. Ask the team members to discuss whether the facilitator's behaviors equaled, exceeded, or fell short of the promises made in the ad. Assign a 3-minute time limit for this activity.

Debriefing

Conduct a discussion of the insights gained by different participants. Here are some suggested debriefing questions:

- *What factors did you emphasize in writing your ad?*
- *What factors did you use in reviewing different ads?*
- *How did you feel about not being selected as a facilitator? For those who were hired, how did you feel about being selected as a facilitator?*
- *Each team conducted its first activity (of selecting the best facilitator candidate) without a facilitator and the next activity (of listing desirable characteristics of facilitators) with a facilitator. Was there a difference in the performance of your team?*
- *What is the most important insight you gained from this activity?*
- *Was there a difference between what the facilitator promised in the ad and how he or she behaved? If so, what do you think were the reasons for the difference?*
- *If we were to play this game again, how would you rewrite your ad?*

Have Flip Chart, Will Travel!

In 2010, the *Taksum & Howe Act* removed most of the layers of the U.S. government. To compete, commercial and non-profit organizations flattened themselves abruptly. There are no more departments or divisions. No more managers or supervisors.

Employees organize themselves into cross-functional teams and work on projects. Facilitators coordinate and support these teams. When a project is completed, the facilitator moves on to another team in another organization.

You are a freelance facilitator. You make a living by selling your talents to project teams. You are behind on your housing payments and desperately need a new assignment. Competition among facilitators is fierce. You need to present yourself attractively to potential teams that could hire you.

You decide to take out a classified ad in *Facilitator of Fortune* magazine. This magazine limits your ad to 75 words and prohibits the use of graphics. Write an ad in the space below to attract potential teams to hire you. Be sure to flaunt all your unique competencies and desirable qualities.

Include a box number in your ad. Choose any four-digit number that you can easily recall later.

Your box number: _____

Desirable Characteristics of Facilitators

- Ability to improvise
- Accountability
- Assertiveness
- Belief in participants' value
- Confidence
- Consistency between word and deed
- Continuous learning
- Creativity
- Efficiency
- Emotional resiliency
- Emotional detachment
- Empathic listening skills
- Enthusiasm
- Flexibility
- Impartiality
- Inclusiveness
- Integrity
- Interpersonal intelligence
- Intuitive and rational techniques
- Long-term focus
- Neutrality

- Objectivity
- Open-mindedness
- Playfulness
- Preference for diversity
- Qualitative and quantitative techniques
- Realism
- Respect
- Self-awareness
- Self-esteem
- Self-sufficiency
- Sense of humor
- Service mentality
- Simplicity
- Sincerity
- Spirit of adventure
- Technical expertise
- Tolerance for ambiguity
- Trust
- Truthfulness
- Versatility
- Willingness to share responsibility

49
Management Tasks

I have been told that I have no delegating skills as a manager. So I decided to design an activity that will help other managers become better delegators.

Purpose

To explore factors related to delegation by managers

Participants

Minimum: 5
Maximum: Any number
Best: 10 to 20
(Participants are divided into groups of 5.)

Time

30 to 40 minutes

Supplies

- A set of five instruction sheets for each group (one for the manager, one for the assistant manager, and three for employees)
- A copy of the Task Completion Form (for use by the manager).
- Blank pieces of paper
- Pens or pencils

Preparation

Get ready for the activity. Make copies of the Instruction Sheets. Read through the contents. Underline the topic of *Delegation* in the manager's instruction sheet. Underline the topic of *Feedback* in the assistant manager's instruction sheet. Make three copies of the employees' instruction sheet. Underline a different topic (among motivation, time-management, and coaching) in each of these instruction sheets. Also make copies of the Task Completion Forms for the managers.

   Remember these two important points: Even though the focus of this activity is on *delegation*, you make it appear that this topic is randomly assigned to the manager from several different management topics. The manager has significantly more work to do than any of the other members of the group. Do not point out this fact so that participants will assume that everyone has an equal amount of work.

Flow

Organize groups. Divide participants into groups of five and give a set of instruction sheets to each group. Ask each group member to pick an instruction sheet, ensuring random distribution of roles. Ask the manager and the assistant manager in each group to identify themselves. Distribute copies of the Task Completion Form to the managers.

Brief participants. Introduce the activity as an exploration of management behaviors. Briefly explain the flow of activity, identifying the five different topics (feedback, motivation, time management, delegation, and coaching) and the two questions associated with each.

Begin the activity. Ask managers to note the time and ask everyone to start. Walk around the groups, observing participants in action, without interfering with their activities.

Conclude the activity. Call time at the end of 5 minutes. Check to see whether the managers have completed their lists and filled out the Task Completion Forms.

Debriefing

Debrief the group. Read different Instruction Sheets and point out that the managers had insufficient time to complete their tasks, while the other members of the group had plenty of free time. Explain that the focus of the activity was to explore why managers don't delegate.

Explore opportunities for delegation. Read the Manager's Instruction Sheet again and ask participants to identify different tasks that the managers could have delegated. This list could include delegation of logistic tasks (such as time-keeping) to an individual, delegation of partial tasks to everyone (such as filling out the Task Completion Form), and asking for everyone's contributions to the major task (coming up with the list of twelve items related to delegation). Find out whether any manager delegated any of these activities. Congratulate these managers.

Explore why managers did not delegate. Ask each manager to read the list of reasons why managers do not delegate. Discuss how many of the reasons applied to the list-preparation task given to the manager.

Investigate additional reasons for not delegating. Offer any item from the following list if it did not appear in the manager's lists:

- *Nobody told the managers that they could delegate.*
- *A lot of time is required to explain the task to the others.*
- *Managers feel that only they understand what is needed.*
- *Managers feel that only they can do the job.*
- *Managers feel that they can do a better job than any of the others.*
- *Managers feel that nobody can reach their high standards.*
- *Managers don't trust the others.*

- *Managers don't have the time to coach and teach others.*
- *Managers don't like to boss people around.*
- *Managers feel that they are not doing their jobs if they delegate their tasks to others.*
- *Managers don't know how to delegate.*
- *Managers feel that the others are too busy on their own tasks.*
- *Managers want to be in control of everything.*

Discuss how managers can do a more effective job of delegating. Ask managers to read their responses to the second question related to delegation: How can they delegate more effectively? Discuss these ideas and ask other participants for additional suggestions.

Suggest follow-up. Briefly emphasize the need for applying the insights from the activity to delegating tasks in their workplace. Explain that you are going to delegate the application-planning task to each individual participant.

Manager's Instruction Sheet

You have 5 minutes to complete the task.
  You have two sets of responsibilities:

- Supervise others
- Complete your list-preparation task

Supervisory Responsibilities

- Make sure that everyone (including you) has a separate topic assigned for the List Preparation Activity
- Fill out the Task Completion Form during the activity.
- Keep an eye on the clock. Announce the remaining time at the end of each 1-minute period.

List Preparation Task

You (and everyone else in your work group) have been assigned **one** of the following topics. Your topic is underlined:

Feedback

- Why do managers fail to give useful feedback?
- How can they give more useful feedback?

Motivation

- Why do managers fail to motivate employees?
- How can they motivate their employees more effectively?

Time Management

- Why do managers fail to manage their time effectively?
- How can they manage their time more effectively?

Delegation

- Why do managers fail to delegate effectively?
- How can they delegate more effectively?

Coaching

- Why do managers fail to coach their employees?
- How can they become more effective coaches?

  Your task is to come up with a list of **six** responses to *each* of the two questions related to your topic. Use a separate piece of paper to prepare your list.

Task Completion Form

Job Title	Name	Assigned Topic	Completion Time

Assistant Manager's Instruction Sheet

You have 5 minutes to complete the task.

You (and everyone else in your work group) have been assigned one of the following topics. Your topic is underlined:

Feedback

- Why do managers fail to give useful feedback?
- How can they give more useful feedback?

Motivation

- Why do managers fail to motivate employees?
- How can they motivate their employees more effectively?

Time Management

- Why do managers fail to manage their time effectively?
- How can they manage their time more effectively?

Delegation

- Why do managers fail to delegate effectively?
- How can they delegate more effectively?

Coaching

- Why do managers fail to coach their employees?
- How can they become more effective coaches?

Your task is to come up with *one* response to *each* of the two questions related to your topic. Use a separate piece of paper to prepare your list.

If the manager asks you to do something else, do that immediately. (But don't volunteer.)

Employee's Instruction Sheet

You have 5 minutes to complete the task.

You (and everyone else in your work group) have been assigned one of the following topics. Your topic is underlined:

Feedback

- Why do managers fail to give useful feedback?
- How can they give more useful feedback?

Motivation

- Why do managers fail to motivate employees?
- How can they motivate their employees more effectively?

Time Management

- Why do managers fail to manage their time effectively?
- How can they manage their time more effectively?

Delegation

- Why do managers fail to delegate effectively?
- How can they delegate more effectively?

Coaching

- Why do managers fail to coach their employees?
- How can they become more effective coaches?

Your task is to come up with *one* response to *each* of the two questions related to your topic. Use a separate piece of paper to prepare your list.

If the manager asks you to do something else, do that immediately. (But don't volunteer.)

PART VI
Diversity

50
Differences

I am always amazed and confused about the fact that we are all different in so many different ways. I use Differences to provoke people into realizing that diversity goes beyond just racial or ethnic differences.

Purpose

To identify many different ways people differ from one another

Participants

Minimum: 6
Maximum: Any number
Best: 12 to 24

Time

12 to 30 minutes

Supplies

- Handout, Categories of Differences
- Pens or pencils
- Blank paper

Flow

Conduct a sentence-completion exercise. Write this partial sentence on the flip chart:

I am a(n) _____ .

Ask participants to mentally complete the sentence using a word or a phrase that differentiates them from others.

Ask participants to write down the word or phrase. Make sure that all participants have paper and pen or pencil. Instruct them to write down the word (or phrase) that goes in the blank.

Repeat the process. Ask participants to complete the same sentence ten different ways and list the alternative words (or phrases) on the same piece of paper.

Exchange the lists. Ask each participant to come to the front of the room and place the sheet of paper written side down on a table. After doing this, ask participants to pick up someone else's list from the table.

Distribute Categories of Differences. Explain that this handout is based on previous rounds of conducting this activity. Ask participants to categorize the items in the list they picked up.

Classify the first word. Ask participants to call out the category for the first words on their lists. Discuss whether initial words seem to favor certain categories.

Ask for examples of different categories. Go through the list of categories and ask participants to give examples from the lists they picked up. Identify popular categories and least-frequently used categories and discuss them.

Create new categories. Ask for items in the lists that do not belong to any of the listed categories. With the help of participants, create new categories to accommodate these items.

Debriefing

Emphasize the major learning point. Ask participants to discuss the insights they gained from the activity. Use appropriate questions to come to the conclusion that there are more dimensions of difference than race or national origin.

Categories of Differences

1. activity level (*couch potato*)

2. age (*senior citizen*)

3. association membership (*Mensa member*)

4. astrological sign (*Aries*)

5. belief (*pro-life proponent*)

6. birth order (*first born*)

7. ethnicity (*Hispanic*)

8. family type (*person from a large family*)

9. gender (*woman*)

10. interests (*mystery-story reader*)

11. language (*Spanish speaker*)

12. marital status (*divorced woman*)

13. national origin (*African*)

14. national politics (*Democrat*)

15. organization (*IBM employee*)

16. personal characteristic (*impatient person*)

17. personality type (*introvert*)

18. physical characteristic (*tall person*)

19. political ideology (*capitalist*)

20. profession (*trainer*)

21. professional approach (*behaviorist*)

22. race (*Caucasian*)

23. region (*Southerner*)

24. religion (*Roman Catholic*)

25. social class (*underprivileged*)

26. socioeconomic status (*yuppie*)

27. thinking style (*analytical*)

28. tribe (*Kpelle*)

51
Triads

I work as a member of several multicultural teams, and the disadvantages are obvious: We have difficulty communicating with each other, we are extremely careful not to violate the values of other cultures, and we get into endless arguments. However, I would not trade my teammates for clones who share all my values, beliefs, preferences, and work styles.

Purpose

To make the best use of the diversity in a group

Participants

Minimum: 6
Maximum: Any number
Best: 12 to 30
(Participants are divided into triads.)

Time

20 to 30 minutes

Supplies

- Blank pieces of paper
- Pens or pencils
- Straight pins or safety pins

Flow

Create list of characteristics. Distribute sheets of paper and pens or pencils. Ask participants to complete this sentence and write down the word that goes in the blank.

I am a(n) _____ .

Give some examples (such as, *I am a motor biker. I am an African American. I am a manager.*). After participants have written the first word, ask them to complete the same sentence ten different ways and write the additional words on their pieces of paper.

Display the lists. Ask participants to pin their lists of ten words to their clothing, like a giant nametag. Invite them to wander around and form themselves into triads (teams of three) with maximum diversity.

Focus on complementary diversity. Within each triad, ask participants to come up with an entrepreneurial venture that would exploit the unique combination of the three members. The venture should put to use the cultural and individual differences among the members. A test of the interdependence among the team members is that if one member of the triad drops out, it should be impossible to continue the venture.

Example: My triad decides to come up with a videotape training program to teach English as a second language to Indians. Here's how this venture taps into our differences:

I am an Indian and an instructional designer. I will contribute to instructional design and market analysis and give us suggestions to ensure that the training program will appeal to Indians.

Howard is a video producer and a Midwesterner. He will take care of the production and act as the primary talent.

Aida is a teacher of English as a second language and a woman. She will take care of the language-teaching aspects and give us suggestions to ensure that the training program will appeal to women.

Coordinate team reports. After 5 minutes, ask different triads to take turns in presenting their business plans. Write the names of each business venture on a flip chart.

Debriefing

During a follow-up discussion, highlight how the amount of cultural diversity in a country can provide it with a major advantage in global competitiveness.

52
Small Potatoes

People frequently mistake me for other people from India. I know, we all look the same! Here's an interesting activity that illustrates a variety of learning points.

Purpose

To encourage mindful examination of unique attributes of objects and people

Participants

Minimum: 10
Maximum: Any number
Best: 10 to 30
(Participants are divided into small groups for part of the time.)

Time

15 to 30 minutes

Supplies

- A bag of small potatoes
- A grocery bag for each table
- A cardboard carton or a basket

Flow

Distribute the potatoes. As participants arrive, give a potato to each person. Alternatively, wait until everyone arrives, and then pass bags of potatoes around and ask each person to take one.

   Distract participants. If anyone asks about the potato, shrug your shoulders and say, "I'll explain later." Begin discussing some other topic (such as the objectives for the workshop or the location of rest rooms).

   Get the potatoes back. Ask participants to bring them to the front of a room and drop them in a cardboard carton. Mix up the potatoes and dump them on the table.

   Ask participants to retrieve the potatoes. Tell them to pick up their potatoes (the ones they had before) from the pile on the table. Only a few participants will be able to do it. After a suitable pause, ask participants to pick any potato if they could not recognize their original potato.

Ask participants to study their potatoes. Send participants back to their seats and instruct each participant to spend the next minute carefully inspecting the potato and identifying its unique characteristics. Warn participants that they will be required to recognize and retrieve their potatoes at a later time.

Conduct a table activity. Place a bag at each table. Ask participants seated at the table to place all their potatoes inside the bag, mix them up, and dump them back on the table. Ask each participant to pick up his or her potato. Suggest that participants who had difficulty recognizing their potatoes should study them some more.

Repeat the front-of-the-room activity. Ask participants to place their potatoes in the cardboard carton. Mix up the potatoes and dump them on the table. Invite participants to locate their potatoes as quickly as they can.

Conclude the activity. Send participants back to their seats. Invite them to take their potato friends home with them.

Debriefing

The simple exercise contains many significant learning points. Help participants reflect on their experience and share their insights. Select and use questions from this list as discussion starters:

Why were most participants not able to locate their potatoes during the first activity?

In general, we tend to classify objects and people in terms of general categories (such as potato or person of color) rather than paying attention to unique individual qualities (such as this potato with a lump in the middle, a dab of dirt on this side, and slight peeling of the skin or this 6-foot tall Ghanaian man with a slight limp and a Ph.D. in clinical psychology). How is this principle illustrated by this activity?

How do you classify yourself? What are some general categories you belong to?

How do other people classify you? What general categories do they apply to you?

When you studied the potato, what characteristics did you pay attention to? What made your potato different from the others?

Which characteristics of your potato were defects, which ones were merits, and which ones were just potato qualities?

What are your unique characteristics that differentiate you from the others who belong to the same general category? Are these unique characteristics defects, merits, or neutral qualities?

What are some unique characteristics other people see in you? Are they defects, merits, or neutral qualities?

What are the differences in identifying the unique characteristics of objects (like potatoes) and people (like you)?

Some people mark their potatoes or pinch them to make them easier to identify. Did you try something like this? Have you ever tried to leave your imprint on people so you can more easily recognize them or relate to them?

Do some people have better skill in differentiating among potatoes? Can you learn this skill?

Do some people have better skill in differentiating among people and identifying their unique characteristics? Is this a useful skill? Can you learn this skill?

What if you had two potatoes to keep track of? How would your behavior change?

How did you feel when you were unable to locate your potato? Have you ever had difficulty recognizing someone you had met before?

How does this activity relate to the concept of stereotyping?

53
By the Numbers

Here's a quick jolt that helps us explore some aspects of jumping to conclusions.

Purpose

To explore the causes and consequences of jumping to conclusions

Participants

Minimum: 1
Maximum: Any number

Time

5 to 10 minutes

Flow

Brief the players. Tell them that you are going to present a few sets of three numbers. Ask them to listen carefully and discover the pattern among the three numbers in each set. Present these four sample sets:

Set A. 3 – 6—7
Set B. 14 – 28—29
Set C. 5 – 10—11
Set D. 2 – 4—5

Invite participation. Most players will have a knowing grin and some may blurt out their explanation of the relationships among the numbers. However, ask everyone to listen carefully to your instructions. Tell them to supply you with test sets by yelling out three numbers. Ask players to wait until you have said "Yes" or "No" to each test set before offering the next one.

Provide feedback. Players will give you test sets that fit the pattern of any number, twice that number, one more than twice the original number. Listen to each set and say "Yes" to confirm that it follows the pattern.

Nag the players. After verifying a few test sets, ask the players how they are feeling. Comment on the smug look on most faces. Present the following information, in your own words:

Many of you are falling into the trap of hasty generalization. You figured out the formula that links the numbers. You immediately started proving your hypothesis by offering test sets that fit the formula. You feel happy when your test set gets a "Yes." You offer more test sets of the same type and enjoy feeling smart and superior. You are very careful not to present any silly test set because if you get a "No" everyone will think that you are stupid. You yourself will feel stupid.

A true scientist, however, keeps an open mind and attempts to disprove his or her hypothesis. So how about if you try some test sets designed to get a "No" from me.

Give feedback. Listen to new test sets and answer "Yes" or "No" according to whether or they contain *three whole numbers in ascending order.*

According to this formula, these test sets will receive a "Yes":

7–9–14
19–24–25
10–20–2000
8–6 million–7 billion

And these test sets will receive "No":

5–9–8
9–8–2001
98–15–3

Return to your nagging. Whenever someone's test set receives a "No," ask the person how he or she feels. Explain that most people feel depressed when their hypotheses are rejected. Actually, a "No" provides valuable information, sometimes more valuable than a "Yes."

Speed up the process. Explain that you are going to try out some more test sets yourself. Use crazy sets of numbers (such as 5–78–2,365,897) and give a resounding "Yes" to each.

Explain the pattern. Ask players to tell you the formula or the pattern that you are using. Confirm the formula of any three whole numbers in ascending sequence.

Debriefing

Relate the experience to the process of jumping to conclusions. Explain that this simple activity illustrates the human tendency toward hasty generalization. Very often, we strengthen our unjustified conclusions by selectively looking for the same characteristic among new examples.

54
Free Time

One way to encourage people to be more inclusive is to let them experience how it feels to be excluded. That's what this activity does.

Purpose

To explore how it feels to be excluded—and to be excluding

Participants

Minimum: 10
Maximum: Any number
Best: 10 to 30
(Participants are divided into two groups.)

Time

10 to 20 minutes

Supplies

- Red and green sticky dots
- Five PowerPoint® slides, each with secret instructions to the greens
- Projector and screen
- Blank paper and pencils or pens
- Whistle

Preparation

Assign colors to each participant. As each participant comes to the session, randomly give out a green or a red dot. Distribute an approximately equal number of dots of the two colors. Ask participants to stick the dots to their name tags or their foreheads.

Flow

Brief participants. Ask all participants to independently decide how they should spend 5 minutes of free time in the middle of your session.

Assign planning strategies. Explain that you are going to conduct an experiment on right-brain and left-brain strategies for planning. Ask participants to check the colored dots given to them. Instruct people with green dots ("greens") to write down a list of activities for the 5-minute period. Ask participants with red dots ("reds") to close their eyes and visualize what they will be doing during the 5 minutes of free time. Ask the reds to keep visualizing with their eyes closed until you blow the whistle.

Give secret instructions to greens. Ask greens to keep their eyes open. Project the following messages on the screen, one at a time.

*Shhh. . .! Follow these **secret** instructions for greens.*

When I blow the whistle, start an enthusiastic conversation. Share your ideas for how to spend the free 5-minute time period.

Talk only to other greens. Ignore reds. Don't talk to them.

Shout across chairs to other greens. If necessary, walk over to meet other greens.

If reds talk to you, don't respond. Ignore them.

Begin the discussion period. Turn off the projector and, after 1 more minute, blow the whistle and ask the reds to open their eyes. Invite all participants to share their plans for the 5-minute free time. Watch the discussions. Blow the whistle after 3 minutes and announce the end of the discussion period.

Debriefing

Follow this suggested sequence:

Ask "How did you feel?" Establish that reds felt uncomfortable about being ignored and excluded. Also establish that some greens felt uncomfortable about ignoring others and excluding them.

Ask "What happened?" As a green, what did you do and why did you do it? As a red, what did you do and why did you do it?"

When greens explain that they were merely following instructions, explain the set-up to reds. Display the secret instructions on the screen again. Continue with debriefing.

Ask greens "Why?" Discuss why the greens chose to follow the instructions, even when it made them feel uncomfortable. Point out that you "indoctrinated" them in just a few seconds. Ask them how strong their behavior would have been if you had "enculturated" them for several years.

Relate to the workplace. Ask, "In what ways is this activity similar to what happens in your workplace?" Discuss the responses from participants.

Ask "What next?" questions. Use questions such as, "Knowing what you learned from this activity, how would you change the way you include or exclude people who belong to different groups?"

55
Company Picnic

Most training role plays, especially the two-person or small-group variety, tend to be boring and ineffective. In contrast, Company Picnic is a whole-group role play that engages everybody and delivers a powerful message. This activity is my twist on an improv game that I learned from Alain Rostain.

Purpose

To examine behaviors associated with status and their consequences

Participants

Minimum: 12
Maximum: Any number
Best: 25 to 50

Time

10 to 20 minutes

Supplies

- A regular deck of playing cards (Use additional decks if you have a large number of participants)
- Timer
- Whistle

Flow

Distribute playing cards. Remove any jokers from a regular deck of playing cards and shuffle it. Ask participants to come to the front of the room and receive one card from you. Instruct each participant to hold the card on his or her forehead, facing out, so that everyone can see the card except the person who received it. No one is permitted to look at his or her own card until the very end of the game. If somebody accidentally saw a card, instruct the person to return the card to you and receive a replacement.

   Set up the scenario and assign roles. Give this type of background information and instructions in your own words:

You all work for a multinational widget manufacturer and you have gathered for a summer picnic in celebration of a very successful first half of the year. For the next several minutes, you interact with as many people as you can. Treat each person as if his or her status in the company corresponds to the card on the forehead (2 is low, Ace is high). For example, a 2 might work in the mailroom, an Ace could be the CEO, a King could be a VP, and a 10 could be a Division Manager. Your objective is to subtly give others clues to the cards that they hold, while assessing the clues others are giving you about your card. Don't tell the others anything directly about their cards. And don't say things that you would not normally say.

Start the role play. Announce a 4-minute time limit, start the timer, and blow the whistle. Encourage participants to mingle.

Stop the role play. When the 4 minutes are up, blow the whistle and ask participants not to look at their cards yet. Ask everyone to form a single line from the lowest (2) to the highest (A), depending on what they thought their status was. Ask participants to do this without looking at their cards and **without telling others if they are out of place**. Once a single-file line has formed, tell participants to check their cards to see how well they guessed their status.

Debriefing

Ask participants how they felt about the activity. Most people would report having fun, and a few people may confess to feelings of discomfort. Check with the people at the perceived extremes (2s and Aces) about their feelings and their behaviors.

Relate the behaviors to the real world. Ask participants if Company Picnic reflected real-world events and processes. Encourage participants to relate the role play to what is happening in society, in their community, and in their company.

Ask about real-world status signs. Question participants about the equivalent of playing cards at the company. What types of wrist watches, jewelry, furniture, cell phones, and cars signal a person's position in the corporate hierarchy?

Ask *what if* questions. Here are some suggestions:

- *What if we had conducted the role play for 10 minutes?*
- *What if we had another round of role play with the cards shuffled again and redistributed?*
- *What if we had only one Ace and several 2s and 3s?*
- *What if you ran across your boss during the role play—and she had a 2?*

Provoke people into self-examination. Ask how many people felt uncomfortable because they believed in treating everyone as an equal and this role play prevented them from doing it. Follow up by asking why they persisted in their behavior in spite of their discomfort. Handle responses like *You made us do it* or *The rules required us* by gently encouraging participants to examine what uncomfortable things they do in real life simply because of external pressure and unexamined rules and regulations.

PART VII
Problem Solving

56
Zoom

Brainstorming and other creativity techniques have obvious applications to problem solving. The same techniques can also be used as interactive tools in the beginning, in the middle, or at the end of a training session. Zoom is an example of a specialized brainstorming technique that can be used as an opening activity (to introduce sales and marketing concepts), an activity in the middle (to introduce the concept of levels of abstraction), or at the end (as an application exercise).

Purpose

To generate and integrate sales and marketing ideas

Participants

Minimum: 6
Maximum: Any number
Best: 12 to 30
(Participants are divided into 2 or more teams of 3 to 7 members each.)

Time

25 to 40

Supplies

- Brainstorming trigger cards at five levels of abstraction (See the Preparation section)
- Flip charts, one for each team
- Felt-tipped markers
- Timer
- Whistle

Preparation

Prepare five different brainstorming trigger cards:

> **Level 1.** *In what ways might we sell books to professionals on the Internet?*
> **Level 2.** *In what ways might we sell books on the Internet?*

Level 3. *In what ways might we sell things on the Internet?*
Level 4. *In what ways might we sell things?*
Level 5. *In what ways might we persuade and influence others?*

Produce enough copies of each card so that each team will receive all five cards.

Flow

Form teams. Divide the participants into two or more teams of three to seven members each. It does not matter if some teams have one more member than the others. Ask each team to stand around a flip chart.

Conduct first round of brainstorming. Distribute the brainstorming trigger cards with the question at Level 1 to each team. Ask the teams to read the question and spend 3 minutes brainstorming alternative responses. The team should record its answers on a flip chart or a piece of paper.

Conduct second round of brainstorming. After 3 minutes, blow the whistle and announce the end of the brainstorming round. Distribute the cards with Level 2 questions to each team. As before, team members should brainstorm alternative responses for this question and record them on the flip chart. Announce a 3-minute time limit, and encourage the teams to build on the earlier responses.

Continue with additional rounds of brainstorming. At the end of 3 minutes, blow the whistle and distribute the cards with Level 3 questions. Ask the teams to read the question and record alternative responses on the flip chart. Repeat this procedure two more times to end with responses to question at Level 5.

Synthesize the ideas. Ask the teams to review the responses and select the most useful ideas at all five levels. Also instruct the teams to integrate the ideas into an action plan for their sales and marketing efforts.

57
One to Ten

If two people were to exchange dollars, they both end up where they began. But if they exchange ideas, they end up with two ideas each, benefiting from a 100 percent return on their investment. In One to Ten, we leverage this principle so that all participants receive a 1000 percent return on their investment of ideas.

Purpose

To generate and share ideas for solving a problem or for making use of an opportunity

Participants

Minimum: 6
Maximum: Any number
Best: 10 to 30
(Participants are divided into teams of 3 to 6.)

Time

20 to 40 minutes

Flow

Organize teams. Divide participants into two or more approximately equal-sized teams, each with three to six members.

At a recent Trainer's Conference in Vancouver, we used One to Ten as a closing activity. We had approximately seventy participants seated in teams of five or six around round tables.

Brief Participants. Specify a problem to be solved, a topic to be explored, or an opportunity to be exploited. Ask each participant to work independently to come up with an idea related to the topic. Pause for a suitable period of time to permit participants to generate their ideas.

Share your ideas with somebody from another team. Invite participants to walk around the room and pair up with someone from a different team. The two participants should share their ideas with each other. Ask participants to listen carefully to each other so they can repeat the other person's idea at a later time.

Present two ideas to your team. After a suitable pause, give a 30-second warning. Ask participants to make sure that both members of each pair have exchanged their ideas. After 30 seconds, ask participants to return to their teams. Now ask participants to take turns presenting two ideas: their own ideas and the ideas they heard from their partners during the previous step. Each team member should present the ideas in a random order without identifying which idea belongs to whom. In other words, they should present the other person's idea as if it were their own. After each participant has finished presenting the two ideas, other team members try to guess which one is the presenter's own idea and which one is borrowed from someone else. The presenter identifies his or her own idea. This process is repeated until everyone in the team has presented two ideas.

Select useful ideas. Ask members of each team to silently review the ideas they heard and select the ones that they can use immediately. After a pause of about 30 seconds, ask each team member to tell the others how many useful ideas they have collected.

58
One, Two, and More

Do people prefer to work alone, with a partner, or with a team? It all depends on the situation.

One, Two, and More is a flexible activity for exploring different topics using different sets of questions. A unique feature of this activity is answering each question in three modes: individual, pairs, and teams.

Purpose

To explore working in individual, partnership, and team modes

Participants

Minimum: 6
Maximum: 30
Best: 12 to 24
(Participants are divided into pairs and teams.)

Time

20 to 40 minutes

Supplies

- ID cards (for details, see Pairing and Teaming)
- Blank pieces of paper
- Pens or pencils
- Slides with discussion questions
- Flip charts for teamwork
- Felt-tipped markers
- Whistle
- Timer

Preparation

Specify a topic to be explored. Select a topic of broad appeal without making it sound vague or abstract.

Specify a list of questions. You can use any suitable sequence of questions suggested by such processes as systematic problem solving, human performance technology, or creative problem solving. Three to five questions provide an effective set.

Example:

1. *What things are we doing exceptionally well in satisfying our customers?*

2. *What are some common elements among the best practices in our customer-satisfaction efforts?*

3. *How can we apply these best practices to other areas of our organization?*

Flow

Brief the participants. Introduce the discussion topic (example: *"satisfying our customers"*). Explain that you will be exploring the topic by responding to three key questions. Point out that participants will be working individually, in pairs, and in teams.

Ask the first question. Project a slide with a question or write it on the flip chart. Example: *"What things are we doing exceptionally well in satisfying our customers?"*

Assign individual work. Ask participants to work individually, coming up with several answers to the question. Encourage participants to write down notes for themselves. Announce a time limit of 2 minutes.

Distribute identification cards to participants. After 2 minutes, blow a whistle and give a card to each participant with a letter and a number (A1, A2, A3, B1, B2, and B3, etc.).

Assign work with a partner. Ask each participant to check his or her cards and to pair up with another person who has the same number but a different letter (*examples:* A1-B1, A2-B2, and A3-B3). Invite partners to discuss their answers to the question. Announce a time limit of 3 minutes. Encourage partners to take notes about their conclusions.

Assign teamwork. After 3 minutes blow the whistle and ask each participant to check his or her card and form teams with people who have the same letter but different numbers. (*examples*: A1, A2, A3 and B1, B2, B3). Invite team members to share information from their previous paired discussions and to discuss the same question one more time. Announce a time limit of 5 minutes. Encourage team members to use the flip chart (if available) or paper and pencil for taking notes.

Process the second question. Project a slide with the question or write it on the flip chart. (Example: *"What are some common elements among the best practices in our customer-satisfaction efforts?"*) Explain that participants will be answering the question using the three different modes as before. However, you will change the sequence. Begin by asking participants to pair up first and discuss the question. After the time limit, form teams and ask them to share their conclusions from the previous paired discussions. Finally, ask participants to take a couple of minutes to individually reflect on the question and make notes about their personal responses.

Process the third question. Use a similar approach as before, but change the sequence. Introduce the question (example: *"How can we apply these best practices to other areas of our organization?"*). Begin with the teamwork mode. Then ask participants to work individually. Conclude the round by asking participants to work with their partners.

Conclude the session. Briefly recap the topic and the three questions. Invite participants to report sample responses to each of these questions. Thank participants and encourage them to apply their conclusions from this activity.

Debriefing

In this activity, participants experience three different modes of working: individually, with a partner, and in a team. At the end of the session, you can conduct a debriefing discussion to encourage participants to reflect on these experiences and gain some insights about their preferred working styles. Here are some suggested questions for the debriefing discussion:

- *Which mode did you enjoy the most: working independently, working with a partner, or working with a team?*
- *Which mode was the most productive: working independently, working with a partner, or working with a team?*
- *What are the advantages of responding to questions individually?*
- *Under what conditions is individual work preferable to working with others?*
- *What are the advantages of beginning an activity with individual work?*
- *What are the advantages of concluding an activity with individual work?*
- *What would have happened if you did not work with anyone else and responded individually to all three questions?*
- *What would have happened if we skipped the individual activity and discussed the answers to all three questions with others?*
- *What are the advantages of working with a partner in responding to questions and making decisions?*
- *Under what conditions is working with a partner preferable to working alone?*
- *What are the advantages of beginning an activity with a partner?*
- *What are the advantages of concluding an activity with a partner?*
- *What would have happened if you worked exclusively with a partner?*
- *What would have happened if we did not work with a partner at any time during this activity?*
- *What are the advantages of working as a team?*
- *Under what conditions is teamwork preferable to individual work or working with a partner?*
- *What are the advantages of beginning an activity with teamwork?*
- *What are the advantages of concluding an activity with teamwork?*
- *What would have happened if you worked exclusively in teams while discussing all three questions?*
- *What would have happened if we skipped teamwork and worked on all three questions individually? What if you worked with a single partner throughout the activity?*
- *Which would you prefer: working with the same partner or with different partners? Why?*
- *Which would you prefer: working with the same team members or with different team members? Why?*

Pairing and Teaming

Use the table below for creating cards for pairing and teaming.

If you have an odd number of participants, give a card to yourself so you will pair up with one of the participants and become a member of a team. Be careful not to dominate the discussion when you are participating in paired work or teamwork.

Number of Participants	Cards	Number of Pairs	Number of Teams	Members in Each Team
6	A1, A2, A3, B1, B2, B3	3	2	3
8	A1, A2, A3, A4, B1, B2, B3, B4	4	2	4
10	A1, A2, A3, A4, A5, B1, B2, B3, B4, B5	5	2	5
12	A1, A2, A3, A4, A5, A6, B1, B2, B3, B4, B5, B6	6	2	6
14	A1, A2, A3, A4, A5, A6, A7, B1, B2, B3, B4, B5, B6, B7	7	2	7
16	A1, A2, A3, A4, B1, B2, B3, B4, C1, C2, C3, C4, D1, D2, D3, D4	8	4	4
18	A1, A2, A3, A4, A5, B1, B2, B3, B4, B5, C1, C2, C3, C4, D1, D2, D3, D4	9	4	4–5
20	A1, A2, A3, A4, A5, B1, B2, B3, B4, B5, C1, C2, C3, C4, C5, D1, D2, D3, D4, D5	10	4	5
22	A1, A2, A3, A4, A5, A6, B1, B2, B3, B4, B5, B6, C1, C2, C3, C4, C5, D1, D2, D3, D4, D5	11	4	5–6
24	A1, A2, A3, A4, A5, A6, B1, B2, B3, B4, B5, B6, C1, C2, C3, C4, C5, C6, D1, D2, D3, D4, D5, D6	12	4	6
26	A1, A2, A3, A4, A5, B1, B2, B3, B4, B5, C1, C2, C3, C4, D1, D2, D3, D4, E1, E2, E3, E4, F1, F2, F3, F4	13	6	4–5
28	A1, A2, A3, A4, A5, B1, B2, B3, B4, B5, C1, C2, C3, C4, C5, D1, D2, D3, D4, D5, E1, E2, E3, E4, F1, F2, F3, F4	14	6	4–5
30	A1, A2, A3, A4, A5, B1, B2, B3, B4, B5, C1, C2, C3, C4, C5, D1, D2, D3, D4, D5, E1, E2, E3, E4, E5, F1, F2, F3, F4, F5	15	6	5

59
Double Negatives

Do you remember that *the negative of a negative is a positive* from your algebra classes? We use this principle in the Double Negatives activity for generating ideas. This technique is effective because your brain gets excited whenever you do something negative and mischievous.

Purpose

To brainstorm a set of ideas for achieving a goal

Participants

Minimum: 2
Maximum: Any number
Best: 10 to 40
(Larger groups of participants are divided into 2 to 5 groups, each with 4 to 6 members.)

Time

20 to 40 minutes, depending on your goal and the number of participants

Supplies

- Blank pieces of paper
- Pens or pencils
- Flip chart
- Felt-tipped markers

Preparation

Specify your goals. Write a goal related to a problem or an opportunity.

Example: *Workshop participants should return on time after a coffee break.*

Write the *laog*. A *laog* (pronounced *lay-augh*) is the exact opposite of the goal. In most cases, you can create the laog by replacing the verb in your goal with its antonym.

Example: *Workshop participants should **not** return on time after a coffee break.*

Flow

Form teams. If you have two to seven participants, ask them to work as a single team. With more participants, divide them into two to five teams, each with four to six members. It does not matter if some teams have an extra member.

Ask participants to brainstorm strategies for achieving the laog. Ignore your original goal and present the laog. Ask them, in a serious voice, to write down a list of ideas for achieving the laog. You will probably get some funny looks from participants.

Here are different ideas from a recent group for ensuring that the workshop participants will not return on time after a coffee break:

Make the early participants wait for the latecomers.
Repeat what you have already done for the benefit of the latecomers.
Punish participants who come back early.
Reward the latecomers.
Make sure that the participants have nothing to look forward to after the coffee break.
Encourage participants to check their voice mail and catch up with their telephone calls during the break.
Ensure that the latecomers will not miss anything important.
Accept the habit of being late as a cultural difference. Be politically correct and avoid imposing your cultural values on the others.
Give infrequent breaks so that the participants have a lot of things to do.
Give such short breaks that nobody can return on time.
Give such long breaks that people get distracted.
Conduct your workshop in a distracting environment.
Come back late from your coffee break. Set an example for being late.
Don't specify a definite return time. Let the participants decide when they should return.
Make sure that your presentations are so boring that participants don't want to return to the session.

Demonstrate how to reverse the ideas. Ask a participant (or a team) to give you one of their ideas for reaching the laog. Write this idea on the flip chart. Work with the participants to come up with the opposite of this idea and write it also on the flip chart.

Original idea: *Make the early participants wait for the latecomers.*
Reversal: *Get started on time. Don't wait for the latecomers.*

Demonstrate how to come up with more than one reversed idea. Sometimes you may reverse a strategy in more than one way. Demonstrate how to do this on the flip chart.

Original idea: *Punish the early participants.*
Reversal 1: *Reward the early participants.*
Reversal 2: *Punish the latecomers.*

Edit your list of reversals. When you reverse your ideas for achieving your laog, you end up with ideas for achieving your goal. Examine each idea and rewrite it to make it more specific and practical.

Reversal 1: *Punish the latecomers.*
Edited idea: *Ask each latecomer to sing a song.*

Expand your list. Your edited list of ideas may suggest additional ones. Keep adding ideas to the list.

Debriefing

Encourage a debriefing discussion of this activity. Use questions such as the following:

- Many people find brainstorming for negative ideas to be more energizing than the traditional brainstorming for positive ideas. Did you experience this phenomenon? What makes this type of reverse psychology work with most people?

- Let's apply the Double Negatives approach to the use of this technique. Quick, come up with one strategy for *not* using Double Negatives. Now reverse this idea at least twice.

- Double Negatives is a problem-solving tool. You can also use it as a training tool. What are the advantages of using Double Negatives for training?

- Are there any potential hazards in using Double Negatives as a training tool? What are these hazards and how can you remove or reduce them?

60
Letters and Numbers

Purpose

To come up with ideas that will appeal to various stakeholders

Participants

Minimum: 9
Maximum: Any number
Best: 16 to 20
(Participants organize and reorganize themselves into two teams.)

Time

15 to 30 minutes

Supplies

- Team Allocation Table for the facilitator
- Blank pieces of paper
- Pens or pencils
- Timer
- Whistle
- Flip-chart pads
- Felt-tipped pens
- Masking tape

Flow

Brief the participants. Explain that you are going to facilitate a structured brainstorming activity in two parts. Specify the goal for brainstorming (example: *How can we increase our market share?*).

 Form teams. Use the Team Allocation Table to select the appropriate set of Team Allocation Cards. Distribute these cards, one card for each participant. Point out that each card contains a combination of a letter and a number. Ask the participants to find others with the same *letter* and form themselves into teams. Depending on the total number of participants, you may have three to six teams.

Assign roles. Explain that each team will represent a specific stakeholder. Assign the roles according to this list:

Team A = customer
Team B = designer
Team C = marketer
Team D = manufacturer
Team E = distributor
Team F = sales people

Use as many roles as you have teams. Depending on the total number of participants, there may be three, four, five, or six different roles.

Generate ideas. Ask members of each team to brainstorm strategies for achieving the goal from the point of view of the role assigned to them. Ask teams to generate several ideas, discuss these ideas, and select the ten best ideas. Request someone in each team to record the ideas. Announce a 9-minute time limit for this activity.

Form mixed teams. After 9 minutes, blow the whistle and stop the activity. Tell participants that you are going to reorganize them into a new set of teams. Ask participants to check their Team Allocation Cards once more and find others with the same *number* to form new teams.

Generate ideas. Ask members of the new teams to continue brainstorming for achieving the original goal. Ask participants to maintain their loyalty to the stakeholder roles from the previous round but try to focus on satisfying the needs and preferences of other stakeholders. Encourage participants to recall and share their ideas from the previous round and keep an open mind toward other perspectives. As before, ask teams to select the ten best ideas and record them on a sheet of flip-chart paper. Announce a 9-minute time limit for this activity.

Present lists of ideas. Blow the whistle at the end of 9 minutes, and ask teams to post their lists on convenient areas of the wall. Invite all participants to take a gallery walk and review the lists from other teams.

Personal action plans. Invite each participant to select one or two of the ideas from the wall posters that they want to play a role in advocating and implementing.

Debriefing

Conduct a debriefing discussion of insights gained by different participants. Here are some suggested questions for this debriefing:

- *What were the differences in your thinking (and in your discussions) between the two rounds? Which one did you enjoy more?*

- *How different was the stakeholder role from your "real" role in the workplace? Did you have any difficulty in playing the role assigned to you?*

- *What would have happened if participants were asked to play their real-world roles during the first round? What are the advantages and disadvantages of working in your natural role?*

- *Did you have any difficulty in carrying over your role from the first round to the second round? How did you balance the needs of your stakeholder role with the needs of all stakeholders?*

- *Did any team member during the second round become too stubborn in maintaining his or her role from the previous round? How did other team members react to this type of behavior?*

- *During the activity, what insights did you gain about the problem, about yourself, and about the way people interact when they are solving problems?*

- *What insights did you gain by brainstorming and evaluating ideas from different stakeholder perspectives?*

- *What did you learn about the similarities and differences among the needs, perceptions, and preferences of different stakeholder groups?*

- *This activity can be used for problem-solving purposes or for training purposes? What training topics and objectives can benefit from the use of this activity? How would you ensure effective learning among your participants?*

- *How would you conduct this activity if there were only five participants in the group?*

Team Allocation Table

Team Allocation Cards

Participants					
9	A1, A2, A3	B1, B2, B3	C1, C2, C3		
10	A1, A2, A3, A4	B1, B2, B3	C1, C2, C3		
11	A1, A2, A3, A4	B1, B2, B3, B4	C1, C2, C3		
12	A1, A2, A3, A4	B1, B2, B3, B4	C1, C2, C3, C4		
13	A1, A2, A3, A4, A5	B1, B2, B3, B4	C1, C2, C3, C4		
14	A1, A2, A3, A4, A5	B1, B2, B3, B4, B5	C1, C2, C3, C4		
15	A1, A2, A3, A4, A5	B1, B2, B3, B4, B5	C1, C2, C3, C4, C5		
16	A1, A2, A3, A4	B1, B2, B3, B4	C1, C2, C3, C4	D1, D2, D3, D4	
17	A1, A2, A3, A4, A5	B1, B2, B3, B4	C1, C2, C3, C4	D1, D2, D3, D4	
18	A1, A2, A3, A4, A5	B1, B2, B3, B4, B5	C1, C2, C3, C4	D1, D2, D3, D4	
19	A1, A2, A3, A4, A5	B1, B2, B3, B4, B5	C1, C2, C3, C4, C5	D1, D2, D3, D4	
20	A1, A2, A3, A4, A5	B1, B2, B3, B4, B5	C1, C2, C3, C4, C5	D1, D2, D3, D4, D5	
21	A1, A2, A3, A4, A5	B1, B2, B3, B4	C1, C2, C3, C4	D1, D2, D3, D4	E1, E2, E3, E4
22	A1, A2, A3, A4, A5	B1, B2, B3, B4, B5	C1, C2, C3, C4	D1, D2, D3, D4	E1, E2, E3, E4
23	A1, A2, A3, A4, A5	B1, B2, B3, B4, B5	C1, C2, C3, C4, C5	D1, D2, D3, D4	E1, E2, E3, E4
24	A1, A2, A3, A4, A5	B1, B2, B3, B4, B5	C1, C2, C3, C4, C5	D1, D2, D3, D4, D5	E1, E2, E3, E4
25	A1, A2, A3, A4, A5	B1, B2, B3, B4, B5	C1, C2, C3, C4, C5	D1, D2, D3, D4, D5	E1, E2, E3, E4, E5
26	A1, A2, A3, A4, A5, A6	B1, B2, B3, B4, B5	C1, C2, C3, C4, C5	D1, D2, D3, D4, D5	E1, E2, E3, E4, E5
27	A1, A2, A3, A4, A5, A6	B1, B2, B3, B4, B5, B6	C1, C2, C3, C4, C5	D1, D2, D3, D4, D5	E1, E2, E3, E4, E5
28	A1, A2, A3, A4, A5, A6	B1, B2, B3, B4, B5, B6	C1, C2, C3, C4, C5, C6	D1, D2, D3, D4, D5	E1, E2, E3, E4, E5
29	A1, A2, A3, A4, A5, A6	B1, B2, B3, B4, B5, B6	C1, C2, C3, C4, C5, C6	D1, D2, D3, D4, D5, D6	E1, E2, E3, E4, E5
30	A1, A2, A3, A4, A5, A6	B1, B2, B3, B4, B5, B6	C1, C2, C3, C4, C5, C6	D1, D2, D3, D4, D5, D6	E1, E2, E3, E4, E5, E6

61
Long Words

As a magician, I sometimes use an accomplice in the audience to help me perform intriguing effects. Long Words is not a magic trick, but it uses an accomplice to drive home an important point.

Incidentally, the original name for this game was Proactive Planning. However, this name gives away an important secret. So I changed it to the current bland name.

Purpose

To emphasize the importance of long-term planning

Participants

Minimum: 2
Maximum: Any number
Best: 10 to 20
(Participants work individually.)

Time

10 to 20 minutes

Supplies

- Handout, How to Play Long Words
- Pens or pencils

Preparation

Handouts with suggested words. Run off a copy of the handout for each player. On each copy of the handout, somewhere on the margin, write any two of the following words, using different words for different handouts:

agreements, anteaters, apartments, arraignments, arrangements, enterprise, entertainers, estrangement, generators, impersonate, interpreter, interrogate, magistrate, mainstream, pragmatism, pre-arrangement, presentations, presentiment, programmers, protesting, rearrangements, regenerate, regeneration, remonstrate, renegotiates, representation, retirement, ringmaster, segmentation, stagnation, tangerines, transparent, and transporting

A secret accomplice. Long before conducting the game, find a suitable accomplice. Explain to this person that you are going to play a word game in three rounds. Give the person a copy of the handout and ask him or her to read it. Make sure that he she has understood how to play the game. Tell the person that you are going to teach him or her a secret strategy that will guarantee victory. Write these three words on the margin and ask your accomplice to use them in that order for the three rounds of the game:

I
MANAGEMENT
REPORTERS

Explain to your accomplice that he or she will lose the first round but most likely win the next two rounds.

Flow

Distribute copies of the handout. Ask participants to read the instructions.

Explain the scribbles on the margin. Tell participants that some handouts may contain words scribbled by previous players. Suggest that participants may use those words but they may come up with longer words.

Conduct the first round. Blow the whistle, pause for 30 seconds to signal the start of the first round, and blow the whistle again to conclude the round. Ask participants to show their words to each other (hiding the words written on the margin). Declare the player with the longest word as the winner for the first round. You may have more than one winner for the first round. Your accomplice will definitely lose this round.

Conduct the second round. Repeat the procedure. Your accomplice will win this round—unless some other player has figured out a similar strategy.

Conduct the third round. Repeat the procedure one more time. Your accomplice will win this round also.

Identify the game winner. Congratulate your accomplice for having won the most rounds.

Debriefing

Confess to the participants that you had shared the winning strategy with an accomplice. If anyone else had come up with a similar strategy, congratulate the person for his or her proactive thinking. Ask participants to think back on the experience and to analyze the winning strategy. Ask appropriate questions to elicit these learning points:

- *It is important to come up with proactive plans rather than reactive ones for immediate results.*
- *Limited time tempts us to ignore proactive planning.*
- *We don't have the patience to read and reflect on all the details in an instruction sheet.*
- *You may win the battle, but lose the war.*
- *Sometimes you may have to lose early to win later.*
- *We are tempted to cash in lucky breaks (such as the "left-over" words on the margin) without thinking about long-term consequences of our actions.*

How to Play Long Words

A, A, E, E, E, E, G, I, M, M, N, N, O, P, R, R, R, S, T, T

Study the twenty letters listed above. Some letters (A, E, M, N, R, and T) are repeated more than once, and some letters (B, C, D, F, H, J, K, L, Q, U, V, W, X, Y, and Z) are missing.

You (and all other players) have the same twenty letters.

This game is played in three rounds. You win each round of the game if you create the longest word using as many of these letters as possible. The letters that you use during each round will not be available for the subsequent rounds.

Round 1. When you hear the whistle, begin making up words. You have 30 seconds to come up with an English word using any of the letters above.

Write your word here: _____

Stop when you hear the whistle again.

Cross out the letters used for making your word. You should not use these letters in future rounds of the game.

Round 2. When you hear the whistle again, start the second round.

Write your word here: _____

Stop when you hear the whistle again. Cross out the letters used for making your word. Do not use any of the crossed-out letters in the next round.

Round 3. Let's play another round of the game as before.

Write your word here: _____

62
New Anagrams

I frequently have trouble thinking inside the box. Unfortunately, the default mode for my brain is to automatically reject obvious solutions and come up with innovative alternatives. As a result, I sometimes end up with a convoluted solution instead of an easy one. New Anagrams is a jolt that punishes people who are too smart—and creative—for their own good. Unfortunately, I cannot benefit from this jolt because I know the secret!

Purpose

To come up with simple solutions to a problem, even after being rewarded for more complex and creative solutions

Participants

Minimum: 1
Maximum: Any number
Best: 10 to 30
(Participants work individually.)

Time

5 to 15 minutes

Supplies

- Blank pieces of paper
- Pens or pencils
- Flip chart
- Felt-tipped markers
- Timer
- Whistle

Flow

Brief the participants. Explain that you are going to solve several anagram puzzles. Tell participants that they can choose to solve these puzzles individually, with a partner, or with a team. They can also change their minds between one puzzle and the next.

Demonstrate how to solve an anagram puzzle. Write these two words on the flip chart with a plus (+) sign between them:

NEW + BEET

Tell participants "Rearrange the seven letters in this pair of words to spell one word."

Pause while participants work on the puzzle. It is possible that someone will blurt out the solution or exclaim, "I've got it."

After a suitable pause, give the solution: BETWEEN.

Present the next puzzle. Write these two words on the flip chart as before:

NEW + SITS

Tell participants, "Rearrange the seven letters in this pair of words to spell one word." Also instruct participants to stand up if they have solved the puzzle.

Wait for 20 seconds or until someone stands up (whichever comes first). Announce the solution: WITNESS.

Repeat the procedure. Use these pairs of words. (Try your hand at solving the anagrams before checking the solutions.)

NEW + SETS
NEW + SOAP
NEW + LIDS
NEW + RODS

Always repeat the same instruction:

"Rearrange the seven letters in this pair of words to spell one word."

After presenting each pair of words, wait for 20 seconds or until someone stands up before announcing the solution.

Give the final test. Tell participants that you are going to give them another pair of words as the final test. Write these words on the flip chart:

NEW + DOOR

Repeat the standard instruction:

"Rearrange the seven letters in this pair of words to spell one word."
(Try your hand at solving this anagram before checking the solution.)

Pause for about 50 seconds as participants struggle with the task and become frustrated.

Announce the solution (amidst groans and complaints from participants).

Debriefing

Have a discussion about what participants learned. Ask appropriate questions to help them discover this point:

Sometimes we try too hard and become too smart for our own good. Instead of following the simple directions, we think outside the box and complicate our lives unnecessarily.

Here are some additional insights earlier participants came up with. Share them with your group and invite them to react to each of them:

- *There is an advantage to taking other people's statements literally.*
- *We impose unnecessary constraints upon ourselves.*
- *When we are successful, we become complacent.*
- *Early success makes you ignore alternative strategies.*
- *The harder we try, the tougher the problem becomes.*
- *When we are in a hurry, we ignore alternative approaches.*
- *Different people get bored by different activities.*

Invite participants to come up with real-world examples of these principles.

Solutions

NEW + SETS: WETNESS
NEW + SOAP: WEAPONS
NEW + LIDS: SWINDLE
NEW + RODS: WONDERS (or DOWNERS)

Solutions (for the "final test"):

NEW + DOOR: ONE WORD

63
Similes

This activity gives participants several opportunities to think outside the box.

Purpose

To explore how initial success usually hampers creative thinking

Participants

Minimum: 1
Maximum: Any number
Best: 10 to 20
(Larger groups of participants are divided into teams of 4 to 8.)

Time

10 to 20 minutes

Supplies

- **Letter tiles.** Cut 20 1/2-inch square tiles from card stock. Copy these letters on the tiles, one letter per tile: A B C D D E G H L N O O P R S S T U U Y. Use block capital letters only.
- Prepare one set of tiles for each team of participants. Place each set of 20 tiles in an envelope.

Flow

Distribute the letter tiles. Give an envelope with the tiles to each team. Ask the teams to take the tiles out of the envelope and arrange them in a roughly alphabetical order.

Brief the participants. Explain that a simile is an explicit comparison between two things, linked by the word *as* or *like* as in *tough as nails* or *poor as a church mouse.* Announce that you will present an incomplete simile and the teams will spell the missing word using the letter tiles.

Present the first simile. Say,

Blank as a bug in a rug. What word goes in the blank? Spell this word using your letter tiles.

Pause for appropriate period of time and announce the correct answer: *snug.*

Continue with other similes. Repeat the process with these similes, one at a time, substituting a blank for the word in parentheses: *(busy) as a beaver, (cute) as a button,* *(dead) as a doornail, (good) as gold, (pure) as the driven snow,* and *(sly) as a fox.* With each simile, announce the correct answers after a suitable pause.

The teams will have no difficulty in responding rapidly and correctly. You are giving them easy problems to ensure immediate success. This will set them up for the challenge in the next step.

Spring the challenge. Without changing the procedure, present this incomplete simile: *Blank as a fiddle.* Pause for the teams to spell the correct word with their letter tiles.

The "obvious" correct answer is *fit.* However, the tiles do not include the letters *f* or *i.* Since the teams have fallen into a routine thinking pattern by this time, they are unlikely to come up with a rapid solution. However, there are (at least) three different ways to complete the simile with the letter tiles:

1. Create a new simile. The task is to come up with a simile—not a cliche. Spell the word *loud* (or *costly* or *raucous*) to suggest these similes:

   loud as a fiddle

   costly as a fiddle

   raucous as a fiddle

2. Spell ELT with the letter tiles.

   # E L T

   Then hide parts of the bottom horizontal lines of E and L with two other letter tiles, turned upside down with their blank sides showing.

3. Turn all twenty tiles upside down so that their blank sides show. Create the letters F, I, and T by arranging the blank tiles like this:

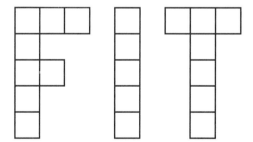

Elicit alternative answers. Wait for a couple of minutes to see whether any team comes up with one of these (or some other) acceptable answers. If the teams flounder for a long time, drop suitable hints (such as *"Your simile does not have to be a cliché"* or *"Can you convert an E into an F"?* or *"Think of the blank sides of the tiles as pixels"*). Whenever a team comes up with an answer, show it to the other teams. Encourage the teams to come up with alternative solutions.

Debriefing

Ask the participants what would have happened if you started with *"Blank as a fiddle"* as the first item. Encourage a discussion of how initial success results in mindless routines that hamper creative problem solving. Invite participants to identify habitual routines in their work processes and figure out creative strategies for handling them.

64
Assumptions

When it comes to creativity and problem solving, "don't make unnecessary assumptions" is an excellent piece of advice. Unfortunately, however, many trainers and managers make the silly assumption that when you tell people not to make unnecessary assumptions, they will immediately realize their stupidity, master the new principle, change their behavior patterns, and live happily ever after. In reality, you need to provide people with repeated experiences of dysfunctional assumptions before they move away from their state of denial. Assumptions does that by entrapping people several times.

Purpose

To increase the awareness of the assumptions you make and the impact of these assumptions

Participants

Minimum: 1
Maximum: Any number
Best: 10 to 50
(Participants work individually to solve puzzles.)

Time

30 to 45 minutes

Supplies

- LCD projector
- Screen
- Flip chart
- Felt-tipped markers
- Blank pieces of paper
- Pens or pencils
- Timer
- Whistle

Flow

Present the first puzzle. Write these three-letter chunks on a flip chart or project them on the screen. Tell participants that the letters are printed on tiles and ask them to rearrange *the six tiles to spell three words.* Ask participants to stand up when they have solved the puzzle.

MAN SON
LES ECT
OBJ AGE

Pause for the solution. This puzzle is a fairly easy one and most people will solve it rapidly. After a suitable pause, confirm the solution:

MANAGE
LESSON
OBJECT

Check assumptions. Ask these three questions:

What assumptions did you make before solving the puzzles? (Typical response: *There must be a catch somewhere.*)
Did these assumptions help you or hinder you?
What assumptions are you making after solving the puzzle? (Typical responses: *This stuff is easy. I must be a genius!*)

Present the second puzzle. Write these three-letter chunks on a flip chart or project them on the screen. Tell participants that the letters are printed on tiles and ask them to rearrange *the six tiles to spell three words.* Ask participants to stand up when they have solved the puzzle.

ATT END
RET ION
RIT IRE

Pause for the solution. This puzzle is tougher than the first one. Pause for about 30 seconds and then confirm the solution:

ATTRITION
RETIRE
END

Check assumptions. Ask these three questions:

What unnecessary assumptions did you make before solving the puzzles? (*All solution words must be six letters long.*)
Did these assumptions help you or hinder you?
What assumptions are you making after solving the puzzle? (Typical responses: *The facilitator is cheating. I will avoid this mistake in the future.*)

Present the third puzzle. Write these three-letter chunks on a flip chart or project them on the screen. Tell participants that the letters are printed on tiles and ask them to rearrange *the six tiles to spell three words.* Ask participants to stand up when they have solved the puzzle.

ACT FAT
HER NIH
NOI WIT

Pause for the solution. This will frustrate most participants. Pause for about 30 seconds and then confirm the solution (even if no one has solved it):

ACTION
FATHER
WITHIN

There will be an immediate howl of protest. Remind them that all the three-letter chunks were on tiles and explain that you simply turned two of these tiles upside down to change the sequence of letters:

NIH -> HIN
NOI -> ION

Check assumptions. Ask these three questions:

What unnecessary assumptions did you make before solving the puzzles? (Letters cannot be turned upside down.)
Did these assumptions help you or hinder you?
What assumptions are you making after solving the puzzle? (Typical responses: *That was a cheap trick. I will be more vigilant next time.*)

Present the fourth puzzle. Write these three-letter chunks on a flip chart or project them on the screen. Tell participants that the letters are printed on tiles and ask them to rearrange *the six tiles to spell three familiar words.* Emphasize the slight variation in the usual instruction. Ask participants to stand up when they have solved the puzzle.

AMI EEF
LIA RDS
RWO THR

Pause for the solution. Pause for about 30 seconds and then confirm the solution:

THREEFAMILIARWORDS

Check assumptions. Ask these three questions:

What unnecessary assumptions did you make before solving the puzzles? (Typical responses: *There should be a blank space between words. Words should end after a tile.*)
Did these assumptions help you or hinder you?
What assumptions are you making after solving the puzzle? (Typical responses: *There cannot be any more ways to trap us.*)

Present the fifth puzzle. Write these three-letter chunks on a flip chart or project them on the screen. Tell participants that the letters are printed on tiles and ask them to rearrange *the six tiles to spell three words.* Ask participants to stand up when they have solved the puzzle.

ONE WAY
HOW ANY
THI ACP

Pause for the solution. Pause for about 30 seconds and then confirm the solution:

ANYONE
ANYHOW
ANYWAY

Check assumptions. Ask these three questions:

What unnecessary assumptions did you make before solving the puzzles? (Typical responses: *"ACP" cannot be a part of any English word. Each tile can be used only once. Each tile has to be used.*)
Did these assumptions help you or hinder you?
What assumptions are you making after solving the puzzle? (Typical responses: *There must be some other reason that I am failing repeatedly.*)

Present the sixth puzzle. Write these three-letter chunks on a flip chart or project them on the screen. Tell participants that the letters are printed on tiles and ask them to rearrange *the six tiles to spell three words.* Ask participants to stand up when they have solved the puzzle.

ARL TAI
TCG EKH
NET DTS

Pause for the solution. Pause for about 30 seconds and then confirm the solution:

ARL
TAI
TCG
EKH
NET
DTS

If some participants don't get it, ask them to read the three words vertically: attend, racket, lights.

Check assumptions. Ask these three questions:

What unnecessary assumptions did you make before solving the puzzles? (Typical responses: *These cannot be English words. All words should be written horizontally, from left to right.*)
Did these assumptions help you or hinder you?
What assumptions are you making after solving the puzzle? (Typical responses: *This misery has got to stop sooner or later.*)

Present the seventh puzzle. Write these three-letter chunks on a flip chart or project them on the screen. Ask participants to rearrange *the letters in the six tiles to spell three words.* Repeat the instruction because it is slightly (but significantly) different from the previous instruction. Ask participants to stand up when they have solved the puzzle.

CUR SEE
POT ARY
REU OND

Pause for the solution. Pause for about 30 seconds and then confirm the solution:

RESCUE
POETRY
AROUND

Remind participants that your instructions asked for rearranging the letters, and not the tiles as in the previous round.
Check assumptions. Ask these three questions:

What unnecessary assumptions did you make before solving the puzzles? (Typical responses: *It's the same instruction as before.*)
Did these assumptions help you or hinder you?
What assumptions are you making after solving the puzzle? (Typical responses: *There will be a coffee break soon.*)

Present the eighth puzzle. Write these three-letter chunks on a flip chart or project them on the screen. Ask participants to rearrange *the six tiles to spell three words.* Ask participants to stand up when they have solved the puzzle.

MAI VAL
CON SON
CHE GAR

Pause for the solution. Pause for about 30 seconds and then confirm the solution:

MAISON
GARCON
CHEVAL

Check assumptions. Ask these three questions:

What unnecessary assumptions did you make before solving the puzzles? (Typical responses: *They should all be English words.*)
Did these assumptions help you or hinder you?
What assumptions are you making after solving the puzzle? (Typical responses: *The next one will be easy.*)

Debriefing

Apologize to the participants for torturing them. Conduct an informal debriefing discussion by asking participants to discuss the activity and come up with the learning point they got from it. Summarize the key point that you are trying to make: It is easy to make unnecessary assumptions that prevent us from solving the problem. Explain that although you used eight different variations of the puzzle, there are probably many more types of unnecessary assumptions we can make. Invite participants to come up with more diabolical variations on this theme, and share them with you.

65
Criteria

I am a compulsory buyer of electronic gadgets—and once I buy the latest gizmo, I have no trouble explaining to my accountant why I could not live without it. This personal neurotic behavior is the basis for Criteria as a decision-making activity.

Here's my rationalization of "choose first, justify later" behavior: When planning to buy a computer, for example, logical people begin with a set of criteria and select the best computer from among the alternatives that meet the criteria. The problem with this rational approach is that you are not sure about the initial set of criteria and you may end up with buyer's remorse after your final selection. In Criteria, you turn the procedure upside down.

Purpose

To identify factors that contribute to your perception of quality or desirability

Participants

Minimum: 6
Maximum: Any number
Best: 10 to 30
(Participants are divided into teams later in the game.)

Time

15 to 45 minutes, depending on the complexity of choices

Supplies

- A collection of items, objects, or descriptions. (In a recent game, for example, we used descriptions of a dozen different MP3 players.)
- Flip chart
- Felt-tipped markers
- Masking tape

Flow

Distribute the items. Give seven to twelve items to each participant. If you have a larger number of items, distribute different sets of items to different participants.

In our sample game, we gave the same set of twelve product descriptions to all players.

Assign an individual task. Ask participants to select the best item. Keep your request somewhat general to avoid suggesting any specific criteria. If participants ask for details, ask them to use their own judgment. Announce a suitable time limit for completing the task.

We asked participants to review the twelve items and to select the three best ones within 5 minutes.

Assign a teamwork task. At the end of the time limit, ask participants to organize themselves into equal-sized teams of three to six members. Within each team, ask participants to reflect on why they selected what they selected and come up with a list of criteria. Encourage teams to generate a list of different criteria that they intuitively or explicitly used in the selection process.

Here are some of the criteria that the teams came up with: price, features, flash memory, manufacturer, availability, hard-drive capacity, durability, design, supported formats, color, weight, and features.

Ask teams to organize the criteria. Invite them to remove duplicate criteria and to organize the remaining criteria into logical categories. Give a sheet of flip-chart paper to each team and have its members record their organized lists.

One team organized the criteria into three groups: value, capacity, and versatility.

Conduct a display-and-review activity. Ask teams to tape their flip-chart records to the wall. Invite participants to review other teams' outputs.

Conduct an application exercise. Ask teams to select the most important criteria and apply them to select the best alternative.

The teams went through the same twelve alternatives and applied the three to five criteria for comparing them and selecting the best one. Many participants were surprised how their selection turned out to be very different from the original selection—and yet they did not feel any self-reproach.

Debriefing

To ensure effective learning from this activity, conduct a debriefing discussion. Use questions like these to structure the discussion:

- In general, do you make your choices in an impulsive or deliberate fashion?
- Is there a difference in the way you make choices at home and on the job? What is the reason for any difference?
- In what situations is it more effective to make a rapid selection? In what situations should you work in a systematic fashion?
- What were some of the popular criteria that were used by most people in your team? What were some of the unique ones?

66
Karma

"Enjoy the moment" is a valid piece of advice. "Think of the future" is another valid piece of advice. Karma gives participants practice in choosing between these two guidelines in making a series of decisions.

Purpose

To explore the impact of choosing to live in the moment or letting future consequences determine your decisions

Participants

Minimum: 2
Maximum: Any number
Best: 10 to 20
(Participants are divided into pairs.)

Time

15 to 30 minutes

Supplies

- A set of 10 black playing cards (Ace through 10 of spades or clubs) and 10 red playing cards (Ace through 10 of hearts or diamonds) for each pair of players. (You can assemble two sets of these cards from a standard deck of playing cards.)
- Blank pieces of paper
- Pens or pencils

Flow

Brief the participants. Demonstrate the rules of the game by playing a sample game with a volunteer from the audience. Assume the role of the dealer and let the volunteer make the decisions. Play the game according to the rules as explained below.

Finding a partner. Ask each participant to find a partner. Give each pair of partners a set of ten black and ten red cards. Select one player to be the dealer and the other player to be the decision-maker for the first round.

Explain the basic objective. Tell the participants that this is primarily a solitaire game that is played for ten rounds. The object of the game is to accumulate a high score at the end of the tenth round. Explain that participants usually accumulate a score of about 50 points.

Conduct the first round. Ask the dealers to hold the packet of black cards face down, shuffle them, and ask the decision-maker to take any card and turn it face up.

Reasonable enjoyment. If the card selected by the decision-maker has a value of 1 through 5 (counting Ace as 1), then this value is recorded on the player's score sheet as the enjoyment score for the first round.

Reckless enjoyment. If the card selected by the decision-maker has a value greater than 5, it is labeled a *temptation* card. The decision-maker has a choice of enjoying or resisting it.

- If he or she chooses to enjoy it, the value of the card is recorded on the score sheet as the enjoyment score for the first round. In this case, the dealer takes some cards from the shuffled packet of red cards (held face down) and inserts them in the packet of black cards. The number of red cards depends on the magnitude of temptation: If the decision-maker accepted a 6, one red card is added to the black packet. If she accepted a 7, two black cards, and so on. (The number of red cards equals the value of the temptation card minus 5.)

- If the decision-maker resists the temptation card, he or she does not receive any enjoyment points for the round. No red cards are added to the packet of black cards.

Continue the game. Play continues in the same fashion. The value of any black card less than 6 is added to the decision-maker's enjoyment score for the round. In the case of a temptation card, the player has the choice of accepting it (which results in adding points to the score and red cards to the packet) or resisting it (which results in no addition of points to the score or red cards to the packet).

Deal with red cards. During any round, if the player selects a red card, its value is subtracted from the decision-maker's current total of enjoyment score.

Reflect on the past. During any round, the decision-maker may choose to reflect. This involves not picking any card but taking the packet from the dealer, inspecting all of the cards, and removing any one red card. The reflection move does not add to the enjoyment score but reduces the likelihood of receiving points during future rounds.

Conclude the game. Game ends after the tenth round. The decision-maker's total enjoyment score becomes his or her score for the game.

Switch the roles. The decision-maker of the first game becomes the dealer for the next game. The game is repeated as before.

Debriefing

To ensure that participants don't treat Karma as merely a recreational activity but gain useful insights from it, conduct a debriefing session. Use questions like these to structure the discussion:

- *How does this game reflect your professional life?*
- *How does this game reflect your personal life?*

- *Does the second decision-maker let the first player's score influence her choices and her perception of the final score? Why do you think this happens? How does this reflect the real world?*

- *When you came across the first temptation card, what did you decide to do? Why?*

- *How would you have reacted if your score ever became negative?*

- *What was your decision during the last round? Did it differ significantly from your behavior during the earlier rounds?*

- *Did you ever reflect? What made you decide to do so?*

- *Decision-makers play in a reckless fashion during the last round. They don't resist temptations during this round. Do you agree or disagree with that statement?*

- *If the packet contains several red cards, are you likely to reflect or to grow more reckless? Why do you think so?*

Variations

No one to play with? You can play the game all by yourself by taking on both roles.

Don't have a deck of playing cards? Buy a deck (or several decks) as soon as you can. In the meantime, play our automated version on the computer by visiting http://thiagigroup.com/karma/.

PART VIII
Critical Thinking

67
$5 Exercise

I'm sure that you have handled several $5 bills recently. But have you ever paid attention to the bill? Do you remember whose portrait is on this bill? $5 Exercise is a quick activity that emphasizes the importance of being mindful with common objects.

Purpose

To increase awareness of how mindlessly we go through life

Participants

Minimum: 2
Maximum: Any number
Best: 10 to 20
(Participants are divided into pairs.)

Time

7 to 10 minutes

Supplies

$5 bills (or any equivalent local currency)

Flow

Pair up participants. Ask participants to find partners and sit (or stand) facing one another. If one participant is left over, you become the partner.

Show the money. Ask each pair of partners to produce a $5 bill. If any of the pairs cannot find a $5 bill, lend them one or ask them to use some other bill. Ask partners to hold a single bill by its opposite corners so that each participant can see only one side of the bill.

Begin questioning. Ask partners to take turns asking questions about the side of the bill they can see.

Sample questions:

How many times is the number 5 printed on my side?
How many times is the word "five" printed on my side?
How many digits does the serial number have?

What building is shown on my side?

Which direction is Abraham Lincoln facing?

How many pillars does Lincoln Memorial have?

Complete the sentence found on my side: This note is legal tender for all debts . . .

Give answers. As soon as one partner asks the question, the other partner must give an immediate answer. Correct answers earn 1 point. Incorrect answers or no answers earn no points. In this case, the questioner should immediately give the correct answer.

Switch partners and sides. Stop the question-and-answer activity after a few minutes. Ask participants to walk around and find new partners who worked on the other side of the $5 bill during the previous round. As before, ask the partners to sit or stand facing each other and hold the $5 bill in such a way that they can see only one side. This side should be the opposite of the side each participant saw during the previous round.

Continue questioning. Ask the partners to use the same procedure as before for asking questions, answering, and scoring points. Conclude the round after about 2 minutes.

Debriefing

Conduct a quick debriefing. Ask participants to discuss how familiarity breeds mindlessness. Use these types of questions:

- *What work-related supplies and tools do we take for granted?*
- *What are the dangers of ignoring familiar objects and people?*
- *What could we gain by paying attention to these objects and people?*

68
Double Talk

What are you thinking right now? Are you talking to yourself while you are reading this page? Is your self-talk distracting you from paying attention to the content? Double Talk is a somewhat humorous jolt—with a serious message.

Purpose

To increase the awareness of distracting self-talk and its consequences

Participants

Minimum: 4
Maximum: Any number
Best: 10 to 30
(Participants work in pairs.)

Time

7 to 15 minutes

Flow

Pairing partners. Ask participants to pair themselves up. In each pair, ask the taller participant to assume the role of a listener and the other participant to become the IV.

Assign a task for the IVs. Explain that the IV is to sit close to the listener and to whisper a string of disconnected distractions that the person is likely to be thinking about. Recommend that IVs use topics that are highly interesting (*Should I buy a lottery ticket?*) or disturbing (*What if they decide to rightsize again?*) or bothersome (*Did I turn the stove off this morning?*) or intriguing (*What exactly does Sheila see in him?*) or guilt-provoking (*I forgot Doug's birthday again. I am an idiot!*). Also suggest that the IV should use first-person singular and run-on sentences in a stream-of-consciousness mode.

Make a presentation. Give a short fact-filled presentation on some dry topic. Do this for 2 to 3 minutes. Ask the IVs to ignore you and to begin whispering.

Stop your presentation. Thank the IVs for their imaginative contributions and ask them to stop whispering. Ask the listeners to jot down some of the words, ideas, and topics mentioned by the IV. Pause for a minute.

Test participants. Ask a series of short-answer questions based on the content of your presentation. Ask all participants (both listeners and whisperers) to decide whether or not they know the answers.

Debriefing

Point out that everyone's listening and learning performance was less than perfect. Both listeners and whisperers missed some of the important points that you made.

Explain that IV stands for the *Inner Voice* and that the whispers simulate self-talk. Conduct a quick debriefing to elicit the point that talking to yourself and listening to yourself reduce learning effectiveness.

Variations

If time permits, repeat the activity with the other player as the IV. Encourage the listeners to tune out the whispers and to focus on your presentation.

If you want to be more dramatic, assign two IVs (one for each ear) to each listener.

69
Audio Tic-Tac-Toe

My friend is worried that her declining ability to recognize faces, remember telephone numbers, recall words, and to concentrate on the content of conversations are all precursors to Alzheimer's. I think that this is just a minor symptom of age-related cognitive decline that can be halted and reversed by exercising one's brain. An effective way to exercise the brain is to play games that require the use of your memory.

Participants don't have to be old to play Audio Tic-Tac-Toe, but there must be at least three people to play it.

Purpose

To exercise participants' short-term memory

Participants

Minimum: 3
Maximum: Any number
Best: 12 to 30
(Participants are divided into groups of 3.)

Time

5 to 15 minutes

Supplies

- Audio Tic-Tac-Toe Spreadsheets
- Pens or pencils

Flow

Form triads and assign roles. One participant is *recorder* who has the *Audio Tic-Tac-Toe "Spreadsheet."* The recorder marks every move called out by the other two participants (called *contestants*) in this spreadsheet, but keeps it hidden.

Explain the play procedure. Contestants visualize the spreadsheet and take turns calling out the box where they want to put their symbol.

Example:

She says, "My first X goes in box A3."
I say, "My first O goes in box B2."
She responds with, "My second X goes in box C1."
I say, "My second O goes in box A1."
She says, "Box C3."
I say, "Aha! My third O goes in box B3."
She says, "My fourth X goes in box C2. And I win!"

Explain how to win (or lose). The recorder does not say anything until all the boxes are filled or a contestant claims victory.

A contestant wins if:

- He or she places a symbol in three boxes in a straight line (as in the usual game of tic-tac-toe)
- The opponent tries to place his or her symbol in a box that already contains a symbol
- The opponent incorrectly claims victory

Play the game. Ask participants in each triad to start the game and play it. Monitor this activity and give help if needed.

Continue the game. At the end of each game, the next player assumes the role of recorder. Game proceeds as before.

Debriefing

The main point of this activity is that different factors affect our short-term memory. Ask participants to suggest and discuss techniques for reducing distractions and focusing on the game. Invite them to explore the impact of external factors (such as the presence of the audience and conversations in the background) and internal factors (such as anxiety and lack of confidence). Also ask participants how they would identify and remove distractions that hamper their ability to concentrate on work-related tasks.

Variations

This is just the game to play during long drives. Make sure, however, that the driver is not the recorder.

And after you have mastered this version, move on to the next levels: Use a 4 by 4 grid, a 5 by 5 grid, and so on.

Audio Tic-Tac-Toe Spreadsheet

	A	**B**	**C**
1	A1	B1	C1
2	A2	B2	C2
3	A3	B3	C3

70
Memory Test

This activity does not require any extraordinary mental feats. It just helps participants discover four basic (and interesting) facts about memory.

Purpose

To understand four factors that improve recall

Participants

Minimum: 1
Maximum: Any number
Best: 10 to 30
(Participants work individually.)

Time

5 to 7 minutes

Supplies

- Blank pieces of paper
- Pens or pencils

Flow

Brief participants. Tell them that you are going to administer a simple memory test. You will read a standardized list of words. Participants should listen carefully to these words without writing them down. Later, you will test to see how many words they can recall.

Present words. Read the following list of words. Pause briefly between one word and the next. Do not change the sequence. One of the words (*night*) is repeated three times.

    dream
    sleep
    night
    mattress
    snooze
    sheet
    nod

tired
night
artichoke
insomnia
blanket
night
alarm
nap
snore
pillow

Slightly distract the participants. Talk about something else for a minute. You may explain your plans for the rest of the training session or the agenda for the session or your favorite TV show. Spend about 60 seconds doing this.

Administer the recall test. Ask each participant to take a piece of paper and write as many of the words from the list you read as possible. Pause for about 40 seconds.

Debriefing

Explain your intent. Reassure participants that you are not interested in finding out how each person performed on the test. Instead, you are going to use this test activity to explore four basic principles about memory.

Present the four principles. Here are four important principles about memory. Explain each of them, using data from participants' performance on the test:

- **Primacy and recency effects.** Ask participants to raise their hands if they recalled the words *dream* and *pillow*. Explain that people easily remember the first and the last items in a series. Most participants would have written *dream* and *pillow* because they were the first and the last word in the list.

- **Surprise effect.** Ask participants to raise their hands if they recalled the word *artichoke*. Explain that people remember things that are novel or different. Most participants would have written *artichoke* because it is very different from the other words in the list.

- **Repetition effect.** Ask participants to raise their hands if they recalled the word *night*. Explain that people remember things that are repeated. Most participants would have written *night* because you repeated it three times.

- **False-memory effect.** Ask participants to raise their hands if they recalled the word *bed*. Reveal that this word was not on your list. Explain that the brain closes logical gaps in what it hears, sees, or reads, and frequently remembers things that did not take place. Most participants would have written *bed* because it logically belongs to this list (even though you never read it).

Encourage action planning. Ask participants how they would use these four principles to help them remember new terms and ideas in the training session. Give examples such as, *"To compensate for the primacy and the recency effects, pay particular attention to ideas presented during the middle of the training session. Make use of the repetition effect by repeating these ideas to yourself several times."*

Critical Thinking   **269**

71
Business Strategies

I keep losing tic-tac-toe games, especially when playing with small children. This is probably because I get distracted about the elegance of the game and keep figuring out how to use its structure for training games. Business Strategies is one of my recent adaptations of tic-tac-toe.

Purpose

To explore the impact of business strategies on customers, employees, and shareholders

Participants

Minimum: 9
Maximum: Any number
Best: 10 to 30
(Participants are divided into teams of 4 to 6.)

Time

30 to 45 minutes

Supplies

- Flip chart
- Felt-tipped markers
- Pads of small Post-it® Notes
- Pens or pencils
- Timer
- Whistle

Preparation

Prepare a 3 by 3 grid. Draw a grid like the sample on a flip chart. Label the three columns *customers*, *employees*, and *shareholders*. Label the three rows with the same words. (See the following sample.)

Business Strategies Grid

	Customers	Employees	Shareholders
Customers			
Employees			
Shareholders			

Flow

Appoint a judge. Before conducting the activity, recruit a senior manager from the organization to act as a judge. At the beginning of the activity, introduce the judge and explain that he or she will select the best item from each box on a 3 by 3 grid.

Organize participants into teams. Create three or more teams, each with three or more members. (It does not matter if some teams have one more or one fewer member.) Ask team members to sit around a table and introduce themselves to each other, if necessary.

Identify the three stakeholder groups. Explain that coming up with effective business strategy involves satisfying three important groups of people: *customers, employees,* and *shareholders.* Briefly explain who members of these three groups are. Point out that it is possible for the same person to belong to more than one group.

Explain the structure of the grid. Draw participants' attention to the fact that the grid has the same labels for the columns as for the rows. Point to the three boxes along the diagonal line from the top left to the bottom right. These boxes have the same label for both the column and the row. (The other six boxes have different labels for the column and the row.)

Explain what goes in the diagonal boxes. Tell participants that they will place ideas for satisfying members of each of the three groups in each box. Point to the top-left box and write "Manufacture high-quality products" as an example of what goes in this box.

Explain what goes in the boxes above the diagonal. Point out that sometimes actions that satisfy one group may also satisfy another group. Point to the three boxes above the diagonal. Tell participants that they will place ideas for mutually satisfying the two groups associated with each box. Point to the top-right box (that belongs to the *shareholder* column and the *customer* row) and write "Give discounts to frequent customers to gain their loyalty" as an example of a mutually satisfying idea. Explain that this action will please both the customers and the shareholders because loyal customers buy more products.

Explain what goes in the boxes below the diagonal. Point out that sometimes what satisfies one group may clash with the needs of another group. Point to the three boxes below the diagonal. Tell participants that they will place clashing ideas that may satisfy one group at the expense of the other in these boxes. Point to the bottom-left box (that belongs to the *customer* column and the *shareholder* row), and write "Give excessive discounts to customers" as an example of a clashing idea. Explain that deep discounts will delight customers but displease shareholders because profit margin will go down.

Explain the contest procedure. Distribute pads of 3-inch by 2-inch Post-its to each team. Tell all participants that they will have 10 minutes to write different items to be placed in the nine different boxes of the grid. Each Post-it should contain only one item. A team may not write a second item for a box until they have written at least one item for each of the nine boxes. After the 10-minute interval, a judge will identify the best item in each box. The team that wrote the highest number of best items will win the contest.

Pause for 10 minutes. Encourage teams to discuss various ideas, write each of them on a note, and post it on the appropriate box of the grid.

Conclude the activity. At the end of 10 minutes, blow the whistle and ask teams to stop writing and finish posting their notes. Ask participants to review the ideas in various boxes in the grid. At the same time, ask the judge to review the items and select the best item from each box.

Announce the results. Ask the judge to read the best idea from each box. Ask each team to keep track of how many times its ideas were selected. At the end of the judge's announcements, identify the team with the highest number of selected ideas. Declare the team to be the winner and congratulate its members.

Debriefing

Conduct a discussion about the relationship among the three groups of stakeholders and the impact of different activities on these groups. Ask participants for guidelines to increase mutually satisfying strategies and to reduce conflicting strategies.

72
Tree

Here's a fast-paced drawing activity that catches participants behaving in a somewhat unthinking fashion. Although very brief, this activity delivers an important message.

Caution

This entrapment activity will backfire if you gloat about catching participants making a mistake. When you point out what *they* failed to do, stress the fact that that *you* have made the same mistake several times. Maintain an appropriate tone of humility.

Purpose

To be mindful of invisible but critical elements of a system

Participants

Minimum: 1
Maximum: Any number
Best: 10 to 30

Time

99 seconds

Supplies

- Blank index cards
- Pens or pencils

Set-Up

Before the training session or during a break, place an index card and a pencil on each person's seat. If this is not possible, distribute paper and pencils to all participants.

Flow

Give instructions. Ask everyone to draw a tree on the index card within 45 seconds. Explain that this tree could be a realistic one or an abstract one. The only critical requirement is that it should be drawn within the 45-second time limit.

Pause. Wait for 45 seconds while participants complete this task.

Explain the learning point. After 45 seconds (it doesn't matter if some of the artists are still working on their masterpieces), begin debriefing. Instead of conducting a time-consuming discussion, present the major learning point this way:

Look at your tree. Look at your neighbor's tree.

How many of drew the roots for your trees? Very few of you did that! I know that I omitted the roots when I first participated in this activity.

So what is holding up the trees without the root system? How do these trees get water and nutrition? You must agree that the root system is an essential component of the tree.

Why did I not draw the roots? Probably because I usually don't see the roots. They are hidden.

How many things do I mindlessly ignore just because they are not visible? Do we disregard critical elements of a system just because they are out of sight? Sometimes the most critical elements in a system are not physical objects but invisible and intangible essentials such as relationships and feelings.

What problems are likely to arise from selective seeing and thinking? How can we remove or reduce the impact of habitually ignoring that which we cannot see?

73
ExEx

Whether you are a marketer, accountant, manager, or salesperson, you can always conduct an experiment in your workplace. Learning the basic principles of experimental research will help you make more logical decisions in all aspects of your work life. This knowledge will also enable you to better evaluate other people's statements about what is effective and what is not. In ExEx (which stands for "Experiential Experimentation") participants learn basic concepts of experimental research—and participate in an experimental research project.

Caution

Participants may become bored and distracted during the 30-minute study period. However, tell them that the objectivity and the reliability of your experiment depend on all participants following the instructions given to them. It is especially important to prevent members of the *hearts* and *spades* groups from interacting with each other during the entire 30-minute period.

Purpose

To understand and apply basic principles and procedures of experimental research methodology

Participants

Minimum: 12
Maximum: Any number
Best: 24 to 120
(Participants are divided into 4 groups. Some groups are divided into pairs.)

Time

60 to 90 minutes

Supplies

- Copies of Handout A, Introduction to Experimental Research (with examples)
- Copies of Handout B, Introduction to Experimental Research (without examples)
- Four Instruction Cards, each associated with a playing card suit, prepared in advance by cutting them apart

- Copies of the questionnaire, consisting of Confidence Scale and Enjoyment Scale
- Pens or pencils
- Flip chart
- Felt-tipped markers
- Timer

Preparation

Prepare two versions of the handout. Prior to play, prepare sufficient number of copies of the handout, Introduction to Experimental Research, with and without examples. The version with examples is labeled as *Handout A* and the version without examples is labeled as *Handout B*.

Assemble playing cards to randomize the subjects. Prior to play, divide the total number of participants by 4, rounding upward if necessary. From a deck of playing cards, take this many cards of *each* suit and place them in a bag or some other convenient container.

Flow

Assign participants to different treatment groups. As participants walk in, ask each person to take a card from the bag. After all participants have done so, ask them to check the suit of the card and go to one of the four breakout rooms (or four corners of the meeting room) assigned to the suit. Ask each participant to pick up an instruction card and a copy of the handout at the location and follow the instructions.

This is what happens in the four different locations:

- In the *spades* location, participants read Handout A independently for 30 minutes.
- In the *hearts* location, participants read Handout B independently for 30 minutes.
- In the *clubs* location, participants read Handout A independently for the first 15 minutes and then discuss its content with a self-selected partner for the next 15 minutes.
- In the *diamonds* location, participants read Handout B independently for the first 15 minutes and then discuss its content with a self-selected partner for the next 15 minutes.

Keep track of time. At the end of 15 minutes, remind participants in the clubs and the diamonds locations to select partners and to discuss the content for the next 15 minutes. (If the number of participants in these groups is odd, create a triad to accommodate the extra participant.) At the end of 30 minutes, ask all participants to return to the common meeting area.

Administer the questionnaire. Ask the participants not to talk to each other. Distribute copies of the questionnaire (which contains two scales) and pens or pencils and ask each participant to independently respond to it.

- The *Confidence Scale* lists ten topics related to experimental research. Participants are asked to circle a number from 1 through 4 next to each topic to indicate how confident they feel about their mastery of the topic.

- The *Enjoyment Scale* contains a single 4-point item that asks participants how much they enjoyed the instructional procedure.

Analyze data. Ask each subject to find the total of the circled numbers in the confidence scale. Then ask the participants in each of the four groups to get together and to compute the average (or *mean*, as experimenters call it) confidence and enjoyment scores. After a suitable pause, draw two 2 by 2 grids on the flip chart and enter the means in the appropriate boxes (or *cells*, in the parlance of experimenters):

Data Analysis Grids

Confidence Scores

	Handout with Examples	Handout Without Examples
Discussion	Clubs' mean confidence score:	Diamonds' mean confidence score:
No Discussion	Spades' mean confidence score:	Hearts' mean confidence score:

Enjoyment Scores

	Handout with Examples	Handout Without Examples
Discussion	Clubs' mean enjoyment score:	Diamonds' mean enjoyment score:
No Discussion	Spades' mean enjoyment score:	Hearts' mean enjoyment score:

Announce the hypotheses. Explain that earlier experiments suggest that the effectiveness and enjoyment of learning increase when:

1. Examples are used in the handout.

2. Learners discuss the contents of the handout with partners.

Therefore, these are the hypotheses investigated in the experiment:

- The subjects in the spades group (that used neither examples nor discussions) should have the lowest mean score in both confidence and enjoyment.

- The subjects in the diamonds group (that used both examples and discussions) should have the highest mean scores.

- The subjects in the other two groups (hearts and clubs) should have medium levels of mean scores.

Test the hypotheses: Ask participants to study the data in the grid and discuss how they relate to these hypotheses.

Debriefing

Use the following types of discussion questions to apply the concepts from the handout to process participants' experience:

- *Who were the subjects in this experiment? What were their important characteristics?*
- *Why did we not ask the subjects to select their own treatment groups?*
- *We used playing cards to assign the subjects to different treatment groups. Was this method truly random?*
- *This experiment had two dependent variables. What were they?*
- *What were the independent variables in this experiment?*
- *What type of experimental design did we use?*
- *What could have been a better experimental design?*
- *Did the experiment confirm or reject the hypotheses?*
- *What conclusions can we draw from the data?*
- *This experiment involves training variables. How can we conduct a similar experiment involving marketing variables?*

Handout A: Introduction to Experimental Research

Why should we learn about experimental research?

Learning the basic principles of experimental research will help you make more logical decisions in all aspects of your work life. This knowledge will also enable you to better evaluate other people's statements about what is effective and what is not.

What is a *hypothesis*?

A hypothesis is an informed guess (or hunch) about cause-effect connections.

Based on participants' behaviors in e-mail games, a researcher has this hypothesis: People who play e-mail games are more likely to send e-mail messages for other purposes.

What is an *experiment*?

An experiment is a research activity in which at least one factor is deliberately "manipulated" by the researcher.

A researcher "manipulates" the work schedule of a group of managers by having them play an e-mail game for 15 minutes a day.

Who is a *subject*?

The people who participate in an experiment are called subjects. In an experiment different subjects may receive different treatments.

We are conducting an experiment on the use of e-mail by women managers. If we use twelve women managers in our experiment, they are our subjects.

What is a *constant*?

All experiments involve several factors that affect the subjects. A factor that is the same for all the subjects is called a constant.

In our sample experiment gender (women) and job type (manager) are constants.

What are *variables*?

A factor that takes on different values for different subjects in an experiment is called a variable.

In our sample experiment, the age and height of women are variables.

What are different types of variables?

A *dependent variable* is a variable related to the results that we are trying to study. This is the variable that is affected by our experimental treatments.

In our sample experiment, the use of e-mail is the dependent variable.

An independent variable is the variable that is manipulated in the experiment. These variables have an effect on the results of the experiment.

In our sample experiment, we have the women managers play an e-mail game for two weeks. The time spent in playing the game is the independent variable.

What does controlling variance mean?

Variance refers to differences in any variable. The goal of experimental research is to eliminate or restrict the influence of factors that produce variance. By controlling variance in an experiment, we are able to make confident statements about the effect of the independent variable on the dependent variable.

How can we control variance by *holding factors constant*?

For example, we can select only those women managers whose IQ scores are between 100 and 110 in our experiment.

There are two major limitations to this strategy:

- The amount of data is reduced because we are using only a selected set of available subjects.
- *In our sample experiment, we cannot use women managers with an IQ score that exceeds 110.*
- We can generalize the results only to a restricted group of people.
- *The findings from our sample experiment are true only for a small group of women managers whose IQ scores range between 100 and 110.*

How can we control variance by *randomization*?

If we are testing two different treatments, we can flip a coin for each subject and assign him or her to a specific treatment depending on whether the coin turns up heads or tails. This is an example of randomization. When an experimenter randomly assigns subject to treatments, it evenly spreads the effects of variables across the groups.

What is an experimental design?

An experimental design is a plan for conducting an experiment. It identifies the dependent and independent variables and shows how these variables are positioned in the experiment. The design also specifies when and where different types of data are collected and measures of the dependent variable are taken.

What is a *test*?

This term is used to describe different types of data collection and measurement procedures.

In our sample experiment, if we count the number of times a woman manager sends e-mail messages in a week, this can be considered a test.

A **pretest** refers to data collection at the beginning of an experiment, before the subjects receive experimental treatments.

In our sample experiment, if we count the number of times women managers send e-mail messages before participating in the e-mail game, this can be considered a pretest.

A **post-test** refers to data collection in an experiment after the subjects receive the experimental treatment.

In our sample experiment, if we ask women managers to participate in an e-mail game for two weeks (which is our experimental treatment) and then count the number of times women managers send e-mail messages, this can be considered a post-test.

What is a post-test-only control-group design?

Sometimes you may want to experiment with a single treatment. In this case, you give the treatment to one group and withhold it from another similar group. After the treatment is completed, you test that group and the other group (which did not receive any treatment) to discover the effect of the treatment.

In our sample experiment, we began with a group of twenty-four women managers. We randomly assigned them to two equal-sized groups of twelve members. The first group (called the experimental group) participates in an e-mail game, spending approximately 15 minutes each day for two weeks. During these two weeks, the second group (called the control group) does not participate in the e-mail game or do anything special related to the use of e-mail. At the end of these two weeks, both groups are "post-tested": We count how many times women managers in either group send e-mail messages. If there is a difference between the post-test scores of the two groups, we can assume that it is due to the two weeks of playing e-mail games by the experimental group.

What is a pretest-post-test control group study?

There is a major flaw in the preceding experimental design: It is possible that the subjects in the experimental group are already performing at a higher level than those in the control group. In a situation like this, we may use a pretest-post-test control group design. In this design, you begin by testing both groups before and after the treatment. Any differences in the increase in performance between the two groups can be attributed to the experimental treatment.

In this design, experimental and control groups are randomly set up as before. Pretest data are collected from both groups before the experimental group begins to play the e-mail game for two weeks. After two weeks (during which time the experimental group played the e-mail game and the control group did not) post-test data are collected from both groups. By computing the increase in the number of e-mail messages between the pretest and the post-test, we can confidently attribute any differences to the impact of playing the e-mail game for two weeks.

Handout B: Introduction to Experimental Research

Why should we learn about experimental research?

Learning the basic principles of experimental research will help you make more logical decisions in all aspects of your work life. This knowledge will also enable you to better evaluate other peoples' statements about what is effective and what is not.

What is a *hypothesis*?

A hypothesis is an informed guess (or hunch) about cause-effect connections.

What is an *experiment*?

An experiment is a research activity in which at least one factor is deliberately "manipulated" by the researcher.

Who is a *subject*?

The people who participate in an experiment are called subjects. In an experiment different subjects may receive different treatments.

What is a *constant*?

All experiments involve several factors that affect the subjects. A factor that is the same for all the subjects is called a constant.

What are *variables*?

A factor that takes on different values for different subjects in an experiment is called a variable.

What are different types of variables?

A *dependent variable* is a variable related to the results that we are trying to study. This is the variable that is affected by our experimental treatments.

An *independent variable* is the variable that is manipulated in the experiment. These variables have an effect on the results of the experiment.

What does controlling variance mean?

Variance refers to differences in any variable. The goal of experimental research is to eliminate or restrict the influence of factors that produce variance. By controlling variance in an experiment, we are able to make confident statements about the effect of the independent variable on the dependent variable.

How can we control variance by *holding factors constant*?

We can eliminate the variance by holding a factor constant.

There are two major limitations to this strategy:

- The amount of data is reduced because we are using only a selected set of available subjects.

- We can generalize the results only to a restricted group of people.

How can we control variance by *randomization*?

If we are testing two different treatments, we can flip a coin for each subject and assign him or her to a specific treatment depending on whether the coin turns up heads or tails. This is an example of randomization. When an experimenter randomly assigns subject to treatments, it evenly spreads the effects of variables across the groups.

What is an experimental design?

An experimental design is a plan for conducting an experiment. It identifies the dependent and independent variables and shows how these variables are positioned in the experiment. The design also specifies when and where different types of data are collected and measures of the dependent variable are taken.

What is a *test*?

This term is used to describe different types of data collection and measurement procedures.

A **pretest** refers to data collection at the beginning of an experiment, before the subjects receive experimental treatments.

A **post-test** refers to data collection in an experiment after the subjects receive the experimental treatment.

What is a post-test-only control-group design?

Sometimes you may want to experiment with a single treatment. In this case, you give the treatment to one group and withhold it from another similar group. After the treatment is completed, you test that group and the other group (which did not receive any treatment) to discover the effect of the treatment.

What is a pretest-post-test control group study?

There is a major flaw in the preceding experimental design: It is possible that the subjects in the experimental group are already performing at a higher level than those in the control group. In a situation like this, we may use a pretest-post-test control group design. In this design, you begin by testing both groups before and after the treatment. Any differences in the increase in performance between the two groups can be attributed to the experimental treatment.

Four Instruction Cards

♣ Instruction Card for Clubs

You have 30 minutes to study *Handout A.*

Study the handout by yourself for 15 minutes. Do not talk to anyone during this period.

Then discuss the content of the handout with a partner for the remaining 15 minutes.

♠ Instruction Card for Spades

You have 30 minutes to study *Handout A.*

Read the handout carefully for 30 minutes.

Do not talk to anyone during the study period.

♦ Instruction Card for Diamonds

You have 30 minutes to study *Handout B.*

Study the handout by yourself for 15 minutes. Do not talk to anyone during this period.

Then discuss the content of the handout with a partner for the remaining 15 minutes.

❤ Instruction Card for Hearts

You have 30 minutes to study *Handout B.*

Read the handout carefully for 30 minutes.

Do not talk to anyone during the study period.

Confidence and Enjoyment Scales

Confidence Scale

Below are thirteen terms associated with experimental research. How confident are you about your ability to explain each of the terms and to give an appropriate example? Circle the number that indicates your level of confidence for each item, using this code:

1 = very unsure
2 = unsure
3 = sure
4 = very sure

1. constant	1	2	3	4
2. control-group	1	2	3	4
3. controlling variance	1	2	3	4
4. dependent variable	1	2	3	4
5. experiment	1	2	3	4
6. experimental design	1	2	3	4
7. hypothesis	1	2	3	4
8. independent variable	1	2	3	4
9. post-test	1	2	3	4
10. pretest	1	2	3	4
11. randomization	1	2	3	4
12. subject	1	2	3	4
13. variable	1	2	3	4

Enjoyment Scale

How enjoyable was your 30-minute study period? Choose one:

1 = very boring
2 = boring
3 = interesting
4 = very interesting

74
Quick Questions

It is a tough thing to encourage participants to reflect on provocative questions and come up with valuable insights. That is what this 99-second activity attempts to do.

Purpose

To compare frequently used interventions for improving human performance with effective interventions for the same purpose

Participants

Minimum: 1
Maximum: Any number
Best: 10 to 30
(Participants work individually.)

Time

99 seconds

Flow

Brief the participants. Explain that you are going to ask two related questions, one for the audience in each side of the room. Participants are to shout out the first answer that comes to mind.

   Ask the first question. Turn to the right side of the room and ask, "What is the most frequently used intervention for improving employee performance?" Pause for about 5 seconds and invite audience members to shout out the answer. When the shouting dies, say, "I heard most people shout 'training.'"

   Ask the second question. Turn to the left side of the room and ask, "What is the most effective intervention for improving employee performance?" As before, wait for about 5 seconds and signal audience members to shout out the answer. Listen carefully and say, "There were many different responses, but very few people shouted 'training.'"

   Explain the key point. Instead of conducting a debriefing discussion for belaboring the point, simply explain this idea in your own words:

Training is the most important intervention. It works effectively whenever there is a lack of skills and knowledge. Training is also one of the most abused interventions. It is frequently used for solving motivational problems and management support problems. In many situations, you

should be using more suitable interventions such as incentives and feedback. These interventions will produce more effective results.

Here's my third question for everybody: How can we effectively use training appropriately and avoid abusing it in situations in which it is not likely to produce effective results? You cannot answer this question in 5 seconds. Take as much time as you want to reflect on this critical question.

75
Triple Nine

The key to such procedures as needs analysis, market research, and evaluation is the ability to find patterns in available information, collect additional information, and come to logical conclusions. Triple Nine is a game with a pocket calculator that gives participants ample practice in this type of logical thinking.

Caution

This activity could be stressful for non-mathematical types. However, it only involves addition. The resulting skills are definitely worth pushing participants slightly beyond their comfort zone.

Purpose

To think logically and achieve a goal with the fewest moves

Participants

Minimum: 2
Maximum: Any number
Best: 10 to 20
(Participants are divided into pairs.)

Time

5 minutes for each match. The game can be replayed any number of times.

Supplies

A calculator for each participant

Flow

Secret number. The first player enters a 3-digit number (a number from 100 to 999) and tells his or her opponent that she is ready.
   Cathy punches in her secret number 297, presses the plus key, and proclaims, "Ready!"
   Add a number. The second player calls out a number that has 1, 2, or 3 digits. The first player adds this number to the original number and then informs his or her opponent:

- How many 9s there are in the total
- Any other digit, but not its position

Ted says, "Add 123." Cathy does so and gets a total of 420. She says, "No 9s and a 4."

Repeat. Continue the process of the second player calling out a number, the first player adding it to the total, and giving information about 9s and one other digit. Keep track of how many moves the second player takes.

Ted says, "Add 555," hoping to change the 4 to a 9 regardless of its position. Cathy adds the 555 and gets 975. She tells Ted, "One 9 and a 5." This is the end of the second move.

Four digits. If the total goes over 999 any time during the play of the game, the first player returns to the previous total. The first player says, "Overflow!" and does not give any additional information. This is counted as a move.

Ted guesses that the 9 is in the hundreds place, although he is not sure of the location of the 5. To make the maximum use of the situation, he asks Cathy to add 44. When Cathy does this, she gets a total of 1019. So she presses the minus key, cancels the last addition, and says, "Overflow." This is the end of the third move.

Ted is not upset because he has collected useful information. His hunch about the 9 in the hundreds place is confirmed. He also figures out that the tens digit (the digit in the middle) is greater than 5 because only then could the total have gone over 1,000. Therefore, the 5 must be in the units place. He calls out, "Add 4." Cathy's total is now 979 and she responds with "Two 9s and a 7."

Ted has figured out the entire number now. To finish off the game, he say, "Add 20." Cathy does so and announces "Three 9s." The first game ends in five moves.

Reverse roles. The game is played again with the roles reversed. The second player in the previous game now selects a secret number and the other player tries to run it up to 999.

Here's the complete game when it is Cathy's turn to guess:

Move 1. Cathy begins by saying, "Add 123." Ted does so and announces, "No 9s and a 1."

Move 2. Cathy figures out that the 1 cannot be in the hundreds place because Ted began with a three-digit number and added 123. So the "1" has to be in the tens or units place. Cathy guesses the latter and says, "Add an 8." Ted does the addition and says, "No 9s and a 2."

Move 3. Cathy takes a moment to process this information. Since she did not get a 9, the units digit was not the one. It must have been in the tens place. Since the units digit wasn't a 1, adding 8 would have made it 10 or more, so the tens place must have gone up to 2. To clinch this digit, Cathy says, "Add 70." Ted reports "One 9 and a 3."

Move 4. Where is this 3? Since this is the fourth round, Cathy does not think it is in the hundreds place. So she says, "Add 6." Her guess is wrong. Ted says, "Still one 9 and a 3."

Move 5. Apparently the 3 was (and still is) in the hundreds place. Cathy says, "Add 600." As she expected, she gets two 9s and a 6.

Move 6. Cathy has the entire number now. She says, "Add 3," and gets her triple 9s.

Match. Two games make a match. The player who gets the triple 9 with the least number of moves wins the match.

Since Cathy needed six moves and Ted only five, Ted wins.

Debriefing

Conduct an informal debriefing discussion by asking participants what they learned from the game about analyzing data, collecting additional information, and recognizing patterns. Invite participants to share work-related situations in which they have to make logical decisions based on incomplete information.

76
Wobegon Test

Garrison Keillor claims that all the children in Lake Wobegon are above average. This is obviously statistically impossible. The irony in this statement reflects the universal tendency to overestimate ourselves and to underestimate others. That is the learning point of this jolt.

Purpose

To increase the awareness of the tendency to overestimate ourselves and underestimate others

Participants

Minimum: 5
Maximum: Any number
Best: 10 to 30
(Participants work individually.)

Time

5 to 10 minutes

Supplies

- Small pieces of paper
- Pens or pencils
- Flip chart
- Felt-tipped markers

Flow

Get personal ratings. In the middle of your next meeting, invite participants to rate their behaviors associated with this statement:

I listen very carefully to what the others say.

Ask participants to use this rating scale:

10 = always
9 = very frequently
8 = usually
7 = often
6 = sometimes
5 = occasionally
4 = once in a while
3 = seldom
2 = rarely
1 = never

Ask each participant to anonymously write down the appropriate number on a small piece of paper, fold it, and give it to you.

Get ratings of other people's behavior. Now ask each participant to think of other participants' listening behaviors and rate this statement (using the same rating scale and the same procedure as before):

Others listen very carefully to what I say.

Display the averages. With the help of the participants, quickly calculate the average value of both sets of ratings. Mark these two averages on a line like this:

1————2————3————4————5————6————7————8————9————10

Debriefing

It is very likely that the "I" average is greater than the "others" average. Ask participants to take a moment to reflect on the implications of this discrepancy.

After a suitable pause, discuss participants' insights. Then ask participants to plan different strategies for jointly raising the "others" average. Encourage them to be individually accountable for the group's average.

PART IX

Corporate Training Topics

Time Management

77
Time Value

Time is money. This game helps players make sure that their time is well-spent.

Purpose

To maximize the value of brief periods of time

Participants

Minimum: 6
Maximum: Any number
Best: 12 to 30
(Participants are divided into 3 to 5 teams.)

Time

40 to 60 minutes

Supplies

- Flip charts
- Felt-tipped markers
- Index cards
- Timer
- Whistle

Preparation

Assemble a panel of judges. Near the end of this game, you need two to five people to determine the winning teams. Enroll a few of your friends and tell them that all they have to do is to listen to half-a-dozen ideas and decide which one is best and which one is the most unique. This activity should not require more than 5 minutes of their time.

Flow

Form teams. Organize the participants into three to five teams, each with not more than seven members. It is not necessary for all teams to be of equal size.

Assign teams to flip charts. Ask each team to stand by a flip chart. Make sure that the teams have plenty of markers.

Announce the first topic for brainstorming. Ask this question: *You have $5 to spend. How can you make sure that you get the maximum value for this money?* Tell the teams that they have 5 minutes to brainstorm alternative responses to this question.

Teams should make sure that all members participate in the discussion and someone writes down their ideas on the flip chart. Each team should generate as many ideas as possible within the 5-minute period. If necessary, they may use several sheets of the flip-chart paper.

Conclude the first brainstorming session. After 5 minutes, blow the whistle. Announce the end of the brainstorming session. Explain that the first session was just a warm-up to get prepared for the second one. Ask the players to flip the pages over and begin with a blank sheet of paper.

Announce the second brainstorming topic. Tell the teams that they have another 5 minutes to brainstorm alternative responses to this new question: *You have 5 minutes of free time to spend any way you want. How can you make sure that you get the maximum value for this time?* Ask the teams to use the same procedure as before.

Conclude the second brainstorming session. After 5 minutes, blow the whistle again. Announce the end of the brainstorming session. Tell the teams that you are now going to award points for their accomplishments.

Identify the winning team in the quantitative category. Begin by asking the teams to count the number of alternative ideas on their lists. Identify the team with the most ideas and declare its members to be the winners in the *quantitative* category.

Identify the winning team in the qualitative category. Bring in your friends and introduce them as the panel of judges. Ask each team to copy the two best ideas from its flip-chart list onto index cards, each on a separate card. Collect these cards, shuffle them, and read the ideas. Ask the judges to select the best one among these ideas. Identify the team that contributed this idea and declare its members to be the winners in the *qualitative* category.

Identify the winning team in the uniqueness category. Explain that one of the goals of brainstorming is to generate unique and unusual ideas. Ask each team to copy the two most unique ideas from its flip-chart list onto two different index cards. Use the same procedure as before and ask the judges to select the least conventional idea. Identify the team that contributed this idea and declare its members to be the winners in the *uniqueness* category.

Thank the judges. Tell the judges that their job is done and they may retire to their chambers. Lead a round of applause for the departing judges.

Debriefing

Introduce the debriefing session. This game requires some in-depth debriefing to ensure that the players discover and share key learning points. Explain the purpose and the format of the debriefing session. Here's a suggested script:

You probably have some interesting things to discuss about your experiences in the game you played. I want to conduct a debriefing session to help you share your insights in a structured fashion.

Conduct the debriefing. Begin with a broad question such as: *What did you learn from this activity?* Encourage the participants to share their insights. Whenever appropriate, insert questions like these into the discussion:

- *What did you do while the judges were making their decision? Did you maximize the value of this brief period of time?*

- *This activity used several time-management techniques. Can you figure out what they were?*

- *Imposing an artificial deadline is a useful time-management technique. We used a deadline of 5 minutes. What would have happened if we did not have any deadlines? What if we had a 2-minute deadline?*

- *Your ideas were evaluated according to three different criteria: quantity, quality, and uniqueness. What if I had specified these criteria at the beginning of the activity? Could you have worked more efficiently? Why did no one ask for the goal, or the criterion, or the scoring system at the beginning? What assumptions did you make?*

- *People claim time is money. We brainstormed ideas for enhancing the value of $5 and 5 minutes. Compare your two original lists. Which ideas are similar between the list for spending money and the one for spending time?*

- *To continue with our brainstorming topics, here's another: You have 5 extra minutes every day. How can you make sure that you get the maximum value for spending this time? How can you build up something valuable over a year?*

Conclude the debriefing session. End with this broad question: *How can you apply your insights back in your workplace?* Encourage the players to select one or two 5-minute value-enhancement strategies for immediate application.

78
Time Savers

One of the reasons that I don't work for a corporation is that I do not want to attend meetings, write reports, and submit expense forms in triplicate. You probably have your own special (but less drastic) techniques for saving time.

Purpose

To share and apply practical strategies for reducing different time wasters

Participants

Minimum: 6
Maximum: Any number
Best: 10 to 30
(Participants are organized into teams.)

Time

45 to 60 minutes

Supplies

- Blank envelopes
- Index cards
- Pens or pencils
- Timer
- Whistle

Preparation

Prepare the time-waster envelopes. Select four or five major time wasters in organizational settings. Write a different time waster on the face of each envelope.

Andy uses this game as a follow-up activity to Time Wasters. He re-uses the list of the top-five time wasters identified in that game:

> *Trying to completely satisfy customers*
> *Having to write too many reports*
> *Lack of planning*
> *Delays in budget approval*
> *Inability to say "No"*

Flow

Organize the players. Divide the players into three or more teams, each with not more than seven members. Teams should be approximately the same size. Seat the teams in a rough circle to facilitate the exchange of envelopes.

Brief the players. Review the time wasters. Explain that the players should brainstorm appropriate strategies to eliminate each time waster, or at least to reduce its impact.

Distribute the supplies. Give one time-waster envelope and several blank index cards to each team. Refer to the index cards as time-saver cards.

Conduct the first round. Ask the teams to brainstorm strategies for handling the time waster on the envelope. These strategies should be recorded as short phrases or sentences on one time-saver card. Announce a 3-minute time limit for this activity and encourage the teams to work rapidly. Explain that the time-saving tips will eventually be evaluated in terms of both their quantity and their practical application.

Conclude the first round. After 3 minutes, blow a whistle and announce the end of the first round. Ask each team to place its time-saver card inside the envelope and pass the envelope, unsealed, to the next team. (The envelope from the last team goes to the first team.) Warn the teams not to open the envelopes.

Conduct the second round. Ask teams to read the new time waster on the face of the envelope (without looking at the time-saver card inside). Tell the teams to repeat the procedure of brainstorming and recording strategies on a blank index card. After 3 minutes, blow the whistle and ask the teams to place their time-saver cards inside the envelopes and pass them to the next team.

Conduct more rounds. If you are pressed for time, move to the evaluation round (see below). If you have ample time, conduct one or two more rounds using the same procedure. However, do not conduct more than four rounds in all.

Conduct the evaluation round. Begin this round just like the previous ones. However, the teams do not brainstorm more strategies. Instead, they open the envelopes and comparatively evaluate the time-saver cards inside. They do this by reviewing individual strategies on each card, and then comparing entire cards to each other. Teams distribute 100 points among the time-saver cards to indicate each card's relative practical usefulness. Announce a 3-minute time limit for this activity.

Present the results. At the end of the time limit, check to make sure that teams have recorded the points on each time-saver card. Select a team at random to present its results. Ask the team to read the time waster from the face of the envelope and then to read the ideas on each card, beginning with the lowest-ranked card. The teams should progress from one card to the next, in ascending order of points.

Determine the winner. After all the teams have presented their evaluations, instruct the teams to place the time-saver cards on a table at the front of the room. Then call for the representatives from each team to collect their response cards. Ask the teams to add up the points on their cards to determine their total scores. Identify the team with the highest score as the winner.

Debriefing

Briefly comment on interesting patterns among the time-saving tips. Also comment on the similarities among the ideas from different teams. As a follow-up activity, ask each player to select a personal set of time-saving tips for immediate implementation.

79
Time Wasters

This game encourages participants to discover factors that contribute to wasted time in the workplace.

Purpose

To identify major time wasters in the workplace and arrange them in order of their impact

Participants

Minimum: 6
Maximum: Any number
Best: 10 to 30
(Participants are organized into 3 or more teams, each with 2 to 7 members.)

Time

30 to 45 minutes

Supplies

- Blank pieces of paper
- Pens or pencils
- Flip chart and felt-tipped markers

Flow

Brief the participants. Explain that several factors encourage (and sometimes force) people to waste time in the workplace. Ask participants to name a common time waster. Comment on this example. Point out that identifying major time wasters in the workplace is the first step to removing them.

Begin with individual brainstorming. Ask participants to spend a couple of minutes to reflect on the major time wasters in the workplace and to independently write down a list, for example:

Telephone calls
Saying "yes" to too many people
Waiting to see the boss

Meetings without agendas
Interruptions

Form teams. Organize the participants into three or more teams, each with two to seven participants.

Assign teamwork. Ask the teams to each spend 5 minutes recording a list of time wasters in the workplace. Encourage the team members to use the ideas they had generated earlier.

Ask the teams to narrow down their lists. Instruct each team to select the top five time wasters.

Prepare a common list. Ask the teams to take turns calling out one of the main time wasters from their lists. Record these time wasters on the flip chart. Encourage the teams to avoid repeating the items already on the list. Continue this procedure until the common list has ten to twelve time wasters.

Ask the teams to select the worst time waster. Explain that you are looking for an item that everyone will see as wasting the most time in the workplace. Ask the participants to review the items in the common list and select, with the other members of their team, the worst time waster.

Explain the scoring system. The teams will receive a score equal to the total number of teams that selected the same time waster. For example, if four teams selected *telephone calls* as the worst time waster, then each team would receive 4 points.

Conduct the first round. Tell the teams to select the worst time waster from the common list on the flip chart. Circulate among the teams, gently speeding up the slower teams. Write down each team's choice on a piece of paper.

Award points and rank the worst time waster. Announce each team's selection. Draw a line through the time waster in the flip-chart list that was selected by the most teams during this round. Place the number "1" in front of this item to identify it as the top-ranked time waster.

Continue the game. Ask the teams to review the list and to identify the next-worst time waster. The teams may select (or re-select) any item from the flip-chart list, as long as it does not have a line through it. After collecting the choices from each team, repeat the scoring and ranking procedure. Continue until the teams have identified the top five time wasters.

Break ties. If there is a tie for the next-worst time waster, award scores as before, but do not rank or draw a line through either of the items. Give the teams 1 minute to prepare a presentation to persuade the other teams to select the same item. Then give each team 30 seconds to make its presentation. After the presentations, ask teams to select a time waster. Award scores and rank the item receiving the most choices. If there is still a tie, draw a line through all the tied items, and give them the same rank.

Conclude the game. Continue with the game until the top five time wasters are identified. Announce the conclusion of the game and ask the teams to add up their scores. Identify and congratulate the winning team.

Award points for the original lists. Ask the teams to retrieve their original lists and compare the time wasters on their list with the final top five list. The original list gets 5 points if it has the top-ranked time waster, 4 points if it has the second-ranked time waster, and so on. Ask the teams to add up the scores for their original lists. Identify the team with the highest score total and congratulate its members for having created the best original list.

Debriefing

Debrief the participants. Ask the participants to compare the items on their original individual lists with the final top five list. Encourage the participants to discuss how their personal perceptions differed from those of the others.

People could also plan ways to prevent time wasters in the workplace.

Training

80
Two Sides of Training

It is useless to ask, "Which is better: online learning or instructor-led learning?" The answer is obvious: "It all depends." The effectiveness of any strategy depends on the context. For example, it depends on the content, objectives, learners, technology, and facilitators. In order to come up with the best strategy, one must explore the advantages and disadvantages of conflicting guidelines. That's what Two Sides of Training helps participants do.

Purpose

To better understand—and use—conflicting guidelines for effective training

Participants

Minimum: 3
Maximum: Any number
Best: 12 to 30
(Participants are organized into triads.)

Time

30 to 60 minutes, depending on the number of factors, including the time allowed for each discussion

Supplies

- Timer
- Whistle

Preparation

Come up with a list of opposing pairs of advice ("dichotomies") related to training. Here's a sample list:

- *Content is important vs. Process is important*
- *We should focus on learning outcomes vs. We should focus on learning activities*
- *The teacher is an expert vs. The teacher is a fellow learner*
- *Learn from doing vs. Learn from reflecting on what you did*

- *Learners cooperate with each other vs. Learners compete with each other*
- *Use high-touch strategies vs. Use high-tech equipment*
- *Learn independently vs. Learn in teams*
- *Present the content through graphics vs. Present the content through text*
- *Develop specific objectives vs. Develop general goals*
- *Focus on facilitating learning vs. Focus on transmitting information*
- *Create a playful learning environment vs. Create a serious learning environment*
- *Provide a well-organized structure vs. Provide the freedom to explore*
- *Plan the lessons carefully vs. Improvise your lessons*
- *Emphasize the underlying theory vs. Focus on practical applications*

Flow

Brief participants. Explain that training is full of contradictory guidelines. Present a sample guideline and discuss how the two opposing guidelines make sense in different contexts. Stress the importance of exploring paradoxical guidelines to better understand the factors that influence training effectiveness.

Organize participants into triads. Divide participants into groups of three. If two participants are left over, ask them to form a triad with you. If only one participant is left over, ask the person to play the role of observer.

Assign roles. Ask each triad to identify the person who most closely resembles you, the trainer. Ask this person to play the role of the *Neutral Listener* for the first round. Assign the roles of the *Right Advocate* and the *Left Advocate* to the other two members. Announce that the Right Advocate for each round will become the Neutral Listener for the next round.

Explain the role of the Neutral Listener. The person in the "middle" of each triad should invite the Advocates to present their positions. While an advocate is making his or her presentation, the Neutral Listener should maintain eye contact, nod, smile, and demonstrate other nonverbal behaviors associated with active listening. However, it is important that the Neutral Observer hide any personal opinions and listen to both Advocates with equal interest.

Explain the role of the Advocates. Each advocate will be assigned one of two conflicting guidelines related to training. Both advocates will prepare presentations supporting their positions and attacking the opposing positions. After 15 seconds, the Neutral Listener will point to one of the Advocates. This person will make a presentation for 60 seconds. Immediately after this, the other Advocate will make a presentation.

Process the first dichotomy. Announce the first guideline for the Right Advocate and the conflicting guideline for the Left Advocate. Ask all advocates to get ready for their presentations. After 15 seconds, blow the whistle and instruct the Neutral Listeners to point to either Advocate to begin the presentation. Pause for a minute. Blow the whistle again and ask the other Advocate to make a presentation. Blow the whistle after another minute. Randomly select a Neutral Listener and ask the person to come to the front of the room and summarize the key points from both presentations.

Conduct a quick debriefing. Ask the Neutral Listeners to report on unusual, interesting, and provocative statements made by the advocates. Briefly discuss these comments.

Continue with additional dichotomies. Thank all Advocates and Neutral Listeners. Ask the Right Advocates in each triad to assume the role of the Neutral Listener for the next round. (The Left Advocate from the previous round will now become the Right Advocate and the original Neutral Listener will become the new Right Advocate.) Announce the next pair of conflicting training guidelines and conduct another round of the activity. Repeat the same process with each dichotomy.

Conclude the session. After you have completed your list of dichotomies, invite participants to suggest other pairs of conflicting training guidelines. Treat them in the same fashion.

Debriefing

Conduct a discussion. Ask participants to comment on interesting incidents during their turns as Neutral Observers. Invite participants to figure out how to creatively select and synthesize contradictory guidelines.

81
Interactive Learning

Most participants enjoy activities that involve walking around and chatting with several other people. This is probably because such behavior is very different from the usual "sit-down-and-keep-quiet" approach to typical classroom training. Interactive Learning taps into this wanderlust and garrulity among participants.

Purpose

To become mindful of the variety of interactive training strategies that are available

Participants

Minimum: 12
Maximum: Any number
Best: 15 to 30
(Participants organize and reorganize themselves into different teams.)

Time

30 to 40 minutes

Supplies

- Handout, Interactive Learning Strategies (participants receive a single page from a 6-page handout)
- Blank pieces of paper
- Pens or pencils
- Timer
- Whistle

Preparation

Photocopy the handouts. Arrange the handouts in sets and do not staple the pages.

Flow

Brief the participants. Explain that learning organizations have a competitive advantage because the people in these organizations continuously learn from—and learn with—each other. Effective adult learning benefits from structured activities and interaction among participants. Tell your participants that they are going to use a structured activity to learn more about the variety of interactive learning strategies that are available.

Distribute handout pages. Give out pages of the handout in the 1 through 6 sequence so that equal numbers of participants receive each of the six pages. Ask each participant to review the interactive learning strategies on the page and select the two that appear to be of maximum value to the organization. Announce a 4-minute time limit.

Form convergent teams. At the end of 4 minutes, blow the whistle and ask participants who had the same page to get together. Instruct participants to share their personal choices and arrive at consensus about the two most valuable interactive learning strategies. When the teams reach consensus, ask them to write their choices on a piece of paper and give them to you. Announce a 5-minute time limit for this activity.

Form divergent teams. After 5 minutes, blow the whistle and ask participants to regroup themselves so that each new team has one member with each different page. Ask participants in each team to take turns and share details about the two selected interactive learning strategies on their page. Instruct participants to compare the different strategies and select six strategies from among all pages. Explain that it is not necessary to select one strategy from each page. When the teams reach consensus, ask them to write their choices on a piece of paper and give them to you. Announce a 7-minute time limit for this activity.

Conclude the activity. After 7 minutes, blow the whistle again and ask different teams to present their choice and explain the reasons. Invite questions and comments from the participants and briefly respond to them.

Interactive Learning Strategies: Page 1

1. *Action Learning* involves a combination of action and reflection by a team to solve complex, strategic problems in a real-world organizational setting. Team members apply existing skills and knowledge and create new skills, knowledge, and insights through continuously reflecting on and questioning the problem definition, the collaborative behavior, and the ensuing results.

2. *Action Research* is a strategy that is similar to *action learning*. A team of participants conducts field research to examine a question. Specially suited for participants who don't know what they don't know, data collected during the research may alter the original question. The team may learn unanticipated principles and procedures because of the volatile nature of open-minded inquiry and objective reflection.

3. *Appreciative Inquiry (AI)* is an alternative to traditional problem solving. Instead of focusing on what is wrong, AI emphasizes positive aspects of a situation. The AI process involves encouraging participants to share stories of positive experiences with each other. The facilitator reviews these stories to identify themes for further inquiry. Participants create and share images of a preferred future and brainstorm ways to create that future.

4. *Assessment-Based Learning Activities (ABLA)* require participants to complete a test, a rating scale, or a questionnaire and receive a score (and other feedback) about their personal competencies, attitudes, or personality traits. In some ABLAs, participants' responses are combined to identify the perceptions, opinions, or characteristics of a team, a workgroup, or an organization. Whenever appropriate, ABLAs encourage interaction and discussion among participants to analyze their responses and to apply the results to future action.

5. *Audio Games* are training activities that primarily depend on playback of recorded audio messages (such as audiotape or streaming audio) to provide the training content, structure the training activity, and collect the player's response. Most audio games use few or no visuals (in the form of text or graphics).

6. *Board Games* borrow structures and play materials from popular recreational games to create highly motivating training events. Board games typically use game cards and dice to encourage individuals and teams to demonstrate their mastery of concepts, principles, skills, and problem-solving strategies.

7. *Card Games* involve pieces of information (such as facts, concepts, technical terms, definitions, principles, examples, quotations, and questions) printed on cards. These games borrow procedures from traditional playing card games and require players to classify and sequence pieces of information from the instructional content.

8. *Cash Games* are a special type of simulation game that involves actual cash transactions. They are not gambling games. Nor do they focus on accounting procedures or financial management. Instead, they explore interpersonal skills (such as *negotiation*) and concepts (such as *cooperation*). These games use cash because it effectively simulates the real world and brings out natural behaviors and emotions in participants.

Interactive Learning Strategies: Page 2

9. *Closers* are activities conducted near the end of a session. They are used for reviewing main points, tying up loose ends, planning application activities, providing feedback, celebrating a successful conclusion, and exchanging information for future contacts.

10. *Coaching Activities* involve an individual facilitator (the coach) supporting the learning and improving performance efforts of another individual (the coachee) through interactive questioning and guidance. The process usually requires the two people to establish goals and the coach to observe the coachee, debrief the activity, offer relevant feedback, and suggest suitable improvements.

11. *Consensus Decision-Making Activities* involve a list of items (usually ten) to be arranged in order of priority. Participants complete the task individually and then reach consensus in teams. Then they compare their priority rankings with expert rankings. In the process, they learn more about factors that contribute to the importance of items and also factors that influence making decisions and reaching consensus in teams.

12. *Corporate Adventure Learning* involves physical activities (such as sailing, rafting, rappelling, rock climbing, exploring wilderness areas, and walking on rope bridges) in challenging indoor or outdoor environments. A trained facilitator ensures safety of participants and conducts suitable debriefing discussions that enable participants to construct knowledge, skill, and value from these exciting experiences.

13. *Creativity Techniques* provide a structure that enables participants to solve a problem or to utilize an opportunity in a creative fashion. These techniques are useful not only for learning new skills and knowledge but also for improving the performance of a team.

14. *Cross-Cultural Dialogues.* Participants review, analyze, and discuss recorded conversations between two people from different cultures. These conversations involve projection of cultural values and result in confusion or frustration on the part of one or both of the speakers. However, the levels of discomfort related to the conversations are so subtle that it requires a careful analysis on the part of the participants to identify it.

15. *Culture Assimilators* are interactive exercises designed to sensitize participants to the values of other culture groups. The exercises are structured around brief descriptions of critical incidents that involve intense feelings, knowledge areas, and cultural differences. Participants read and discuss each critical incident and select the most probable interpretation among multiple-choice alternatives.

16. *Debriefing Games* are interactive strategies that are used for encouraging reflection and dialogue about an earlier activity or event. These games require processing of a common experience to extract key learning points from it. They generally encourage participants to identify and express emotions, recall events and decisions, share lessons learned, relate insights to other real-world events, speculate on how things could have been different, and plan for future action.

Interactive Learning Strategies: Page 3

17. *Disaster Simulations* are activities that require participants to cope with simulations of natural or organizational disasters such as an earthquake or downsizing. In dealing with such disasters, participants learn to make fast, collaborative decisions in complex and rapidly changing situations.

18. *Double Exposure Activities* enhance the instructional value of training videos. In a typical video vitamin, participants watch a videotape and then play one or more games that help review and apply the new concepts and skills.

19. *E-Mail Games* are conducted through the Internet. They may involve the play of electronic versions of interactive training games or specially designed activities that permit asynchronous communication in which people receive and send messages at different times. Typical e-mail games exploit the ability of the Internet to overcome geographic distances and involve participants pooling their ideas and polling to select best ones.

20. *Fantasy Role-Playing Games* require participants to enact individual or team roles, often within a science-fiction or fantasy scenario. These role-play activities focus on skills and concepts related to such topics as leadership, teamwork, and planning. Debriefing after the role play draws parallels between the fictional fantasy and workplace reality.

21. *Field Studies and Expeditions* require participants to explore the environment of another country, culture, or time period. Teams of participants are given a set of objectives to achieve, information to collect, or objects to obtain. In the process of completing these tasks, participants acquire new knowledge about the environment and new skills for relating to the local people.

22. *Framegames* provide templates for instant creation of training games. These generic frameworks are deliberately designed to permit easy replacement of old content with new content. You can use framegames to rapidly develop training activities that suit your needs.

23. *Graphic Analogies Discussion Generators* are based on training designs from Scott Simmerman. These activities use cartoon illustrations to engage, enlist, and involve people in performance-improvement discussions and to stimulate collaboration and creativity. The strategy basically involves asking a group of people to compare elements from a generic illustration to the organizational context.

24. *Improv Games* are activities adapted from improvisational theater. The actors do not use a script but create the dialogue and action as they perform. When used as an interactive training technique, improv games facilitate the mastery of skills related to such areas as creativity, collaboration, communication, and change.

25. *Instructional Puzzles* challenge the participants' ingenuity and incorporate training content that is to be previewed, reviewed, tested, re-taught, or enriched. Puzzles can be solved by individuals or by teams.

Interactive Learning Strategies: Page 4

26. *Interactive Lectures* involve participants in the learning process while providing complete control to the instructor. These activities enable a quick and easy conversion of a passive presentation into an interactive experience. Different types of interactive lectures incorporate built-in quizzes, interspersed tasks, teamwork interludes, and participant control of the presentation.

27. *Interactive Storytelling* involves fictional narratives in a variety of forms. Participants may listen to a story and make appropriate decisions at critical junctures. They may also create and share stories that illustrate key concepts, steps, or principles from the instructional content.

28. *Item Processing* is an interactive strategy in which individuals and teams generate, organize, and sequence ideas, facts, questions, complaints, or suggestions. As a result of this activity, participants create organized lists of items. More importantly, this activity enables participants to construct meaningful categories and sequences from isolated items. This results in deeper understanding and easier recall of the content.

29. *Jolts* lull participants into behaving in a comfortable way, then deliver a powerful wake-up call. They force participants to re-examine their assumptions and revise their standard procedures. Jolts typically last for a few minutes but provide enough insights for a lengthy debriefing.

30. *Magic Tricks* incorporate a relevant conjuring trick as a part of a training session. Magic tricks provide metaphors or analogies for important elements of the training content. The tricks are also used as processes to be analyzed, reconstructed, learned, performed, or coached for training participants in appropriate procedures.

31. *Matrix Games* require participants to occupy boxes in a grid by demonstrating a specific skill or knowledge. The matrixes provide a structure for matching or classifying individual items or organizing and comparing a set of items. The first participant to occupy a given number of boxes in a straight line (horizontally, vertically, or diagonally) wins the game.

32. *Musical Team Building* involves participants playing on different musical instruments to create synchronized and rhythmic music. The process that leads to the spontaneous and gradual evolution of the final piece of music is debriefed to provide insights into such topics as teamwork, leadership, and communication.

33. *Openers* are activities conducted near the beginning of a session. They are used to preview main points, orient participants, introduce participants to one another, form teams, establish ground rules, set goals, reduce initial anxieties, or stimulate self-disclosure.

Interactive Learning Strategies: Page 5

34. *Pair Learning* is based on the pair programming component of the extreme programming methodology. This strategy involves two people working on the same computer, sharing a single keyboard. All paired learning results in the development of better products. In addition, paired learning between an expert and a novice results in the latter learning new technical concepts and skills. Paired learning between people from different fields (for example, a subject-matter expert and a writer) results in more effective collaboration skills.

35. *Paper-and-Pencil Games* require players to make their moves by writing or drawing something on paper. A typical game may involve players working on a small piece (or a large sheet) of paper. Paper-and-pencil games may incorporate elements of role plays, simulations, creativity techniques, or quiz contests.

36. *PC Simulations* use playing cards to reflect real-world objects and processes. The rules of PC simulations typically encourage participants to discover principles of interpersonal interaction and inductive thinking.

37. *Procedural Simulations* are dress rehearsals of real-world events, such as conducting a raid to rescue hostages, evacuating a burning building, or being subjected to a surprise inspection by auditors from the funding agency. By working through these simulations, participants get ready for real-world events.

38. *Production Simulations* involve the design and development of a product (such as a video segment, a newsletter, a marketing plan, or a jingle). Different teams compete with each other to create the best product. The initial briefing in this strategy involves teams receiving specifications for the final product, along with a checklist of quality criteria. Teams have a budget and a time limit. They can purchase different job aids, reference materials, handouts, sample products, and consultative help to assist them in their production activity. The final products are evaluated by a panel of outside experts who provide feedback along a variety of dimensions.

39. *Reflective Teamwork* involves participants creating a product related to some aspect of teamwork. Teams then evaluate their characteristics and performance by using the products they created.

40. *Role Plays* involve participants assuming and acting out characters, personalities, and attitudes other than their own. These activities may be tightly or loosely structured and may involve a participant assuming multiple roles or reversed roles.

41. *Seminars* use an interactive format that has been popularized by Mortimer Adler. An effective seminar involves a duration of two hours, seating arrangement that permits participants to face one another, and an open mind. The task of the facilitator is to initiate the discussion with open questions, engage participants with two-way conversations, and to sustain a meaningful discussion.

Interactive Learning Strategies: Page 6

42. *Structured Sharing* represents a special type of framegame that facilitates mutual learning and teaching among participants. Typical structured sharing activities create a context for a dialogue among participants based on their experiences, knowledge, and opinions.

43. *Synthetic Cultures* assign participants to artificial cultures with extreme values along a single specific social aspect (such as an obsessive respect for status). Different types of simulations and role plays within this context provide participants with data related to intercultural interpersonal interactions. Debriefing of the participants result in sharing their insights and learning from each other.

44. *Television Games* borrow the structure of popular TV game shows to present the instructional content and to encourage participants to practice skills. They involve selected contestants and the "studio audience," who participate and learn vicariously. TV Games can be broadcast for distance learning, made available on videotapes, or presented live by using computer game shells and graphics.

45. *Textra Games* combine the effective organization of well-written documents with the motivational impact of interactive experiential activities. Participants read a handout and play a game that uses peer pressure and support to encourage recall and transfer of what they read.

46. *The Case Method* involves a written account of a real or fictional situation surrounding a problem. Participants work individually and in teams to analyze, discuss, and recommend appropriate solutions and to critique one another's work. In some cases, the facilitator may recount the actual decisions implemented in the real-world situation on which the case was based.

47. *Thought Experiments* are mental role plays that involve guided visualization. Individual participants mentally rehearse new patterns of behavior or hold imaginary dialogues. Combined with self-reflection, these activities result in increased self-awareness and mastery of new knowledge and insights.

48. *Troubleshooting Simulations* require participants to systematically find the causes of problems and to fix the problems. These simulations can use realistic simulators (as in the case of debugging faulty machinery) or computer printouts of output data (as in the case of slowing down the loss of market share).

49. *Video Feedback* involves each member of a group role playing an interpersonal skill. This is followed by the group members providing positive and constructive feedback to each role player with the intent of helping the person improve his or interpersonal skills.

50. *Web-Based Games* are interactive activities presented on the Internet. A variety of games and simulations can be played on the web by individuals or by teams. Multi-player games permit several participants to interact with each other at the same time.

Outsourcing

82
FGI

Creativity techniques serve an effective instructional purpose also: They force participants to synthesize and apply what they have learned. FGI serves this purpose in an interesting fashion.

Purpose

To integrate factual information, goals, and ideas related to outsourcing

Participants

Minimum: 6
Maximum: Any number
Best: 10 to 20
(If you have more than 20 participants, organize them into two parallel groups and play separate games.)

Time

30 minutes to 1 hour

Supplies

- Post-it® Note pads
- Flip charts
- Felt-tipped markers
- Timer
- Whistle
- Masking tape

Preparation

Prior to the activity, ask participants to read articles, online pages, and books on outsourcing.

Flow

Specify the training goal. Explain that you are going to conduct an activity that will help participants to synthesize, integrate, and apply the information they have accumulated about outsourcing.

Give and receive sample goals, facts, and ideas. Explain that the name of the activity is FGI and the acronym stands for facts, goals, and ideas. Begin by briefly explaining the three terms and providing a couple of examples of each:

Facts: Bits of information related to the topic. A fact may be about procedures, products, people, or places.

Typical U.S. manufacturing companies now outsource 70 to 80 percent of the components in their finished products.

The salary of a programmer in India is approximately one-tenth the salary of a comparable programmer in the U.S.

Goals: Statements that specify desirable situations or conditions. Goals may include objectives, criteria, metrics, or standards to be achieved. They may refer to a final result or to intermediate outcomes.

Maintain high standards of confidentiality of customer information.

Reduce labor cost by 50 percent or more.

Ideas: Elements of an action plan.

Begin with a business case for outsourcing.

Select elements of the business process that can benefit the most from outsourcing.

Invite the players to give you a couple of goals, facts, and ideas related to outsourcing. Write them down on a flip chart.

Recording initial sets of items. Set up three flip charts and label them *Goals, Facts,* and *Ideas.* Ask participants to record different goals, facts, and ideas on individual Post-it Notes and stick them to the appropriate flip charts. Explain to participants that they can write any number of items in any order and attach them anywhere on the appropriate flip chart.

Encourage the teams to intermix the three lists. After a few minutes, blow the whistle to get the participants' attention. Ask them to review the items posted on each flip chart and generate additional items that belong to the other flip charts.

Goal statement: Avoid negative media publicity.

Related ideas: Carefully think through the impact of outsourcing on current employees and the community.

Communicate the business realities, challenges, and opportunities behind the outsourcing decision to all employees in a timely fashion.

Related facts: Current employees are often hired by the service providers.

Politicians exaggerate the negative public perception of outsourcing.

Observe a silent review period. After about 3 minutes, blow the whistle again. Ask the team members to silently review their lists for the next minute, coming up with additional items to be included. Announce the end of the 1-minute review time and ask participants to continue the task.

Start the editing activity. After another appropriate period of time, blow the whistle again. Organize participants into three teams and assign each team to one of the flip charts. Ask each team to review the items on its flip chart, remove duplicates, and arrange the remaining items in some logical order. Announce a 3-minute time limit.

Conclude the editing activity. Blow the whistle after 3 minutes and ask teams to post their flip charts to convenient locations on the wall. Invite everyone to review all three collections of items.

83
Outsourcing

I love to argue and debate, and I guess that is a natural reaction. But there must be some-thing wrong with me because it does not matter which side I take. I can happily argue about either side of an issue. I attribute this neurotic behavior to the fact that I believe that every issue has good things and bad things associated with it and that the truth lies somewhere in the middle. Outsourcing uses the strategy of asking people at the two sides of a hot issue to present their views and letting the participants work out the reality.

Purpose

To acquire a balanced view of some of the causes, consequences, and implications of outsourcing

Participants

Minimum: 6
Maximum: Any number
Best: 10 to 30
(Participants are organized into teams of 4 to 7.)

Time

30 minutes to 2 hours, depending on how deeply you want to explore the topic of outsourcing

Supplies

- Audio or videotape player
- Blank pieces of paper
- Pens or pencils
- Timer
- Whistle

Preparation

Prepare a list of questions. Ask some typical potential participants for their questions related to outsourcing. Collect and edit the list of questions. (A sample list is provided at the end of this activity.) Select a set of provocative questions that are relevant to the participants.

Find two outspoken authorities to represent the two sides. Tell these experts that you are going to conduct an interview on the topic of outsourcing—and record this interview. Explain that it is acceptable (and desirable) for them to take an unbalanced view that reflects one side or the other.

Record and edit the interviews. Conduct the two interviews independent of each other, but use the same set of questions. Record the interviews on audio- or videotapes. Edit the responses (without altering the sense and the tone of the responses) and sequence them in such a way that different authorities alternate in being the first person to give the answer to different questions. Select five or six questions that elicit the major differences of opinions.

Flow

Brief the participants. Explain that the purpose of the activity is to hear both sides of the issue of outsourcing, identify the differences in perceptions and opinions, and attempt to reconcile these differences.

Play the responses to the first question. Ask participants to listen and to take notes from the alternative responses from the two experts.

Organize teams. Organize participants into teams of four to seven people. Ask teams to analyze the answers and reconcile them. Invite them to discuss the similarities and differences between the two answers. Announce a 3-minute time limit.

Invite a team to present its conclusions. Randomly select one of the teams. Ask the spokesperson from this team to present the results of its discussion and to specify their conclusions. Invite any other team with significantly different conclusions to present its views.

Repeat the process. Play the response to the second question. Ask teams to analyze the responses and arrive at conclusions. Invite a team at random to present its conclusions. Continue by playing the other questions and responses, one at a time, and asking teams to process the responses as before.

Debriefing

Ask teams to come up with one-sentence summaries of their key conclusions. After a brief pause, invite teams to present the summary conclusions. Add your own comments and thank participants for the contribution.

Questions About Outsourcing

1. How do you define outsourcing?
2. What are different types of outsourcing?
3. What are the causes of increased outsourcing?
4. How does technology impact outsourcing?
5. Is outsourcing inevitable?
6. What are recent trends in outsourcing?
7. What do employees gain and lose through outsourcing?
8. How do employees currently react to outsourcing?
9. What do the customers gain and lose through outsourcing?
10. How do customers currently react to outsourcing?
11. What do the stockholders gain and lose through outsourcing?
12. How do stockholders currently react to outsourcing?
13. What happens to the countries that use outsourcing?
14. What happens to the countries that provide outsourcing services?
15. What are the short-term effects of outsourcing?
16. What are the long-term effects of outsourcing?
17. What can we do to keep our people employed?
18. What are the political implications of outsourcing?
19. How should we modify our education, training, and retraining programs to cope with and leverage outsourcing?
20. What are the ethical implications of outsourcing?
21. How do we ensure effective outsourcing?
22. How do we maintain quality, security, and confidentiality standards while outsourcing?
23. How do we keep our industry strong while using increasing outsourcing services?
24. How does outsourcing affect our competitive advantage?
25. What are some good books on this topic?

Change
Management

84
Trifurcation

Rule 1 in creativity: *Never stop with the first idea.* You need at least another alternative. And three is better than two. Trifurcation ensures that you have a Plan B and Plan C at different levels.

Purpose

To generate a series of topical statements related to effective implementation of organizational change

Participants

Minimum: 1
Maximum: Any number
Best: 6 to 15
(Participants are divided into 3 teams.)

Time

30 minutes to several hours, depending on the complexity of the topic

Supplies

- Trifurcation Forms, 10 copies for each team
- Pens or pencils
- Flip charts
- Felt-tipped pens

Flow

Specify the goal. Draw a large replica of the trifurcation form on a flip chart. In the middle triangle write a goal that you are trying to achieve. Number this goal statement as "1."

Here is a goal statement related to change management:

Implement organizational change in an effective fashion.

Specify three first-level statements related to the goal. The triangle with the goal statement is surrounded by three other triangles of the same size. With the help of participants, in each of these three triangles, write a statement related to achieving the goal. You may use any of these techniques to generate first-level statements:

- Logical subdivisions of the goal
- Complementary strategies
- Alternative strategies
- Chronological steps
- Different points of view
- Strategies for satisfying different customers
- Strategies related to different products
- Strategies focusing on different aspects of the goal
- Strategies related to different time spans
- Strategies related to different standards or criteria

If you come up with more than three statements, reduce them to three by combining some of the items. If this is not possible, arbitrarily select three statements.

If you come up with only two statements, you are not trying hard enough. Divide one of the statements into two components.

The change management goal lends itself to these three obvious statements using a chronological division:

Appropriate strategies before the implementation of the change
Appropriate strategies during the implementation of the change
Appropriate strategies after the implementation of the change

Labeled these statements 1, 2, and 3, in chronological order.

Organize teams. Assign participants to three equal-sized teams. Ask the first team to copy Statement 1 in the middle triangle of a trifurcation form. Similarly, ask the second and the third teams to copy Statements 2 and 3 (respectively) in the middle triangle of their trifurcation forms.

Create next set of statements. Ask each team to think about the statement of the middle triangle. Working collaboratively, ask team members to write three second-level statements, one in each of the three outer triangles. These statements should be different from each other, but they all should be related to the statement in the middle triangle. Also the three statements should be of equal complexity and importance. Ask members of the first team to label its three statements 11, 12, and 13. The other teams label their new statements 21, 22, and 23 and 31, 32, and 33 as appropriate.

When all three teams complete their task, you should have a total of nine second-level statements associated with the original goal.

Here are the second-level statements associated with Statement 11 (Appropriate strategies before the implementation of the change):

11. Increase the awareness of the proposed change among all employees.
12. Reassure employees about the impact of the change.
13. Provide accurate and realistic details about the change.

Create third-level statements. Now ask each team to copy each of its three second-level statements in the middle triangles of the three new trifurcation forms. As before, ask teams to work collaboratively to write three sets of third-level statements, one in each of the three trifurcation forms. When they have finished, ask teams to number their statements, adding 1, 2, or 3 to the statement numbers.

When all three teams have completed their task, there should be a total of twenty-seven third-level statements associated with the original goal.

Here are the third-level statements associated with the Statement 11 (increase the awareness of the proposed change among all employees):

111. Prepare a 99-second statement that captures the critical elements of the proposed change.
112. Create a website with basic information about the proposed change.
113. Come up with a catchy and memorable slogan related to the proposed change.

Show the complete picture. This activity began with a single goal and three first-level statements associated with the goal. Later, each team took one of the first-level statements and expanded it into three second-level statements and nine third-level statements. Ask participants to tape their trifurcation forms to the wall in the appropriate sequence. Ask all participants to review the scope and structure of all statements.

Debriefing

Ask participants to suggest suitable revisions to consolidate the work done by different teams and to remove redundancies. Beginning with the third-level, discuss details of implementing each level and integrating them to effectively achieve the goal.

Trifurcation Form

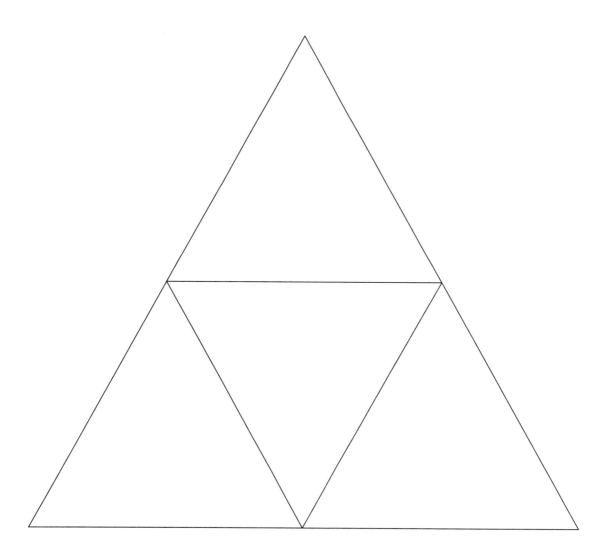

85
White Water

Technological progress continues to catch us by surprise. We create more efficient keyboards, and computers begin accepting voice commands. We design better books, and PDAs display multimedia presentations. We invent better mousetraps, and ultrasonic sirens chase away household pests. White Water simulates a chaotic future in which constantly changing goals demand flexibility and agility.

Purpose

To practice coping with continuous change and ambiguous directions

Participants

Minimum: 10
Maximum: 50
Best: 10 to 30
(Participants are divided into 3 to 10 teams.)

Time

30 to 60 minutes

Supplies

- General Instructions, one copy for each team
- Six Product Specifications, one for each round, one copy for each team (cut the instructions into separate strips so participants will not look ahead)
- Instructions for Judges
- Blank sheets of paper
- Pens or pencils
- Timer
- Whistle

Flow

Form teams. Divide participants into three to ten teams, each with three to seven members. It does not matter if some teams have an extra member.

Assign team roles. Randomly select one team to be the judges. All other teams play the role of Advisory Committees created by a large publishing company.

Distribute instruction sheets. Give each team (including the team of judges) a copy of the General Instructions. Ask team members to review the information. Clarify the instructions by answering questions from participants.

Brief the judges. While the other teams are reviewing the instructions, distribute copies of Instructions to Judges to each member of the judging team. Go through these instructions and clarify any items as needed.

Begin the activity. Distribute a copy of the first Product Specifications *to each team*. Explain that teams have 5 minutes to come up with their lists of suggestions. Start a timer.

Stop the activity. After 3 minutes, blow the whistle to get the participants' attention. Explain that you are interrupting their activity because there has been a significant change in the project. Before explaining the change, ask teams to give you copies of the list of suggestions in its current form.

Begin the second round. Distribute copies of the Round 2 Product Specifications. Ask the teams to restart their activity.

Rate suggestions from Round 1. Give copies of the lists of suggestions from Round 1 to the judging team. Ask the teams to rate the activities within the next 3 minutes.

Shift to the next round. After 3 minutes or when the judges have rated the list of suggestions from Round 1, blow a whistle to attract participants' attention. Explain that some more significant changes have taken place. Collect the lists of suggestions in their current form and give them to the judges.

Distribute the results of Round 1. Explain that the scores range from 2 to 10. Return the lists of suggestions to the appropriate teams so they can check their scores.

Proceed to the next round. Distribute copies of the Round 3 Product Specifications. Repeat the instructions as before.

Repeat the procedure. After 3 minutes, stop the activity. Return the previous lists of suggestions with scores awarded by the judges. Give out the next Product Specifications and ask teams to come up with fresh lists of suggestions. Repeat this process until the end of Round 6.

Debriefing

Begin debriefing. After collecting the lists from Round 6 and handing them over to the judges, begin debriefing the Advisory Committee teams. Use these types of questions:

- *How did you feel about the frequently changing scope of the project?*
- *How does the situation in this simulation reflect what happens in your workplace?*
- *What are some of the causes of these frequent changes in specifications?*
- *Are these frequent changes likely to increase or decrease in your workplace?*
- *What strategies did you use to cope with the constantly changing specifications?*
- *What advice do you have for people in similar situations?*

- *Under what conditions is it better to build on the results of your previous activity?*
- *Under what conditions should you ignore everything that happened before and begin from scratch?*

Announce the final results. Return the lists from Round 6 with the scores to the appropriate teams. Ask teams to add up their scores and announce the total. Identify the team with the highest total score. Discuss the implications of these scores.

Conclude the debriefing. Ask the judges for the comments. Ask each participant to come up with two or three personal action ideas for coping with frequent changes in the workplace.

General Instructions

You are a member of an Advisory Committee established to provide suggestions to a large U.S.-based publishing company.

The publisher has definite plans for a new product and a specific target market based on systematic market research. You will be provided a list of specific details.

Your task, as a team, is to provide five to ten specific suggestions (each expressed in one to three sentences). Your suggestions should provide guidelines for improving the competitive position and potential profitability of the product.

Please record your suggestions legibly on a single side of a piece of paper.

You have 5 minutes to come up with your suggestions.

Product Specifications

Round 1

Context: Retired people are traveling in larger numbers.

Product: Travel guide to the top thirty vacation destinations around the world.

Target Market: Affluent U.S.-American senior citizens.

Round 2

Your organization has undergone some major changes. This has resulted in changes to the product specification. Please revise your list of suggestions to accommodate these changes.

Your task and time limit are the same as before.

Context: A Japanese publishing company has acquired your publishing company.

Product: Travel guide in seven different languages.

Target Market: Young middle-class professionals in Asia.

Round 3

Context: Your publishing company has organized a multimedia group.

Product: A CD-ROM version of the travel guide.

Target Market: Computer-literate professionals around the world.

Round 4

Context: Your company has opened a web portal.

Product/Service: Website with updated vacation travel destinations.

Target Market: Same as before, with a focus on young professional women.

Round 5

Context: The R&D group has developed a virtual-reality kiosk with a motion-activated tread-mill, helmet-mounted 3-D goggles, data gloves, data shoes (that enable the wearer to feel different ground surfaces), along with temperature and odor control.

Product/Service: High-fidelity virtual travel to popular vacation destinations.

Target Market: Affluent people who can pay the hefty fee.

Round 6

Context: Extended use of virtual-reality equipment creates psychotic episodes. In the meantime, human gene repair using nanomachines has been proven to indefinitely extend human life span.

Product/Service: Training workshops on detecting and repairing gene impairments.

Target Market: Physicians interested in updating their professional skills.

Instructions to Judges

You will receive a list of suggestions from each team.

Compare these lists and arrange them in order from the best to the worst.

Give 10 points to the best list and 2 points to the worst list. Assign a suitable number of points (between 2 and 10) to each of the other lists.

You will have 3 minutes for rating the lists.

You will be repeating this judging procedure six times, each time with different lists of suggestions.

Workplace
Violence

86
Workplace Violence

Whenever I use instructional puzzles, participants get addicted to them. Designing puzzles, however, is usually a time-consuming job. On the positive side, designing instructional puzzles forces me to review the content and recall key ideas. Workplace Violence is an activity in which participants design their own puzzles, exchange them with each other, and solve them.

Purpose

To summarize important strategies for preventing workplace violence

Participants

Minimum: 4
Maximum: Any number
Best: 10 to 30
(Participants are divided into pairs.)

Time

10 to 20 minutes (plus 10 to 30 minutes of pre-work)

Supplies

- Handout, How to Solve Twisted Pair Puzzles
- Prepared twisted pair puzzles. Copy each of the six puzzles onto an index card. Record a random identification number on the back of each card.
- Blank pieces of paper
- Pens or pencils
- Timer
- Whistle

Flow

Pre-work. Ask participants to search the Internet and review online information about controlling, preventing, and handling workplace violence. Playfully warn them that success in the training session will depend on their completing this task conscientiously.

Learn about twisted pair puzzles. Distribute copies of the handout to each participant. Ask participants to read the handout and learn how to solve—and create—twisted pair puzzles. Announce a 4-minute time limit for this activity.

Ask participants to pair up. Explain that each pair will be working together throughout the activity. If you have an odd number of participants, create one group of three.

Create a twisted pair puzzle. Distribute blank pieces of paper and pens or pencils. Ask each pair to cooperatively come up with a guideline for preventing workplace violence. Then ask the pairs to convert the guidelines into twisted pair puzzles and write them on index cards. Announce a 5-minute time limit for this activity.

Give finishing touches to the puzzle cards. After 5 minutes, blow the whistle and confirm that each pair has created a twisted pair puzzle on an index card. Ask the pairs to record four-digit identification numbers on the backs of their cards.

Exchange and solve puzzles. Ask each pair to exchange their card with another pair and solve the puzzle. Ask participants not to mark up the puzzle card, but put the identification number on a blank sheet of paper and write the solution. When done, ask pairs to exchange the puzzle cards with some other pairs and continue solving more puzzles. Announce that exchanging and solving puzzles will continue for 10 minutes.

Avoid waiting. If a pair has solved a puzzle but does not have any other pair ready to exchange a puzzle, ask them to come to you. Exchange the puzzle for one of the five prepared puzzles. Repeat this procedure to ensure that all pairs are busy solving puzzles.

Conclude the activity. After 10 minutes, blow a whistle and ask everyone to stop solving puzzles. Find out which pair has solved the most puzzles and congratulate them.

Follow-Up

After the session, collect all the puzzle cards. Select the best ones and use them as prepared cards during the next round.

How to Solve Twisted Pair Puzzles

This is a twisted pair puzzle:

HIISST ADEISTTW AEILPPRUZZ

To solve a twisted pair puzzle, unscramble the first set of letters to discover two words. Decide which word comes first and which word comes next. Then unscramble the next set of letters to discover the third and the fourth words. Repeat this process until you have unscrambled all sets of letters, discovered all the words, and reconstructed the original sentence.

An Example

Here's a sample twisted pair puzzle:

AGIKLNOPRSWY

Since there is only set of letters, this is a two-word sentence.

Working with the letters, I identify the word *WALKING*. That leaves these letters: *OPRSY*. I create the word PROSY with these letters, not sure whether it is a legitimate word. Even if it is, *PROSY WALKING* or *WALKING PROSY* does not sound like much of a sentence. So I decide that *WALKING* is not one of the two words.

Next I try *PARKING*. That left *LOSWY* to be formed into a single word. Still no luck.

I work with the word *ASKING*. Using the remaining letters, I create two words: *PRY* and *OWL*. For a moment I decide that the hidden sentence is *PRY ASKING OWL*. Then I remember that the sentence can have only two words.

I keep playing with other words, intuitively feeling that one of the words should end in *-ING*. After several minutes of torture, I end up with the correct sentence: *PLAYING WORKS!*

Your Turn Now

Go back to the twisted pair puzzle at the top of this page. See whether you can solve it, two words at a time. (Here's a hint: Look at the sentence above each of them.)

How to Create Them

It is easy to create a twisted word puzzle:

1. Type a sentence. *Confrontations are healthy.*

2. If the sentence has an odd number of words, rewrite the sentence so it has an even number of words. *Confrontations can be healthy.*

3. Divide the sentence into pairs of words. *Confrontations can | be healthy.*

4. Take the letters in each pair of words and arrange them in alphabetical order. Print the resulting set of letters in capital letters: *AACCFINNNNOOORSTT ABEEHHLTY*.

   Your puzzle is ready!

1. ACIKLLLNOSST DNOOORS AADEHLTT
   AFFOSTT AACDEGIILNNRSU
   AABDHMNOORST AAABEEKRRS

2. ACDEEFIIIIINNOSSTTU AGOSTT
   ADEEELMNOPSY AEIIOPRSSSSTV EGOSSTTU

3. AEEIKMSTX ABCCEEEILMORSS
   AABEGGINNRRRY ADEFINNRRTUU
   AACEEGIILLNRSS

4. AACEEEILNPRSSTT EEEFLMMOOPRSY
   ABGIILLNNSTY CDEEEEIPRSV
   CEHINORSTTUW BEFLLOOPRTU
   AAAEGLOPRRSSSST

5. ACEIILLNRSSTTUY AACEHIMRSTW
   DEGINOPSSST AACDGHIIINNTTT AEEHRTY
   AEIINNOOPRT

6. ACCEEEIINRRSSTUY AACEEILLLOPPRSTY
   DEEGGIINNNRUV AADELNRY
   GHIMNNOORRSU

Solutions (for the facilitator's eyes only)

1. Install locks on doors that lead to staff areas, including bathrooms and break areas.

2. Issue identification tags to employees and visitor passes to guests.

3. Make exits more accessible by rearranging furniture and clearing aisles.

4. Separate clients from employees by installing deep service counters with bullet proof glass separators.

5. Install security cameras with posted signs indicating that they are in operation.

6. Increase security patrol, especially during evening and early morning hours.

PART X
Review

87
2-Minute Sprints

This fast-moving framegame was inspired by my visit to the trading floor of the Chicago Board of Trade. I use this game as a review activity near the end of training sessions. It is especially effective with factual content as in the case of product-knowledge presentations.

Purpose

To review the content presented through an earlier lecture or reading assignment

Participants

Minimum: 6
Maximum: Any number
Best: 12 to 25
(Participants are organized into groups of 3 or 6.)

Time

15 to 30 minutes

Supplies

- Instruction sheet, How to Play Sprints
- A large number of index cards, each with a number and a question that requires a short answer
- An answer sheet with question numbers and the correct answers
- Timer
- Whistle

Flow

Demonstrate the play of the game. Distribute copies of the handout, How to Play Sprints. Pause briefly while participants read this handout. Ask for three volunteers to come to the front. Explain that you will be the Game Master for this round. Give four question cards to each player. Start the timer and ask your players to yell out card numbers and answers. Demonstrate the procedure by referring to the answer sheet, giving feedback, and replacing the question cards. Stop the game after 2 minutes, help the players to compute their scores, and identify the winner.

Organize groups. Divide participants into two to five groups. Each group should have three to six players. Explain that these groups are not teams: The players in each group compete with each other. In each group, identify a player to be the first Game Master.

Distribute supplies. Give a deck of question cards and a copy of the answer sheet to each Game Master.

Begin the first round. Start the timer and blow the whistle. Ask the Game Masters to conduct the game with their groups.

Conclude the first round. At the end of 2 minutes, blow the whistle again and ask players to stop. Instruct each player to count the number of correctly answered cards. This is the player's score for the first round. Congratulate the highest scorer in each group for winning the first round.

Conduct the second round. Ask Game Masters to collect all cards, shuffle them, and give the deck to the player on their left. This person is now the new Game Master. Conduct the game as before.

Repeat the procedure. Continue playing additional rounds of the game until every member of each group has had a turn at being the Game Master.

Conclude the game. After the final round, identify the player (or players) in each group who won the most rounds. Congratulate these winners.

How to Play Sprints

Receive cards. One of you will be selected to be the Game Master. Obtain four question cards from this person. Review the questions on these cards and come up with answers.

Answer a question. If you know the answer to any of the questions, yell out the *card number*. Keep yelling the card number until you get the attention of the Game Master. When the Game Master recognizes you, give the answer to the question. If you don't know the answer, make a guess.

Replace the card. If the Game Master says that your answer is correct, place the card in front of you. If the Game Master says that your answer is incorrect, give the card to the Game Master. In either case, take another question card from the Game Master.

Continue playing. Repeat the process, trying to answer as many question cards as possible within the 2-minute period.

Calculate your score. When the Game Master concludes the round, count the number of question cards that you answered correctly. This is your score for the round. If you have the highest score, you win this round.

Continue playing. New Game Masters will conduct other 2-minute sprints. Repeat the same procedure during each game (including when you are the Game Master).

88
Cross-Examination

The waiter parked us at a table for two, handed us the menus, and disappeared. Steve and I got bored reading the menu repeatedly. So we held up copies of the menu and quizzed each other about the items and prices. That was the origin of the Cross-Examination game.

Purpose

To demonstrate the mastery of a document by correctly answering questions on the content

Participants

Minimum: 2
Maximum: Any number
Best: 10 to 30
(Participants are divided into pairs.)

Time

20 to 40 minutes, depending on the complexity of the handout and the density of print

Supplies

- A two-page handout. If you have the document available in an electronic format, change the font size so that each side has approximately the same amount of content.
- Blank sheets of paper
- Blank index cards
- Pens or pencils
- Timer
- Whistle

Flow

Distribute the handout to all participants. Tell the participants that there will be a quiz on the contents of the handout and encourage them to read it carefully. Suggest that they should take notes, underline key words, memorize important facts, and make up their own questions. Announce a suitable time limit and start the timer.

Pair up the participants. At the end of the assigned time, blow the whistle. Ask each participant to find a partner and sit (or stand) facing one another. (If one participant is left over, you become his or her partner.)

Assign pages. Ask each partner to toss a coin. The winner owns the first page of the handout and the other participant owns the second page. Each partner holds up the handout so that only one page is visible, while the other page faces the other player. Each partner also takes an index card to keep track of the points earned by the other player.

Begin grilling. Ask partners to take turns asking questions about the content on their sides of the handout. The other player gives an immediate answer. If the answer is correct, the questioner makes a mark on the index score card to award a point to the other player. If the other player gives an incorrect answer or does not answer at all, the questioner reads the relevant part of the handout to give the correct answer.

Continue playing. Monitor the group as they take turns asking and answering questions. Encourage the partners to match the nature of question and its difficulty level with each other. For example, if one partner asks a difficult question with a two-part answer, the other partner should ask a similar question from the other side of the handout.

Conclude this round. Blow the whistle after 3 to 5 minutes. Ask the partners to add up the points awarded to the other player, write the total score on the index card, circle it, initial it, and give it to the other player.

Review the handout again. Explain that participants will have an opportunity to ask questions from the other side. Suggest that they review the handout to get ready for the second round. Give participants an appropriate time limit.

Get set for the second round. Ask participants to walk around and find new partners who worked on the other page during the previous round. As before, ask the partners to sit or stand facing each other and hold their handouts in such a way that they can see the new side.

Repeat the grilling procedure. Ask the partners to use the same procedure as before for asking questions, answering, and scoring points. Suggest that the partners exchange their score cards and use the other side for keeping track of the points for this round. At the end of a suitable time period, ask the partners to complete their score cards.

Determine the winner. Ask the participants to add up their scores from the two rounds. Congratulate the highest-scoring individual or individuals.

89
Open Book

Someone told me that the future belongs not to the person who knows the answers but to the person who knows *where to find the answer.* In most training sessions that I conduct, I distribute copies of a hefty reference manual. I don't waste everyone's time by lecturing about the contents of the manual, but I do encourage participants to become familiar with the structure of the manual so that they can refer to it easily and efficiently. Open Book is a quiz game that helps me achieve this purpose.

Purpose

To familiarize participants with a pertinent reference manual so they can locate and use just-in-time information in the workplace

Participants

Minimum: 10
Maximum: Any number
Best: 10 to 30
(Participants organize themselves into teams later in the game.)

Time

30 to 40 minutes

Supplies

- Copies of a reference manual pertinent to the participants' organization (1 copy for each participant)
- Index cards
- Pens or pencils
- Timer
- Whistle
- Flip chart (for keeping score)
- Set of prepared questions, each on an index card (see Preparation below)

Preparation

Prepare a set of questions related to the topics covered in the reference manual. Write each question on one side of an index card and the page reference on the back. Include at least one question for which the manual does *not* provide the answer.

Flow

Brief participants. Distribute copies of the reference manual. Explain that this manual contains answers to most questions about the training topic.

Assign individual tasks. Tell participants that they have a 10-minute "scanning" assignment. During this time, they should review the manual and figure out its structure. Participants do not have to read about any specific topic in detail or memorize information. However, they should be thoroughly familiar with the organization of different chapters, the topics covered in each chapter, the table of contents, the index, and the system of side headings so they can rapidly find answers to questions.

Generate questions. Distribute ten blank index cards to each participant. As a part of the reading assignment, ask each participant to write *at least* five and *not more than* ten questions that can be answered by referring to the manual. These questions should not be "trick" questions but should represent the types of questions that a participant may have in the workplace. Participants should write each question on one side of an index card and provide a page reference on the back of the card.

Announce a time limit. Explain that participants have 10 minutes to complete the task. Indicate that the more questions a participant generates, the more chances he or she will have to receive high scores later in the game. Start the timer and blow the whistle to begin the scanning and question-writing activity.

Organize teams. At the end of 10 minutes, blow the whistle and ask participants to stop scanning and writing. Ask participants to organize themselves into three or four teams of approximately equal size.

Assign team task. Ask the members of each team to share their question cards, remove duplicate questions, and select the five best questions. Announce a 3-minute time limit. Start the timer and blow the whistle.

Get ready for the quiz show. At the end of 3 minutes, blow the whistle and collect the five question cards from each team. Tell participants that you are going to conduct a quiz show using the question cards they generated, along with a few additional questions that you had prepared. This will be an open-book quiz, and whichever team locates the correct information first will give the answer, reading from the manual or paraphrasing the information. Each team will now have 5 minutes to get themselves ready for the quiz program. Recommend that team members help each other become more familiar with the structure and the content of the documents during this time.

Prepare for the quiz show. Review the questions generated by participants. From these questions and the ones that you prepared earlier, select ten good questions that refer to different parts of the manual. Make sure that these questions represent the types of questions that an advanced participant will have in the workplace. In your set of questions, include the one for which the manual does *not* contain relevant information.

Begin the quiz show. Briefly explain the following procedure in your own words:

I will read a question.
Teams can refer to the manual.
First participant to stand up gives the answer.
Each correct answer earns a point.
For some questions, the manual may not contain any relevant information. In this case, the first person to stand up and proclaim that the answer cannot be found in the documents wins the score points for that question.

Conduct the quiz show. Read the first question. Identify the person who stood up first. Listen to the answer. Award score point. Update the flip-chart scoreboard. If necessary, discuss the answer and clarify any misconceptions. Repeat the procedure, inserting the question without the answer as the fourth or fifth question. Continue for 10 minutes.

Identify the winning team. Congratulate members of the team with the highest score.

90
Review Cards

This is a variation of the previous activity, but with an element of chance. When it comes to designing games for training, games of chance discourage smarter players from mastering new skills and knowledge. On the other hand, games of pure skill discourage weaker players from trying harder once they fall behind. An effective training game strikes a balance between chance and skill. And that's what Review Cards does.

Purpose

To recall and apply facts, concepts, principles, and procedures related to a training topic

Participants

Minimum: 10
Maximum: Any number
Best: 10 to 20
(Participants are organized into teams of 5 to 7.)

Time

20 to 45 minutes

Supplies

- Index cards
- Pens or pencils
- Number 10 business envelopes
- Timer
- Whistle

Preparation

Assign reading materials. Prior to the training session, distribute copies of one or more handouts related to the training topic to all participants. Playfully warn the participants that you will not cover the content during the training session, but instead conduct a quiz contest.

Flow

Part I: Generating Questions

Organize participants into teams. Assign five to seven participants to each team. It does not matter if some teams have one more player than the others.

Ask teams to generate question cards. Distribute blank index cards to each team and ask participants to write thirty or more review questions related to the content covered in the handout, one question on each card. This is an "open-book" activity and participants can refer to the handouts.

Give specifications for the question cards. Explain that the question should be written on one side of the card and the correct answer on the other side. Offer these guidelines:

- *Focus the questions on important learning points.*
- *Avoid trick questions, humorous questions, and trivial questions.*
- *Go beyond mere recall of facts. However, avoid questions asking for opinions.*
- *Use short-answer questions. Avoid true-false or multiple-choice formats.*
- *Write the correct answer on the other side of the card. If a question has more than one correct answer, list all acceptable answers.*

Time the activity. Announce a 10- to 15-minute time limit for writing questions. At the end of this time, blow the whistle to stop the activity.

Part II: Distribution of Question Cards

Add bonus instructions. Ask each team to select any ten question cards and write "Take an extra turn!" on the answer side of the card, below the answer.

Add bad-luck cards. Ask the teams to write "Lose your turn!" on both sides of six blank cards and add them to the set of question cards.

Prepare question-card sets. Ask each team to make sure that all the cards are arranged with the question side up. Distribute an envelope to each team. Ask teams to shuffle the cards and place their packets inside their envelopes with the question side facing the opening of the envelope.

Distribute the question-card sets. Take the envelope from each team and give it to the next team. Ask team members to place their envelopes on the table with the opening facing up.

Part III: Playing the Game

Start the game. Announce that the game will last for 10 minutes. At the end of the time, the person with the most question cards won (by giving correct answers) wins the game. Also inform the participants that this part is a "closed-book" activity. No participant is permitted to refer to the handout or to any notes.

Answer the question. Select one participant from each team to be the first player. Ask this participant to take the top card from inside the envelope, without exposing any other card. This person places the card on the table (hiding the answer), reads the question, and gives an answer.

Win the card. Players now turn the card over and check the "official" answer on the other side. If correct, the player wins the card and adds it to his or her collection. (If the answer is incorrect, the question card is placed on a discard pile.)

Continue the game. If the answer side of the card contains the instruction, "Take an extra turn!" the same player picks another question card. Otherwise, it is the next player's turn. The game proceeds as before.

Lose a turn. Whenever a player picks a card with the instruction, "Lose your turn!" the turn passes to the next player. (The card is placed in the discard pile.)

Challenge answers. After a player reads a question and gives the answer, any other player may yell "Challenge!" if he or she thinks that the answer is not correct. The first player to do so becomes the official challenger and gives an alternative response. The question card is turned over to verify the answer.

- If the original answer is correct, the player wins the card and collects another card from the challenger (for making an invalid challenge).

- If the challenger is correct, he or she wins the card and collects another card from the original player (for giving an incorrect response).

If the original player or the challenger has not won any cards from earlier rounds, no penalty card is collected.

Conclude the game. The game ends when all the question cards have been picked up or when the allotted time of 10 minutes is used up. At this time, the participant with the most cards in each group wins the game.

91
Tougher

Video games are so addictive because the difficulty level increases as you keep making progress. I tried to capture this element in a training game by using the simple tic-tac-toe framework. Tougher is the result.

Purpose

To answer questions by recalling relevant facts and content

Participants

Minimum: 2
Maximum: Any number
Best: 10 to 40
(Participants are divided into pairs.)

Time

5 to 15 minutes

Supplies

- **Question cards:** Sets of 20 to 30 cards with a review question on one side and the correct answer on the other (One set for each pair)
- Blank pieces of paper
- Pens or pencils

Flow

Organize players into pairs. Ask players to pair up and sit facing each other. Make sure that everyone has several pieces of paper and pencils (or pens).

Distribute question cards. Give each pair a packet of question cards. Explain that the cards contain a review question on one side and the correct answer on the other side. Ask participants to turn the cards with the question side up, shuffle them, and place the packet in the middle of the table.

Get ready to play the game. Ask each pair of participants to draw a tic-tac-toe grid on a piece of paper and decide who will be the first player. Ask each participant in the pair to select a unique symbol to use.

Explain how the game is played. Present these rules in your own words:

1. *First player selects a box he or she wants to occupy. The other player picks a question card from the middle of the packet and places it on the table.*

2. *First player immediately gives an answer to the question.*

3. *Both players check the answer on the back of the card.*
   - *If the answer is correct, the player puts his or her symbol on the selected box. The question card is placed on a discard pile.*
   - *If the answer is incorrect, the player does not put a symbol on the selected box. The card is placed (with the question side up) at the bottom of the packet of question cards.*

4. *Game continues with players alternating turns.*

5. *During the later rounds of the game, if the player has already occupied a box, he or she has to answer two questions correctly to occupy another selected box. During subsequent rounds, the player has to answer as many question cards as the number of boxes currently being occupied plus one more. In other words, to occupy the second box, a player has to answer three questions correctly; to occupy the third, four questions; and so on. (It does not matter how many boxes are occupied by the other player.)*

Explain how the game ends. Each game ends when one player occupies three boxes in a straight line—horizontally, vertically, or diagonally. If all the boxes are filled without anyone occupying three boxes in a straight line, then the person who occupies the most boxes is the winner. (In this version of tic-tac-toe there are no tied games.)

Explain how the games continue. At the end of each game, players start a new game. During the continuation, players alternate taking the first turn. Players keep track of how many games they have won. When the time limit is reached (or when all question cards have been correctly answered), the player who won the most games becomes the champion.

Conduct and conclude the game. Announce a suitable time limit. Start the games. Blow the whistle at the end of the time. Identify the winners in each pair and congratulate them.

92
Fast Grab

This is one of my favorite review games. It works effectively with any type of content, but especially with factual information. During the first part of Fast Grab, teams generate lists of questions. During the second part, contestants at each table participate in a quiz game in which the first person to grab an object earns the right to answer a question. If the answer is correct, the contestant receives 1 point.

Purpose

To review training content

Participants

Minimum: 6
Maximum: Any number
Best: 12 to 30
(Participants are organized into teams and reorganized into contest groups.)

Time

30 to 60 minutes, depending on the amount of content

Supplies

- Index cards
- Pens or pencils
- A grabbit (an object that can be easily grabbed, such as an empty bottle or a pop can) for each table
- A bowl of poker chips (or pennies) for each table
- A whistle

Flow

Generate questions. Organize participants into teams of three to seven. Ask members of each team to prepare a set of questions (and answers) based on the content of a handout or on a previous lecture presentation. Each question should be written on one side of an index card and the answer should be written on the back. Encourage teams to generate as many questions as possible because the team with the most questions will probably score more points during the second phase of the game. Assign a suitable time limit for this question-construction activity. At the end of this time, collect all question cards and shuffle the packet.

Organize the contest. At each table, ask participants to count off 1, 2, 3, and so on. Assemble participants with the same number and assign them to different "contest" tables. Ask the contestants to sit around the tables without handouts or notes.

Set up contest tables. Ask contestants at each table to place the grabbit in the middle of the table and to adjust it so that it is at the same distance from everyone. Also place a bowl of poker chips at each contest table.

Explain the play procedure. You will read the question from the top question card. The first contestant to grab the grabbit can answer the question. If correct, this person will win a poker chip.

Read the first question. Ask the contestant who grabbed the grabbit to immediately begin answering the question. The contestant need not shout out the answer, since only the others at the table need to hear it.

Announce the correct answer. Pause for an appropriate period of time. Blow a whistle to signal the end of the response time. Read the correct answer. Ask the other contestants at each table to decide if the grabber's response is the same as (or sufficiently similar to) the answer you read.

Explain the scoring procedure. If the answer is correct, ask the grabber to take a poker chip from the bowl. If the answer is not correct, ask the grabber to return a poker chip to the bowl. If the grabber does not have any poker chips (as in the case of the first question), there is no penalty for giving an incorrect answer.

Continue the game. Read one question at a time, avoiding duplicate questions (written by members of different teams). Pause for the responses and read the correct answers.

Conclude the game. After 7 to 10 minutes, announce the end of the contest. Ask contestants to return to their teams and combine their poker chips. Identify the team with the most poker chips and declare it to be the winning team.

93
Top Choices

At the end of the training session, it is always a good idea to remind participants how much they have learned and how much they have experienced. A boring way to do this is to review the session with PowerPoint® slides. Top Choices provides you a much more interesting alternative.

Purpose

To review and recall topics and activities

Participants

Minimum: 5
Maximum: Any number
Best: 10 to 20
(Participants work individually, in pairs, and in teams.)

Time

10 to 20 minutes

Flow

The most important thing. Ask participants to think back on everything they learned in your training session. Then ask them to identify the most important thing they learned. After a suitable pause, invite any volunteers to respond. After each response, ask the participant to explain why he or she thought it was the most important thing.

The most exciting activity. Ask participants to think back on the activities they participated in. Ask them to narrow down to the most exciting activity. After a suitable pause, ask participants to stand up and find partners. Ask the partners to share their responses with each other. If the partners selected the same activity, ask them to discuss the reasons for their choice. If the partners selected different activities, ask them to persuade each other to change their choices.

Ask partners to present their responses. After a suitable pause, ask participants to sit down. Select a participant at random and ask him or her to declare the most exciting activity. Ask for alternative choices from other participants.

The most surprising topic. For the next round, ask participants to recall various topics and ask them to select the most surprising one. After a brief pause, ask participants to stand up, form themselves into teams of four or five, and discuss their responses. Encourage each team to come to a consensus. After another pause, invite different teams to announce their choices.

Conduct additional top-choice selections. Repeat the procedure with other superlatives such as those listed below. After appropriate pauses, alternatively use individual, pair, and team reports.

The *most controversial* topic
The *most complex* concept
The *most practical* idea
The *funniest* experience

94
Key Points

Here's a final review activity that is more effective than the usual walk through the PowerPoint® slides one more time.

Purpose

To review and recall topics and activities

Participants

Minimum: 5
Maximum: Any number
Best: 10 to 20
(Participants work individually and in teams.)

Time

20 to 30 minutes

Supplies

- Key idea cards (several index cards with different key ideas from the training session)
- Blank index cards (four cards per participant)
- Pens or pencils
- Flip-chart paper (one sheet for each team)
- Felt-tipped markers
- Masking tape

Flow

Prepare initial set of key idea cards. Before the session, prepare a set of key idea cards, each card with a different key idea from the training session. Prepare at least two key idea cards for each participant. If you cannot come up a sufficient number of different key ideas, use duplicates.

Brief the participants. Say to participants, *"I'd like to conclude the training session with a review activity. This activity should help us recall key points from the session."*

Ask participants to write cards. Hand out four blank index cards to each participant. Ask them to write down a key idea from the training session on each card. Give some sample key ideas to the group.

Re-distribute the cards. After about 3 minutes, collect cards from participants. Add your prepared cards to this pile. Mix the cards well and give three cards to each participant. Ask participants to study the statements and arrange them according to their personal preferences.

Exchange cards. Arrange the remaining key idea cards on a large table at one side of the room. Tell the participants that they may discard cards from their hands and pick up replacements. Participants must work silently; they should not to talk to each other during this phase of the game. At the end of this exchange, each participant should have three cards that may or may not include cards from their original set.

Swap cards. Instruct participants to exchange cards with each other to make their hands better reflect their personal opinions. In this phase, any participant may swap cards with any other participant; every participant *must* exchange at least one card.

Form teams. Ask participants to compare their cards with each other's cards and to form teams with people holding similar key idea cards. There is no limit to the number of participants who may team up together, but a team may keep no more than three cards. It must discard all other cards, and the three cards it keeps must meet with everyone's approval.

Prepare a poster. Distribute blank sheets of flip-chart paper and felt-tipped markers to each team. Ask each team to prepare a graphic poster that reflects its three final cards. This poster should not include any text. After 5 minutes, ask each team to read its three cards, display its poster, and explain the symbolism.

95
Whispers

Here's an activity that helps participants after a training session, workshop, or conference compare notes.

Purpose

To reflect on a training experience and share insights with each other

Participants

Minimum: 3
Maximum: Any number
Best: 10 to 30
(Participants are divided into groups of 3 to 7.)

Time

10 to 30 minutes, depending on the number of questions

Supplies

A prepared set of debriefing questions from the list provided at the end of this activity

Flow

Brief participants. Ask them to think back on the training session they attended. Explain that you are going to ask a series of questions. Encourage participants to answer these questions truthfully—and to preserve the confidentiality of the answers.

   Add additional details. Explain that each participant will try to guess the answers of another participant in the group. This is to encourage people to learn more about each other and to expand their points of view.

   Encourage reflection. Request that each person take time to think of the answer to each question—without blurting it out.

   Ask the first question. Select the most appropriate question from the list. Ask this question and wait for participants to come up with answers.

   Ask for predictions. Instruct each person to turn to the player on his or her *left* and whisper a prediction of the response from the player on his or her *right.*

Ask for responses. Tell participants in each group to take turns in giving their personal responses to the question.

Score the prediction. If a participant's response matches the prediction, then ask the predictor to give himself or herself 1 point.

Continue the game. Ask one question at a time. You may ask questions from the prepared list or ad-lib spontaneous questions that probe previous responses. During later rounds of the game, you may invite participants in each group to take turns coming up with their own questions.

Conclude the game. Stop the game when you have used up the allotted time. Thank participants for their cooperation. Invite them to continue asking themselves more questions about what was learned and answering their own questions.

Debriefing Questions

1. What one word best describes your overall reaction to the training session?
2. What grade would you give to the training session?
3. What was the highlight of the training session for you?
4. Who had the most impact on you during the training session?
5. Approximately how many new ideas did you get at the training session?
6. What's one of the new things that you learned at this training session?
7. What one idea do you plan to implement immediately in your workplace?
8. What was the most exciting event during the training session?
9. What was the most boring event during the training session?
10. What advice do you have for someone who would be attending this training session in the near future?
11. What advice do you have for the trainer?
12. What advice do you have for the organizers of the conference?
13. How would you behave differently during next year's conference?
14. How would you behave differently at your workplace as a result of attending this conference?
15. What is one thing about the conference that you will tell your best friend?
16. What was your primary motivation for attending the conference?
17. What do you think was the primary motivation of most people who attended the conference?
18. What would help you to better implement new ideas from the conference at your workplace?
19. If you had to justify the cost of attending next year's conference to your boss, what would you tell her?
20. If you are not able to attend next year's conference, what one thing would you miss the most?
21. As a result of attending this conference, what one thing would you stop doing in your workplace?
22. What support do you need to apply the new principles that you learned at this conference?
23. If you were writing a news report about this conference, what would the headline say?
24. How does the cost of the conference compare to the benefits gained from it?
25. What was the most threatening message that you heard during the conference?
26. Which buzz word or phrase was used most frequently in the conference sessions?
27. If a six-year old asked you, "What did you learn at this conference?," what would you tell her?

28. With which person back in your workplace are you most likely to talk about the conference?

29. How long do you think it will take for you to implement the new ideas you gained from the conference?

30. What did you do at the conference that you feel most positive about?

31. What did you do at the conference that you feel most negative about?

32. What is one key lesson that you are taking back with you?

33. How can your organization get the most benefit from sending you to the conference?

34. What are some of your unmet expectations of the conference?

35. What one thing made you the most uncomfortable during the conference?

PART XI
Closers

96
Psychic Massage

I t is a good idea to conclude your training session on an upbeat note. That's exactly what Psychic Massage accomplishes.

Purpose

To enhance the self-images of the participants by identifying and presenting their positive qualities in an exaggerated fashion

Participants

Minimum: 5
Maximum: Any number
Best: 10 to 30
(Participants are divided into teams of 3 to 5.)

Time

6 to 12 minutes

Supplies

- Timer
- Whistle

Flow

Form teams. Organize participants into teams of three to five members each. Ask each team to participate in the activity independent of the other teams.

Select the first "victim." Ask each team to identify the member whose first name comes earliest in the alphabet. This participant is the first victim. Ask the victim to turn his or her back to the rest of the team.

Give instructions. Using your own words, explain the rules of this activity:

Team members must talk about the victim behind his or her back.
They must talk loudly enough so that the victim can hear everything they are saying.
They have exactly 1 minute for talking about the victim.

Emphasize this important point. Team members can only make positive, uplifting statements about the victim. If the team members cannot think of anything positive about the victim, they must fake it.

Begin the first round. Blow the whistle to announce the beginning of the first round. Start a timer. Blow the whistle again at the end of 1 minute to conclude the first round.

Identify the second victim. Ask the victim to turn around and face the other team members. The person seated to the left of the original victim becomes the next victim. The next victim turns his or her back on the rest of the team.

Begin the next round. When you blow the whistle, team members talk about the next victim behind his or her back, using the same rules.

Repeat the procedure. Continue the activity until everybody has had a turn being victimized.

Handling extra participants. If one or two teams have an extra member, bring them to the front of the room, one person at a time. Ask the person to turn his or her back to the rest of the participants. Ask all other participants to talk about this person using the same rules as before.

Conclude the session. Proclaim that you definitely have a uniquely talented group of participants.

97
Success Stories

Do you conclude your workshops by asking the participants to develop detailed action plans? This idea is great in theory, but it does not work well in practice because most players are too eager to go home to patiently list milestones, tasks, resources, deadlines, and other such minutia. I prefer a rapid right-brain action-planning exercise that is incorporated into this activity.

Purpose

To create personal visions of successful application of the skills and knowledge acquired in the workshop

Participants

Minimum: 6
Maximum: Any number
Best: 10 to 30

Time

1 to 15 minutes

Flow

Form triads. Ask the participants to organize themselves into teams of three to five. Ask the team members to seat themselves facing each other.

   Brief the participants. Inform them that they are going to participate in a role play. After the groans die down, tell them that each participant will play his or her own role. The only difference is that the role play takes place in the future, twelve months later. So everyone will be a year older and wiser.

   Outline the scenario. Use this suggested script:

You three bumped into each other at O'Hare airport. You have a long layover and you decide to walk down to the bar and catch up with personal news. After a couple of drinks, one of you says, "Hey, remember the workshop we attended last year? Did you ever use any of that stuff in your workplace?" This triggers a wave of nostalgia and you try to outdo each other with your reports of glowing successes.

Provide role-play details. The role play will come to an end after 4 minutes. Participants don't have to take turns. They may talk to each other as in a normal conversation at a bar.

Encourage imaginative exaggeration. Explain that the participants' main goal is flaunt their successes and attribute them to the workshop. They have poetic license to exaggerate how their fame and fortune have taken a quantum leap. Advise participants not to be modest in making up their history of the next year. However, encourage them to relate the brilliant results to specific aspects of this workshop.

Leave them alone. Let participants act out the role play. Walk around various triads, unobtrusively listening to the glowing reports.

Conclude the session. At the end of the 3 minutes, stop the role plays. Invite volunteers to recount details of the startling success stories they heard.

98
Timescapes

At the end of my workshops and training sessions, most participants are in a flaky (that's a technical term) state of mind. Asking them to do a logical and linear action plan at that stage usually meets with a lot of resistance. So I have switched over to Timescapes as a right-brain planning activity.

Purpose

To visualize the potential impact of the newly learned skills and concepts across different time periods

Participants

Minimum: 6
Maximum: Any number
Best: 10 to 20
(Participants organize themselves into pairs.)

Time

20 to 30 minutes

Flow

Find a partner. Ask the participants to organize themselves into pairs. Explain that each pair will discuss several questions and come up with a joint response.

Ponder on the distant future. Ask the first question:

Thirty years from now, what results would your newly learned skills and knowledge have produced?

Encourage participants to imagine broad impacts on personal, professional, organizational, societal, and global areas.

Present a report. After a pause of 2 minutes, ask for a volunteer. Invite this person to report the conclusions reached by her and her partner. Applaud this report and repeat the process with another participant chosen at random.

Repeat with different time frames. Ask the pairs to imagine alternative responses to this question:

What results would you like to have achieved three years from now by applying your newly learned skills and knowledge?

Point out the difference between this question and the previous one. After a pause of 2 minutes, invite presentations from a couple of volunteers.

Repeat with new questions. Use the same procedure with these three questions:

*What should you be doing three **months** from now to best utilize your newly learned skills and knowledge?*

*What should you be doing three **weeks** from now to best utilize your newly learned skills and knowledge?*

*What should you be doing three **days** from now to best utilize your newly learned skills and knowledge?*

Ask the here-and-now question. Ask the participants to work individually to come up with personal responses to the next question:

*What should you do **right here, right now** for the next 3 minutes to ensure powerful future applications of your newly learned skills and knowledge?*

After a 3-minute pause, invite a few volunteers to share their thoughts.

99
Postcard to a Friend

I enjoy facilitating final activities that serve more than one purpose. Postcard to a Friend serves two purposes—and leaves the participants on an upbeat note.

Purpose

To review the training session and identify personal highlights

Participants

Minimum: 5
Maximum: Any number
Best: 10 to 20
(Participants are organized into teams of 3 to 7 later in the game.)

Time

15 to 30 minutes

Supplies

- Picture postcards, preferably, a different one for each participant
- Pens or pencils
- Flip charts (one for each team)
- Felt-tipped markers
- Masking tape

Flow

Brief participants. Present the following scenario, using your own words:

Imagine it is three months in the future, and you received an e-mail note from a friend indicating that she's going to attend this training session. She is curious about your experiences with the session and wants your advice on how to get the most out of it. You are ready to respond to her by sending her a postcard.

Begin the postcard-writing activity. Ask participants to think back on the training session and recall one or two highlights. Also ask them to think about what two pieces of advice they should give their friend. Distribute a postcard to each participant and ask him or her to write a short, friendly note incorporating the highlights and the advice. Announce a 5-minute time limit.

Conclude the postcard-writing activity. Ask participants who have finished ahead of the others to decorate their postcards with doodles. When everyone has completed the task, collect the postcards and thank the participants.

Ask participants to compare notes. Organize participants into teams of three to seven and ask them to share what they wrote on their postcards.

Create joint postcards. Ask each team to write a joint note to the imaginary friend using large letters on a sheet of flip-chart paper positioned horizontally (landscape format). Announce a 5-minute time limit.

Display the joint postcards. After a suitable pause, ask teams to tape their giant postcards to the wall of the meeting room. Encourage the participants to take a gallery walk and review the products from the other teams.

100
SPAM

If you are a trainer, you probably know what a *Smile Sheet* is. It is a short questionnaire that is used immediately after a training session to collect participants' reactions to the event. The Smile Sheet typically focuses on the lowest level of training evaluation and ignores learning outcomes and application of the new skills and knowledge. Participants don't take these questionnaires seriously because they are usually tired at the end of a training program and eager to go home.

Recently, I have started using an alternative evaluation technique called SPAM, which stands for *Socialized Procedure for Application Measurement*. It requires the use of e-mail notes.

Purpose

To think about applications of new skills to the workplace and share application ideas with other participants

Participants

Minimum: 10
Maximum: Any number
Best: 10 to 30
(Participants work in pairs.)

Time

10 to 15 minutes during the session and 10 to 15 minutes after the session

Supplies

- Business cards (with e-mail addresses from each participant) (If these are not available, ask participants to write their names and e-mail addresses on blank pieces of paper)
- Pens or pencils

Flow

Exchange e-mail addresses with partners. Ask participants to pair up and exchange their e-mail address cards with their partners. Stress the importance of not losing the address cards from the partners.

Explain the SPAM procedure. Give these instructions (in your own words):

Sometime during the next week, write an e-mail note to your partner.

In this note, describe how you plan to apply your new skills and knowledge to your workplace.

If you have already begun applying the new skills and knowledge, briefly describe how you have done so.

Add information about your experiences in the training sessions. Specify what you enjoyed and what you disliked during the session.

Send the e-mail note to your partner. Send a copy to me.

If you don't hear from your partner after a week, send him or her a gentle reminder.

Concluding the session. Emphasize the importance of this follow-up activity. Thank everyone for their participation during the session.

About the Author

Sivasailam "Thiagi" Thiagarajan, Ph.D., is *Resident Mad Scientist* at the Thiagi Group, an organization that is dedicated to improving human performance effectively and enjoyably. Thiagi began designing games when he was seven years old and designing training games when he was twenty-four. He has been making a living working as a full-time training game designer for the past ten years. An international consultant, Thiagi has lived in three different countries and has consulted in twenty-one others. He has been the president of the North American Simulation and Gaming Association (NASAGA) four different times and the president of the International Society for Performance and Instruction (ISPI) twice.

Pfeiffer Publications Guide

This guide is designed to familiarize you with the various types of Pfeiffer publications. The formats section describes the various types of products that we publish; the methodologies section describes the many different ways that content might be provided within a product. We also provide a list of the topic areas in which we publish.

FORMATS

In addition to its extensive book-publishing program, Pfeiffer offers content in an array of formats, from fieldbooks for the practitioner to complete, ready-to-use training packages that support group learning.

FIELDBOOK Designed to provide information and guidance to practitioners in the midst of action. Most fieldbooks are companions to another, sometimes earlier, work, from which its ideas are derived; the fieldbook makes practical what was theoretical in the original text. Fieldbooks can certainly be read from cover to cover. More likely, though, you'll find yourself bouncing around following a particular theme, or dipping in as the mood, and the situation, dictate.

HANDBOOK A contributed volume of work on a single topic, comprising an eclectic mix of ideas, case studies, and best practices sourced by practitioners and experts in the field.

An editor or team of editors usually is appointed to seek out contributors and to evaluate content for relevance to the topic. Think of a handbook not as a ready-to-eat meal, but as a cookbook of ingredients that enables you to create the most fitting experience for the occasion.

RESOURCE Materials designed to support group learning. They come in many forms: a complete, ready-to-use exercise (such as a game); a comprehensive resource on one topic (such as conflict management) containing a variety of methods and approaches; or a collection of like-minded activities (such as icebreakers) on multiple subjects and situations.

TRAINING PACKAGE An entire, ready-to-use learning program that focuses on a particular topic or skill. All packages comprise a guide for the facilitator/trainer and a workbook for the participants. Some packages are supported with additional media—such as video—or learning aids, instruments, or other devices to help participants understand concepts or practice and develop skills.

- *Facilitator/trainer's guide* Contains an introduction to the program, advice on how to organize and facilitate the learning event, and step-by-step instructor notes. The guide also contains copies of presentation materials—handouts, presentations, and overhead designs, for example—used in the program.

- *Participant's workbook* Contains exercises and reading materials that support the learning goal and serves as a valuable reference and support guide for participants in the weeks and months that follow the learning event. Typically, each participant will require his or her own workbook.

ELECTRONIC CD-ROMs and web-based products transform static Pfeiffer content into dynamic, interactive experiences. Designed to take advantage of the searchability, automation, and ease-of-use that technology provides, our e-products bring convenience and immediate accessibility to your workspace.

METHODOLOGIES

CASE STUDY A presentation, in narrative form, of an actual event that has occurred inside an organization. Case studies are not prescriptive, nor are they used to prove a point; they are designed to develop critical analysis and decision-making skills. A case study has a specific time frame, specifies a sequence of events, is narrative in structure, and contains a plot structure—an issue (what should be/have been done?). Use case studies when the goal is to enable participants to apply previously learned theories to the circumstances in the case, decide what is pertinent, identify the real issues, decide what should have been done, and develop a plan of action.

ENERGIZER A short activity that develops readiness for the next session or learning event. Energizers are most commonly used after a break or lunch to stimulate or refocus the group. Many involve some form of physical activity, so they are a useful way to counter post-lunch lethargy. Other uses include transitioning from one topic to another, where "mental" distancing is important.

EXPERIENTIAL LEARNING ACTIVITY (ELA) A facilitator-led intervention that moves participants through the learning cycle from experience to application (also known as a Structured Experience). ELAs are carefully thought-out designs in which there is a definite learning purpose and intended outcome. Each step—everything that participants do during the activity—facilitates the accomplishment of the stated goal. Each ELA includes complete instructions for facilitating the intervention and a clear statement of goals, suggested group size and timing, materials required, an explanation of the process, and, where appropriate, possible variations to the activity. (For more detail on Experiential Learning Activities, see the Introduction to the *Reference Guide to Handbooks and Annuals*, 1999 edition, Pfeiffer, San Francisco.)

GAME A group activity that has the purpose of fostering team spirit and togetherness in addition to the achievement of a pre-stated goal. Usually contrived—undertaking a desert expedition, for example—this type of learning method offers an engaging means for participants to demonstrate and practice business and interpersonal skills. Games are effective for team building and personal development mainly because the goal is subordinate to the process—the means through which participants reach decisions, collaborate, communicate, and generate trust and understanding. Games often engage teams in "friendly" competition.

ICEBREAKER A (usually) short activity designed to help participants overcome initial anxiety in a training session and/or to acquaint the participants with one another. An icebreaker can be a fun activity or can be tied to specific topics or training goals. While a useful tool in itself, the icebreaker comes into its own in situations where tension or resistance exists within a group.

INSTRUMENT A device used to assess, appraise, evaluate, describe, classify, and summarize various aspects of human behavior. The term used to describe an instrument depends primarily on its format and purpose. These terms include survey, questionnaire, inventory, diagnostic, survey, and poll. Some uses of instruments include providing instrumental feedback to group members, studying here-and-now processes or functioning within a group, manipulating group composition, and evaluating outcomes of training and other interventions.

Instruments are popular in the training and HR field because, in general, more growth can occur if an individual is provided with a method for focusing specifically on his or her own behavior. Instruments also are used to obtain information that will serve as a basis for change and to assist in workforce planning efforts.

Paper-and-pencil tests still dominate the instrument landscape with a typical package comprising a facilitator's guide, which offers advice on administering the instrument and interpreting the collected data, and an initial set of instruments. Additional instruments are available separately. Pfeiffer, though, is investing heavily in e-instruments. Electronic instrumentation provides effortless distribution and, for larger groups particularly, offers advantages over paper-and-pencil tests in the time it takes to analyze data and provide feedback.

LECTURETTE A short talk that provides an explanation of a principle, model, or process that is pertinent to the participants' current learning needs. A lecturette is intended to establish a common language bond between the trainer and the participants by providing a mutual frame of reference. Use a lecturette as an introduction to a group activity or event, as an interjection during an event, or as a handout.

MODEL A graphic depiction of a system or process and the relationship among its elements. Models provide a frame of reference and something more tangible, and more easily remembered, than a verbal explanation. They also give participants something to "go on," enabling them to track their own progress as they experience the dynamics, processes, and relationships being depicted in the model.

ROLE PLAY A technique in which people assume a role in a situation/scenario: a customer service rep in an angry-customer exchange, for example. The way in which the role is approached is then discussed and feedback is offered. The role play is often repeated using a different approach and/or incorporating changes made based on feedback received. In other words, role playing is a spontaneous interaction involving realistic behavior under artificial (and safe) conditions.

SIMULATION A methodology for understanding the interrelationships among components of a system or process. Simulations differ from games in that they test or use a model that depicts or mirrors some aspect of reality in form, if not necessarily in content. Learning occurs by studying the effects of change on one or more factors of the model. Simulations are commonly used to test hypotheses about what happens in a system—often referred to as "what if?" analysis—or to examine best-case/worst-case scenarios.

THEORY A presentation of an idea from a conjectural perspective. Theories are useful because they encourage us to examine behavior and phenomena through a different lens.

TOPICS

The twin goals of providing effective and practical solutions for workforce training and organization development and meeting the educational needs of training and human resource professionals shape Pfeiffer's publishing program. Core topics include the following:

Leadership & Management

Communication & Presentation

Coaching & Mentoring

Training & Development

E-Learning

Teams & Collaboration

OD & Strategic Planning

Human Resources

Consulting

What will you find on pfeiffer.com?

- The best in workplace performance solutions for training and HR professionals

- Downloadable training tools, exercises, and content

- Web-exclusive offers

- Training tips, articles, and news

- Seamless on-line ordering

- Author guidelines, information on becoming a Pfeiffer Affiliate, and much more

Discover more at www.pfeiffer.com